AMONG ORANGUTANS

THE BELKNAP PRESS OF

HARVARD UNIVERSITY PRESS | CAMBRIDGE, MASSACHUSETTS AND LONDON, ENGLAND | 2004

AMONG ORANGUTANS

RED APES AND THE RISE OF HUMAN CULTURE

CAREL VAN SCHAIK   photographs by PERRY VAN DUIJNHOVEN

Permission to reproduce photographs has been granted by the following individuals: Sri Suci Utami Atmoko, p. 98 (below right); Charles Backman, p. 181 (left); Herman Rijksen, pp. 30, 72, 77, 78, 98 (above left, *detail;* below left, *detail*), 125; and Chris Schurman, pp. 23, 98 (above center, *detail*). Photographs on pp. 18 (above), 37, 40 (above), 98 (below center, *detail*), 140, 209 are by Carel van Schaik. Illustration on p. 8 is from Nicholaas Tulp, *Observationes Medicae* (1652). Illustration on p. 9 is from Alfred Edmund Brehm, *Brehm's Tierleben* (1876). Illustrations on p. 89 are by J. Gerlier (above; 1878) and PhotoDisc collection (below). All other illustrations are the work of Perry van Duijnhoven.

Library of Congress Cataloging-in-Publication Data

Schaik, Carel van.

    Among orangutans : red apes and the rise of human culture / Carel van Schaik, Perry van Duijnhoven.

      p. cm.

    Includes bibliographical references (p.) and index.

    ISBN 0-674-01577-0 (cloth : alk. paper)

    1. Orangutan.   2. Culture.   I. Title.

QL737.P96S28 2004

599.88′3—dc22   2004052254

To the memory of Idrusman

and to
Herman Rijksen,
Mike Griffiths, and
Willie Smits,
who have led the struggle for
orangutan conservation

CONTENTS

PREFACE

I wrote this book to tell the story of the orangutan that emerged from the mists of a Sumatran swamp. It is a different beast from the solitary recluse we know from other places. The swamp has revealed our red cousins to be every bit as sociable, as technically adept, and as culturally capable as their African relative, the chimpanzee.

The story of the new orangutan is worth telling because it will change how we view ourselves in relation to our closest relatives and how we reconstruct human evolution. In the coming chapters, I will show how the initially independent strands of work on life history and infant development, tool use and intelligence, and culture all fit together in unsuspected ways. I argue that we can use our findings on orangutans to shed light on a major question: what are the origins of human intelligence, technology, and culture?

But there is also another reason for this book. As I write these lines, the province of Aceh continues to be engulfed in armed conflict that put an end to all field research in the region, and my best friend in the region is dead, murdered by either insurgents or government provocateurs. Elsewhere, the orangutan's forests are being cleared or degraded by logging; mothers are shot, their infants traded. The window on our past opened up by the study of these close relatives is rapidly closing again. I fervently hope that telling the orangutan's tale may help to avert the unfolding tragedy. We cannot let them go quietly.

*   *   *

I had a lot of help in the research and in writing this book. Finishing a book is a good time to remember the people who made it all possible. First and foremost, I want to thank Idrusman (Yus), assistant, teacher, companion, and friend for almost twenty years. Yus was by my side when we discovered the orangutans of Suaq. To his memory we dedicate this book. Among the other team members, Ibrahim, the wise, and Dolly, the practical, have been with the project or structures that support it ever since. S. Poniran, then head of the Gunung Leuser National Park, saw the need for the station at Suaq and made it happen. Sayed Mudahar had the dream of finding harmony between forest and people, and Ali Bashya Amin kept the dream alive. The station was supported by the Leuser Development Programme, the brainchild of Pak Sayed, Herman Rijksen, and Mike Griffiths. Mike's home was always open, his counsel always judicious, and his cool car available when needed most; I thank him for years of hospitality and friendship. Then there was Yarrow Robertson, whose love for Leuser is matched by his determination to save as much of it as humanely possible; and Katherine Monk, who fought to save Suaq when everyone else was giving up.

A long-term field project is impossible without a steady flow of funding, and I was extremely fortunate to have the continuous support of the Wildlife Conservation Society (formerly the New York Zoological Society), arguably the most visionary and certainly most thoroughly field-based of all international conservation organizations. John Robinson, Mary Pearl, Alan Rabinowitz, and Josh Ginsberg all believed in the project and kept it afloat over the years. In the final stages, the financial support of the L. S. B. Leakey Foundation helped to broaden our base.

The Suaq project benefited from the hard work of many assistants and students: Beth Fox, Ian Singleton, Arnold Sitompul, Azhar, Bahlias Putri Gayo, Ibrahim bin 'Mohammad, Zulkifli, Ishak, Mukadis, Asril, Syamsuar, Rudy H., Iwan, Fahrulrazi, Abdussamad, Michelle Merrill, Nuzwar, Nurwahidah, and Irma.

Mentors made me who I am: a naturalist with physics envy. At Utrecht, both Jan van Hooff and Pauline Hogeweg, each in their own way, insisted that I keep an eye out for both unique details and universal laws and taught me the value of combining solid empiricism with audacious theorizing. At Duke, John Terborgh showed me that a naturalist could also be a superb scientist. My colleagues in the Department of Biological Anthropology and Anatomy have helped to turn my naturalist's focus onto the origin of humans. Graduate students, both those who worked at Suaq and those who did not, have kept me on my toes over the years: Filippo Aureli, Meredith Bastian, Rob Deaner, Roberto Delgado, Beth Fox, Peter Kappeler, Elissa Krakauer, Chris Kirk, Becca Lewis, Michelle Merrill, Charlie Nunn, Steph Pandolfi, Ian Singleton, Romy Steenbeek, Liesbeth Sterck, and Serge Wich. Unselfish colleagues have enriched my intellectual life: Kristen Hawkes, Peter Kappeler, Sagar Pandit, Gauri Pradhan, Signe Preuschoft, Anne Russon, Maria van Noordwijk, and David Watts. Herman Rijksen, Tatang Mitra Setia, and Suci Utami have freely shared their deep knowledge of orangutan behavior whenever we had a chance to meet. Several people have kindly commented on my confused drafts: Meredith Bastian, John Cant, Richard Klein, Anne Russon, Karen Strier, Russ Tuttle, Maria van Noordwijk, and Serge Wich. Kaye Brown gave me wise advice on the book's organization and on my writing. I thank them for their efforts, but I have to add the standard claim that, sadly, all errors are mine.

I am grateful to Michael Fisher for sharing our dream of creating a book with both pretty pictures and savvy science, to Maria van Noordwijk for making the index, and to the production team at Harvard University Press for making it all seem easy.

Many of the times when I use *we* in this book, I am referring to Perry van Duijnhoven and myself. Perry took most of the pictures in this book. He has been an amazing friend for years, by my side at the highs and the lows. On surveys, his little car-that-could got us where most others feared to go. Accounts of my adventures with Perry could fill another book.

To all I've mentioned here, as well as others too numerous to mention, I offer my sincere thanks.

THE GREAT APE PARADOX

1

The red ape viewed by the zoo visitor is a gregarious animal: young ones endlessly wrestle in play; adults display infinite tolerance toward youngsters that insolently steal food; and their appetite for sex almost rivals that of bonobos. Zoo orangutans are also technically adept animals. They may spend hours examining any object within reach, and zookeepers know they are champion escape artists (and perhaps escapists too), relentlessly trying to work their way out of the most solidly constructed cage.

Yet, in its home, the steamy jungles of Borneo and Sumatra, the Man of the Forest (the meaning of the Malay *orang hutan*) is known neither for its gregariousness nor for its technological prowess. The red apes emerging from the scientific literature live solitary lives in a sea of green; they are loners who spend their days scarfing down fruits or liana tips by the bushel or tearing the bark off a hapless forest tree. They will meet when attracted to the same strangling fig in fruit, but their social intercourse usually amounts to a few glances thrown askance from a safe distance, and more often than not they pass like ships in the night. Also, their legendary technical talents are not much in evidence. Although they build nests by bending and breaking branches, the highest form of tool use reported in the literature until recently was the use of a broken-off twig as a back scratcher.[1]

The other great apes display a similar contrast in behavior. Forty years ago, Adriaan Kortlandt felt compelled to write about the chimpanzee: "We therefore are confronted with the baffling disparity of a creature that shows in captivity nearly human potentialities in technical intelligence and

Orangutans prefer to be on the outside, looking in.

Learning to count in the Think Tank (National Zoo, Washington, D.C.)

cultural capacities, except for a spoken language and a moral code, but appears in the wild to live an entirely non-human way of life."[2] Some twenty-five years later, in 1987, John Tooby and Irv DeVore asked much the same question.[3]

This, then, is the paradox. The great apes we see in zoos and special research facilities are socially astute and intelligent. Chimpanzees have politics every bit as complex and opportunistic as any dealings on the senate floor.[4] Language-trained animals of all great ape species can use a few hundred signs and maintain a polite conversation.[5] So much like us! And yet, it is not clear at all why they need to be so smart in their natural lives out in the woods, where orangutans in particular seem to be neither sociable nor technologically proficient. Great apes in the wild seem to be overqualified for their jobs! Why?

Has science so far failed to appreciate fully the challenges of their lives in the wild? True, chimpanzees use tools in the wild but, surprisingly, none of the other great apes have shown much evidence of it, whereas many other species do. It is true that apes form coalitions, but so do lots of other animals, including many nonprimates that never display near-human abilities, even when prodded by researchers.

Or is the unusual cleverness of the great apes in zoos and psychology labs perhaps merely an artifact of being exposed to objects and tools and to encouraging company? Perhaps if you raise chimpanzees and orangutans with people, as if they were people, they become, in some meaningful sense, almost like people in behavior and cognition. Cognitive psychologists have recognized this phenomenon and named it "enculturation"[6]— the perfect term, as we shall see. But if the potential is there, waiting to be brought out by us, why is it there in the first place?

This book was written to help solve this paradox. We found many of the answers in an unlikely place studying an unlikely animal: swamp orangutans. The orangutan, Asia's red ape, is as serene as chimpanzees are hyperactive, as reserved socially as the chimpanzee is convivial. Yet, those at Suaq are different from any that have ever been studied before: they live at very high densities, like each other's company, and use a variety of tools. We came to think of them as the Asian chimpanzees. By being so different from other orangutans and so similar to chimpanzees, they have made a great contribution to solving the great ape paradox. They have shown us that their lives in the wild are indeed a lot more challenging intellectually than many of us suspected. We have learned from them that intelligence is linked to a slow life history and is built up piece by piece during development, much of it through social learning, and that culture is a gift—a wonderful byproduct of a fortuitous constellation of preconditions—that allows them to exploit their environment more fully.

These findings also help us to shed light on the vexing question why the great apes did not become more like us. What made one of the numerous lineages of great apes so strikingly different in its behavior that we recognize it as a cultural animal, communicating in symbols, building its whole life around culture, and having moral codes, religion, art, and complex institutions? At the end of this book, we will have a few tentative answers.

A Surprise in the Swamp We almost missed these discoveries. It was the summer of 1993. Too tired to sit up or eat, we were lying on the floor of our ramshackle hut along the Lembang River, reviewing our options. We had been working in this coastal swamp for over a year and had discovered an amazing variety of wildlife as well as the highest primate biomass of any site surveyed so far in Southeast Asia. And, above all, our nest counts indicated that we had by far the highest orangutan density ever recorded. But the struggle to get in and out of the swamp was sapping our strength, and we were reaching the point of exhaustion.

This is why we held our summit in the swamp. All of the members of my team were experienced local naturalists. Together we had been scouring the forests of Aceh, Sumatra's northernmost province, exploring the biodiversity of the remaining intact lowland forests. Ecologically, this site, Suaq Balimbing, had surpassed all our expectations. Unfortunately, working there was hard going. Along the river, the forest was quite passable, at least during the unusually dry period fate had bestowed on us to conduct our first survey more than a year earlier. But upon entering the forest, we almost immediately came upon a backswamp, a fetid place riddled with bare patches of mud and treacherous channels of red-brown water. The sweltering heat of the coastal plain made our sweaty bodies easy targets for the countless mosquitoes of various species. But once we had made our way through this zone, we found orangutan heaven. The forest there was rather open and not too tall, with only one clear tree story, much like the European oak forests of my youth. The mud gave way to muck, the forest gradually becoming a peat swamp. Here, according to our nest counts, orangutan density was off the chart, over ten individuals per square kilometer during the period before our survey—twice the highest recorded density elsewhere.

I had dreamed of finding a site like this, part of a vast expanse of forest where we could follow animals wherever they would roam and observe them amid a dense population. In a large site like this, we could finally unravel the social organization of the orangutan: is there an order to the seemingly haphazard movement of individuals? Do they form a distinct social network, an exploded group, or is there no social unit above that of the individual moving around in its own range, oblivious of the

Backswamp during high water

movements of others? This site would perfectly fit the bill, if it weren't for the terrain.

So here we were trying to plot our future course when Ibrahim, during a lull in the deliberations, casually mentioned that he had seen an orangutan female, Sara, poke and bang into a tree hole with a thick stick. Tool use! We had to stay.

That was 1993, and we stayed until we had to leave, in September 1999. Our swamp was not an easy place to work, but we defied the advice of doctors and relatives and went to live in the unhealthy, strength-sapping place called Suaq Balimbing because what was hell for people was heaven for orangutans. This book is about our journey of discovery.

PLANET OF THE APES

In today's hyperconnected world, it is easy to forget how little we once knew about other parts of the world. Aristotle, and hence Western civilization, did not know that great apes existed. Until just a few hundred years ago, all travel was overland and had to pass through the Sahara or Gobi deserts or the high passes and plateaus of the Himalayas, so only the lightest and most precious items from Africa and Asia ever reached the West. What little was known of remote lands came from a mere trickle of unconfirmed rumors. Accepted "knowledge" included tall tales of man-beasts of unusual strength and sexual depravity. In this information vacuum, Western civilization developed an unencumbered sense of superiority. But among the peoples that share their lands with apes, very few refer to themselves as the crown of creation. In the stories of many cultures, animals are humans to whom fate had dealt a bad hand. In northern Sumatra, for instance, the white-handed gibbon, with its hauntingly beautiful, melancholic song, is the descendant of a girl who had been so badly exploited by her stepmother that she ran away into the forest and wailed in her sorrow every morning. And orangutans were simply people that refused to speak for fear of being put to work.

"A most surprizing Creature" The first European to set eyes on an orangutan may well have been Marco Polo, who spent almost half a year in Aceh, on the northern tip of Sumatra, in the late thirteenth century. His reports are far from conclusive, however, and even a little far-fetched:

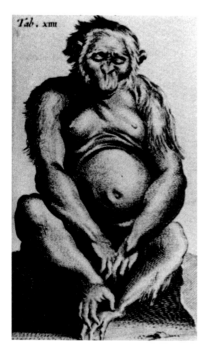

Tulp's "Indian satyr"

naked men with long tails, pygmies with shrunken heads, or cannibals in the hills. All or none of these could be the orangutan.

The first European actually to describe an orangutan, in 1641, may well have been Nicolaas Tulp, the Amsterdam surgeon famously depicted in Rembrandt's *De Anatomische Les (The Anatomy Lesson)*. Most experts say that the female specimen he dissected was a chimpanzee, although some think it is a bonobo.[1] The animal, which died at the court of Prince Frederik Hendrik, had arrived on a ship from Angola, not far from either species' geographic range, and Tulp's description suggests a black great ape. Incongruously, however, he called it an "Indian satyr," an "orang-outang," and also *Homo sylvestris* (the Latin translation of *orangutan*). Are we really to believe that this learned gentleman, who became mayor of Amsterdam, did not know that India was not in Africa or that *orangutan* was a Malay word, at a time when Holland was in the process of setting up its colonial operations in the East? Tulp's own brother-in-law was an officer in the Dutch East Indies Company, after all. What is more, Tulp spiced his description of the animal with tales from Borneo about the beast's lewd behavior.

Presumably Tulp, like others at the time, thought that all great apes— which they called satyrs, after the lecherous creatures of Greek mythology that were half-man, half-ungulate—were one and the same species. Herman Rijksen and Erik Meijaard,[2] however, think the animal he dissected really was an orangutan, hailing from the Angkola region of western North Sumatra. Orangutans from this area may have been darker than those from elsewhere in Sumatra, and Rijksen and Meijaard point to a few more anatomical details in the description that support this interpretation. Moreover, this individual apparently loved to cover itself under a blanket—typical orangutan behavior. So, maybe the first great ape described by science was an orangutan. The illustration accompanying Tulp's description is suitably ambiguous.

Regardless of the specimen's identity, Tulp placed the description of great apes on a scientific footing. Before his description, depictions of orangutans and other great apes were as fanciful a mixture of fact and fiction as the travelers' tales about their behavior. For the first one hundred years or so, illustrations made them look like people, the old wise man of the forest leaning on his stick. In the early nineteenth century, artists under influence of the "Enlightenment" began to look more closely and draw them

By the late nineteenth century, depictions of orangutans had become realistic.

more as they actually were. In fact, the most striking aspect of orangutan morphology is how unspectacular it is. Their most surprising aspect is, instead, their behavior.

Triangulating Human Uniqueness Predictably, the first pickled specimens (followed later by live juveniles) carried to Europe on ships, in the late seventeenth century, caused a sensation among the learned men of the day. Here was a mammal whose anatomical similarity to "Man" was undeniable. Among living organisms, none are more closely related to us than the great apes. Carolus Linnaeus recognized this affinity in his classification of species, although he balked at placing humans and apes in the same family. Maybe the reasons for his reluctance were not entirely scientific, however, for he wrote to a friend that "if I had called man an ape, or vice versa, I should have fallen under the ban of all the ecclesiastics. It may be that as a naturalist I ought to have done so."[3]

About a century later, Charles Darwin returned to the subject of our place in nature. In one of the very last pages of the *Origin of Species,* which appeared in 1859, he wrote coyly that "[i]n the distant future I see open fields for far more important researches." What could possibly be more important than demonstrating evolution through natural selection? Two lines later, he comes to the point: "Light will be thrown on the origin of man and his history."[4] As we know, he left it to Thomas Huxley, that courageous bulldog, to make the claims explicit. After an exhaustive comparison of the anatomy of gorillas, orangutans, chimpanzees, and ourselves, Huxley concluded in 1863 that "the structural differences which separate Man from the Gorilla and the Chimpanzee are not so great as those which separate the Gorilla from the lower apes."[5] His conclusion therefore can be summarized as saying that we are just another African great ape.

In 1871, Darwin finally dared to write his *Descent of Man* and admit that his objective was "solely to shew that there is no fundamental difference between man and the higher mammals in their mental facilities."[6] Humans, then, are African great apes, and we should be able to learn much about human origins and human nature from the study of our close relatives. One way to define human uniqueness, in other words, is by triangulation: estimating our position by the similarities and differences between us and them.

Although Darwin and Huxley had made a compelling case for primatology, somehow their message got lost. The actual birth of the discipline was delayed for many decades, for after the initial shock of Darwin's announcement wore off, the pendulum swung back toward an emphasis on the great distance between the apes and us. Arguments for our differ-

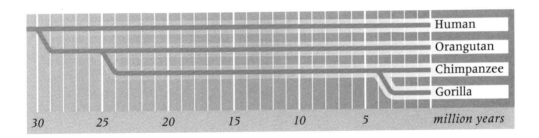

The presumed phylogenetic relationships among humans and great apes in about 1900

ences seemed equally compelling. Imagine this odd police-style lineup: individual males or females of all great apes and humans are arrayed in front of an independent observer, who is then asked to pick the odd man out. Chances are that an objective observer of a collection of females will decide on the human: Upright and flat-footed, largely hairless, short-faced and large-brained, with prominent breasts, buttocks, and thighs, she really stands out among the hairy, bent-over, long-armed, decidedly noncurvaceous ape females. Of course, some of these features (the breasts and buttocks) are secondary sexual characteristics that may confuse the estimation of phylogenetic similarity. Even so, if we line up males, the conclusion must be the same. It is true that males of some species have highly unusual secondary sexual characteristics that would distract an independent observer from the task: the male gorilla has his thick neck and silvery back, and the male orangutan has his moon face and long cape of hair. Nonetheless, it remains pretty easy to pick out the human male, just as flat-footed, upright, short-faced, and large-brained as the human female and just as different in all these features from all ape males. Were we really great apes?

So, at the dawn of the twentieth century, the presumed origin of the human lineage receded further and further back in time, to some 30 million years, so long ago that it is unlikely that biology could ever illuminate the human condition. At the same time, anthropologists focused their energies on defending the bastion of human uniqueness and increasingly denied any role for biology in explaining our behavior (in part for the good reason that biological effects had been abused to support morally questionable causes such as eugenics and immigration quotas).[7] It seemed not unreasonable to conclude that the chasm between great apes and us—with our language, technology, art, culture, morality, religion, humor, as well as war and genocide—was so deep that no biological bridges could be built. During most of the twentieth century, the predominant attitude in the social sciences was that our unique faculties are not the product of regular organic evolution; therefore, no insights would be gained from the study of animals, not even of our closest relatives. In the words of Ashley Montagu:[8] "Man has no instincts, because everything he is and has become he has learned, acquired, from his culture, from the man-made part of the environment, from other human beings." Who needed biology and evolution to explain the properties of this blank slate?

Ironically, this increasingly entrenched attitude was not based on careful research. The early naturalists who collected orangutans rarely did more than watch the behavior of badly wounded animals struggling to escape or small infants kept briefly as pets until they died.[9] Despite increasing opportunity because of expanding university programs and easy access to captive colonies, no Western biologist or anthropologist in the early 1900s came up with the idea of studying primate behavior in the wild. Science was practiced in the laboratory. Observing spontaneously behaving animals outside the strictly controlled laboratory conditions would have been considered utterly unscientific. We simply did not know the first thing about ape behavior, apart from some tantalizing hints that came from psychological experiments by Wolfgang Köhler and Robert Yerkes. After World War I, some young European mavericks took to the field to study the behavior of local animals and founded the discipline of ethology (or behavioral biology), but it took decades for them to get even begrudged respect (Konrad Lorenz, Niko Tinbergen, and Karl von Frisch were belatedly awarded the Nobel Prize for Physiology in 1973). It fell to the intellectual descendants of this generation to at last begin fieldwork on primates, although even they had to face a certain amount of ridicule as butterfly catchers and stamp collectors.

By now, of course, everyone knows the spectacular results that have come in over the last four decades, in particular the remarkable discoveries about chimpanzee tool use, hunting, and warfare, with their charming and chilling correlations to human behavior. These findings have helped to swing the pendulum in the other direction.[10]

Equally instrumental in bringing about a sea change in attitudes about human-ape relations was the molecular work that began in the late 1960s. Increasingly sophisticated, these studies posed ever more effective challenges that in the end overturned received morphological wisdom. The hominid lineage split off from the great ape ancestor not 30 million, not 15 million, but a mere 6–7 million years ago.[11] The convergent strands of compelling behavioral and molecular evidence prompted Jared Diamond to refer to the human as the Third Chimpanzee. If it comes as a shock to anyone to learn that chimpanzees are our closest living relatives, imagine the shock to a chimpanzee to learn that humans, not gorillas, are her closest relatives! In any case, molecular biology has

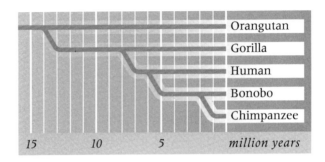

shown that Huxley was right on target: we are just another African great ape, our species represented by a single branch somewhere in the middle of the bushy tree; and we were just like our fellow apes not so very long ago.

As early as 1863, Huxley[12] warned: "It would be no less wrong than absurd to deny the existence of the chasm, but it is at least equally wrong and absurd to exaggerate its magnitude, and, resting on the admitted fact of its existence, refuse to inquire whether it is wide or narrow." The challenge is now, as it was then, to strike a balance. We must ensure that the pendulum comes to rest in the middle. If we overemphasize the differences, there is nothing to be learned from ape behavior, clearly a preposterous position.[13] On the other hand, if we regard humans as mere naked apes and great apes as mere furry humans, we deny the lesson of the lineup: an extraordinary divergence has taken place in the last 7 or so million years. Worse, we would deny ourselves the opportunity to gain an appreciation of the nature of our unique endowment and of the selective processes that brought them about. Indeed, the study of human evolution would be pointless. Seen from this perspective, studies of great apes are of immense value in helping us to triangulate human uniqueness: what do we share, what is unique to us, and, above all, why?

Why Study Orangutans? Identifying our place in nature is by definition a comparative enterprise, beginning with detailed comparisons with our closest living relatives. To the attentive reader of popular accounts of primatology, the chimpanzee story has become very familiar. Over the past four decades, the results of painstaking fieldwork on these African apes have relentlessly chiseled away at the pedestal on which science, or rather social science, had placed humankind. Tool use, tool making, thought and planning, warfare, language, cooperative hunting—all are now believed to have been present (if in simpler forms) among our great ape ancestors. And in the past few years, culture has been added to this list: nonhuman species are recognized to have geographically distinct behavioral variants that are maintained because they are transmitted through social learning (i.e., by nongenetic means). At the same time, this developing picture has helped to bring out more clearly what makes us different, and therefore what has happened during the evolution of that one lineage of bipedal great apes that produced us.

The chimpanzee story has been told often and very well.[14] The story I set out to recount features a character usually considered as one of the extras in the play: the orangutan. Orangutans never took center stage because they are the Asian cousins, not part of the main family line. Moreover, they are elusive: hard to find and easy to lose.

What can the study of orangutans possibly add? A surprising amount, it turns out, and in two different ways. The first is part of the endeavor to define humanity. Orangutans are ecologically much like chimpanzees: both are frugivores with a predilection for extractive foraging. But because the orangutan lineage split off from the African lineage some 14 million years ago, finding a trait shared by chimpanzees and orangutans strongly suggests that it is a basic feature of the great apes, just as its absence, when we have good reason to believe the trait absent, helps us to recognize the more recently derived features of chimps and humans. A case in point is culture-based tool use. If we can demonstrate the presence of material culture in orangutans, this would strongly suggest that the capacity to create and transmit it has been around for many millions of years.

The second reason to study orangutans (or any other primate) is subtler. Having identified the unique features of humans is only the first step. The next step is to ask why these features exist only in humans. We have to identify the factors that favored the changes that took place in the hominid lineage, be they mainly from the outside (in the form of climate change and habitat alteration) or mainly from the inside (in the form of larger brains or slower life histories), though there is always an interaction between the two. To do this right, we need a theoretical framework in which to place our observations of chimpanzees—and, for that matter, of all living primates and other mammals—in order to generate predictions about the selective agents that drove the behavior of our hominid ancestors away from their common great ape base. Theories are more easily constructed when we have variation in the relevant factors: ecology, demography, or social behavior. That is why primatologists study a broad range of species, sometimes even nonprimates.

It is difficult, though, to devise theories about phenomena that have no parallels among most primate species. In such cases, we should of course make sure to study the species that have the phenomenon in question, but it is more important that we try to use the variability within the one or two relevant species to develop causal hypotheses. Culture can serve to illustrate this point as well. Human culture is infinitely more complex than chimpanzee or orangutan cultures or traditions, but by studying variation in the latter, and identifying the underlying causes of this variation, we may develop promising working hypotheses about what set in motion the momentous process that led from great-ape tradition to human culture.

In this book we explore how the new information on orangutans may help us to refine the triangulation process. We will present our conclusions about the evolution of humanness in Chapter 10.

HOMO SYLVESTRIS

3

Orangutans are great apes, and therefore share all the basic great ape features with their African relatives. Physical anthropologists have trouble defining exactly how one recognizes a great ape, but the list usually contains limbs that move rather freely in all directions, the absence of a tail, the habit of building sleeping platforms known as nests, and large body size. Another feature uniting all apes, one that is usually overlooked, is their slow life history: slow development, long lives, and long intervals between successive births.[1] The ancestral great ape was arboreal, and we now know that strict arboreality encourages slow life history. The evolutionary key to slow life history is low mortality of adult animals, and life in the trees is rather safer than on the ground. Arboreal mammals, especially large and rather solitary ones, have far fewer natural enemies, both predators and parasites—assuming of course they are truly at home up in the canopy and manage not to fall.[2]

Some 15 million years ago, in the mid-Miocene, there were numerous kinds of apes.[3] It is thought they are less common now because most were replaced by monkeys, whose four-legged locomotion style better equipped them to cope with gaps in the forest canopy. Monkeys underwent a remarkable adaptive radiation at this time, just as the forests shrank periodically as a result of climate cycles. Captives of the canopy, apes were in trouble. The survivors all invented some way to stay in business. Some—chimpanzees, for instance—became even larger and followed the monkeys to the ground. Gorillas became specialized foragers of fibrous foods on the forest floor, but there was also an Asian ape that did the same: the enor-

Orangutan nest

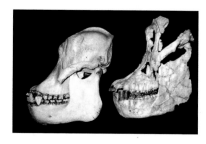

Skulls of the orangutan *(left)* and *Sivapithecus (right)*

Adult female orangutans from Sumatra *(above)* and Borneo *(below)*

mous Miocene *Gigantopithecus*. This genus was in a clade (a set of species sharing a common ancestor) of big Asian apes, which includes *Sivapithecus*. The latter, distributed in a long belt lining the Himalayas, ate hard plant foods, probably nuts.[4] Its skull is a spitting image of the orangutan's. Many scholars surmise that *Sivapithecus* was actually the predecessor of all orangutans (genus *Pongo*).[5]

In Southeast Asia the original canopy-dwelling life style persisted. New finds from Vietnam from the late Pleistocene show a *Pongo* with massive jaws that clearly fed on hard objects[6] such as nuts but was nonetheless a devoted arborealist. Some other Pleistocene Asian apes, the gibbons, are likewise still hanging in there. They are even more adapted to life in the treetops, with their breathtaking leaps and midair turns. The largest of them, the siamang, is less gracile and a bit more sedate in its acrobatics. Hence, some sites in Sumatra harbor three species of apes—all strictly aboreal—more than anywhere else in the world. The most likely reason for the apes' persistence in Southeast Asia is that the dense forests of Indochina and Sundaland (the landmass of the Sunda shelf in the South China Sea) were never broken up to the same extent as the African forests. Safe in their habitat, the apes were able to resist encroachment by the upstart monkeys, who arrived in Southeast Asia relatively late.

Marooned: Orangutan Distribution Today, the orangutan, Asia's only remaining great ape, is found only in the deep forests of the large islands of Borneo and Sumatra. Depending on your taxonomist, they come in one species with two subspecies, each on one island, or two species, a Sumatran *(Pongo abelii)* and a Bornean *(Pongo pygmaeus)*. Local names vary. Ironically, the name *orangutan* is rarely used by native peoples inside the natural range. In Sumatra, *mawas* is most common. On Borneo, a extraordinary variety of names apply, including *maias* or *kahiyu*.[7]

The genetic distance between the Sumatran and Bornean orangutans is remarkably large, reaching values that comfortably separate species in other animals, such as the two species of chimpanzee.[8] This is why the orangutans from Sumatra and Borneo are now often considered two separate species, even though they look fairly similar and produce perfectly healthy and viable hybrids in captivity. Compared with Borneans,

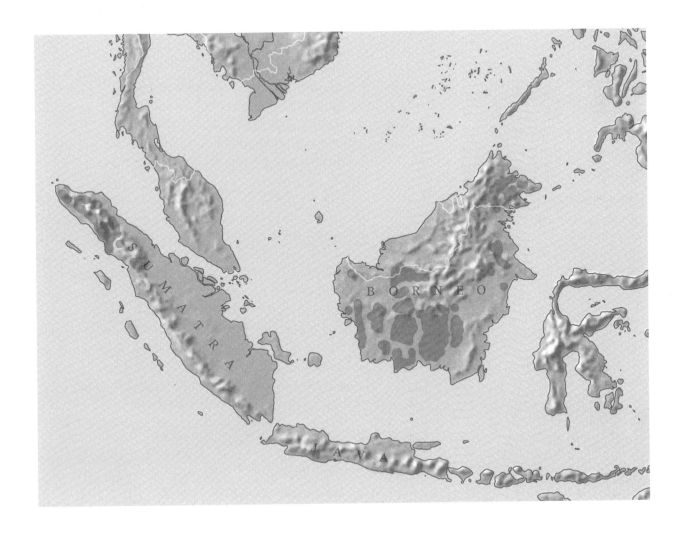

Sumatran orangutans have lighter, denser, and longer fur; lighter, narrower faces; overall more gracile features; and perhaps also shorter thumbs and large toes.

The large genetic distance between the two (sub)species suggests a long separation. Yet Borneo and Sumatra are both part of the large Sunda continental shelf, and the two have been repeatedly connected during glaciations, when sea levels were much lower. How can we explain this large genetic distance?

When the Sunda shelf was dry, it formed an area almost the size of Australia, but it was dissected by major rivers. Unlike monkeys, apes are not good swimmers; indeed, many a zoo ape has drowned in the moats surrounding open-air exhibits. Deep rivers that are so wide that fallen trees

The current geographic distribution of the orangutan

During the last glaciation, Borneo and Sumatra were part of the same land mass: Sundaland.

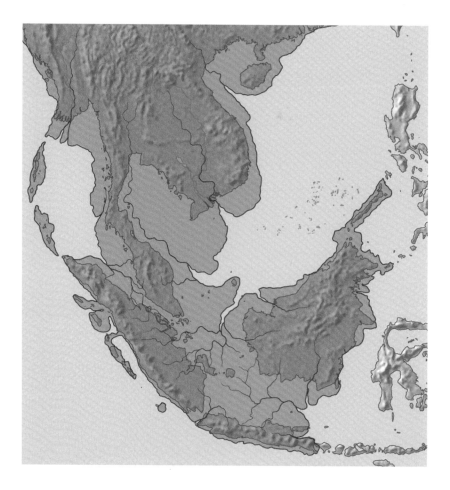

cannot connect opposite banks become impassable for orangutans and thus become genetic barriers. A few large rivers, veritable Sunda Amazons, ran between the two islands and drained to the northeast into the South China Sea and to the east, south of Borneo. That left a low range of hills as the separation. Although orangutans prefer steamy lowland jungles to misty mountains, these hills were not very high—after all, they are below sea level right now. It is more likely that they were covered in very poor heath forests, much like those found on the present-day islands of Bangka and Belitung, and acted as dispersal barriers for that reason. Alternatively, selection on the morphological and physiological features of orangutans on each island has been strong enough to keep the populations genetically distinct, even when there was some migration between them.

Within each island there is also considerable variation. In Sumatra, for instance, furs grade from bright red to rather dark brown, and animals with very long and gracile fingers coexist with those with much stubbier fingers. Recent genetic work has demonstrated the existence of ancient mitochondrial DNA lineages.[9] Because an individual inherits all of its mitochondrial DNA from its mother, such deep differences probably reflect a history of long separation within the Sumatran population. It is possible that the origin of Lake Toba (see map on page 36) led to the long-term separation of a northern and a southern population. Some 150,000 years ago, one of the largest volcanic eruptions ever created this caldera lake, one of the deepest lakes on earth.[10] For millennia, the resulting rocky wilderness, only gradually colonized by algae and lichens, would have been impassable to canopy wildlife.

On Borneo, the variation is even greater but it appears to follow an easily recognized geographic pattern. Colin Groves distinguishes three subspecies on the two sides of the only major mountain range (the Schwaner-Muller mountains) crossing the island, from the southwest to the northeast. In these ancient, worn-down mountains, orangutans are very scarce. Mighty rivers create the separations in the lowlands: the Kapuas River in the west, the Barito River in the southeast, and perhaps the Mahakam River in the east.[11] The subspecies that inhabits the eastern fringe of the island differs from the other orangutans of Sundaland in being more terrestrial, better able to cope with tough, fibrous foods, and perhaps even living a faster-paced life.

Why is it that this magnificent ape, clearly quite capable of making its living in a tropical rain forest, became marooned on these two islands at Asia's fringe? Throughout the Pleistocene era *Pongo,* either the same species or one closely related to today's orangutans, lived on the mainland all the way up to southern China. Climate change may have played a role in the story of this strikingly shrinking range,[12] but, as I will discuss in greater detail in Chapter 7, humans may have had an even more significant effect. On Sumatra, we find orangutans only in the northern tip. On Borneo, too, there are curious absences: no orangutans live in most of Sarawak, in Brunei, or in the large southeastern triangle between the Barito River and the Mahakam River. In these places, the impact of human settlement is apparent: if we overlay the maps of orangutan-eating peoples and the orangutan's current distribution, we find that they form almost exact mirror images.[13]

Young and Old, Male and Female Like all vertebrates, orangutans go through distinct stages: infancy, juvenility, adolescence, adulthood, and old age. Although the stages are easy to distinguish, the transitions are gradual. An infant by definition drinks its mother's milk, but whereas the moment of complete weaning marks nutritional independence, it does not necessarily mean that the weanling has attained full competence in all aspects of feeding and foraging. Very young ones look a bit bald, and what hair they do have may stand out in tufts, earning them the nickname spider-heads. Unlike human babies, they have virtually no body fat, with thin and spindly arms and legs, although they tend to be a bit pot-bellied. Bright rings surround their eyes, and even the darkest ones have blonder fur than their mothers do. Although they gradually lose those features, young ones always look fluffier than adults.

A female weighs about 2 kilograms at birth, perhaps approximately 15 kilograms around weaning at age 7 or so, and perhaps some 30 kilograms by age 15, when they give birth for the first time. These numbers are all estimates because we cannot weigh orangutans in the field. After that, growth begins to slow down considerably and most adult females weigh in at around 35–40 kilograms. It was our impression in the field that orangutan females continue to grow throughout the early part of adult life, not just by filling out and growing longer beards but also by growing taller and wider. This pattern may be common among larger, slow-breeding mammals, in which the transition from growth to adulthood gets blurred.[14] Adolescent sterility, for instance, the period when there is some ovarian activity but not enough for a female to get pregnant, may last several years.

If females don't show a clear-cut termination of growth, orangutan males really keep growing. A young adult female sitting next to a fully developed male is dwarfed by him. The largest males can reach 80 kilograms, but not all sexually mature males are that big. Indeed, many local tribes maintain that there are two species of orangutans: big ones, likely to be on the ground, and regular ones, most often found in the trees. The late-nineteenth-century collector William Hornaday, following local Dayak lore, actually distinguished them as separate species, which he presumed to live side by side. His contemporary Odoardo Beccari wrote: "I do not think that any zoologist at the sight of two orangs of the same age, one with, and the other without cheek-expansions, would hesitate a moment in considering

them distinct species."[15] He himself, however, did not believe they were three separate species, but rather that they originated in different regions and subsequently mixed. Why this confusion?

When we call someone an adult, we mean sexually mature. But in many primates, there is a phase during which the males are able to mate successfully but have not yet acquired all the characteristics of full adulthood. In human men, for instance, musculature, beard growth, chest hair, and other male traits may continue to develop through the early to mid-twenties, for some five to ten years after sexual maturity, although this de-

An adolescent female (Yet, *left*) and a flanged male (Jon, *right*)

lay is highly variable. Similar variability is seen in many primates. Animals in this phase are called subadult, a bit of a misnomer because they are quite capable of siring offspring, and in fact often insist on trying (see Chapter 6). Nevertheless, the term has become so entrenched that it has stuck.

The strange thing about orangutan males is that they tend to remain stuck in subadulthood for quite some time—a true case of arrested development. Every sexually mature male starts out as a subadult, sexually mature but not of full body weight. Subadults typically have high foreheads and pretty beards and are of rather slender build, looking a bit like females. Then there are the truly adult males. They have broad moon-faces, the result of flabby flanges growing out of their cheeks like two halves of a dinner plate. This structure makes them look impressive, but we suspect it also helps to channel the energy of the long call in a particular direction. Being right near an orangutan giving a long call feels a bit like standing in front of the loudspeakers at a rock concert: these calls are loud and you feel it! A series of heavy exhalations produce a sequence of deep, booming sounds[16] that carry up to 1 kilometer in flat terrain, and much farther when the male is on a slope or a ridge. The long call is made possible by a big throat sack that is inflated for the purpose. Long shaggy hairs, especially

A subadult male *(left)* and a sexually mature male *(right)*

on their arms, enhance the visual effect. When they display in the trees, they seem to be wearing a hippie poncho and look much bigger than they really are.

Subadult males grow into adult males, but we're not sure whether all do, and they certainly may take their time, up to a quarter of a century, to begin the transition.[17] But when a male grows up, it is fast, although for the first year or so his long calls will be rather awkward-sounding. The riddle of the long and highly variable subadult phase has stood for decades, but in Chapter 7 we will have a crack at solving it.

Canopy Capers Right before I encountered my first wild orangutan, I saw something that puzzled me. It appeared that a highly localized storm was lashing out at the forest. Nothing of the sort was going on, of course: it was simply a large adult male orangutan coming in my direction. The first thing that struck me, after I had recovered from the shock of seeing this moon-faced red giant, was that he seemed so ridiculously out of place up in the trees. Why, I wondered, does he not come down to the ground? At the same time, however, he also seemed to be extremely adroit up there, as though he were canopy-surfing on a wave of bending trees.

These first impressions help us understand the morphology of the world's largest tree-living mammal, which has arboreal adaptation written all over it.

Most primates walk and sit on top of branches. They leap across gaps between canopies of different trees, propelling themselves with their strong hind legs and using their tails to keep their balance while in midair. Although apes may walk like monkeys when on sturdy horizontal branches, they are so much bigger that walking straight ahead and jumping across gaps as monkeys do would get them into trouble. Instead, they usually move around by resting their weight on multiple supports.[18] The technical term, quadrumanous scrambling, is quite apt because it is as if they have four hands, and all four limbs are mobile in all directions rather than sturdy. That means that they often hang below branches rather than sit on top of them, although much of the time they hang and stand at the same time. The orangutan is an extreme exponent of this "quadrumanous" syndrome, even as great apes go: their arms are fully 40 percent longer than their legs. Their hands and feet are very long, with curved fingers and toes, allowing them to grip branches with a hooklike hold. In effect, they have four hands, because their feet can grip just as securely as their hands. Their long arms can wrap around trunks while they climb up and down trees.

The "four-hands" technique enables orangutans to get to the thin, outer branches of tree crowns, where fruit is often concentrated: a hanging primate, especially if it can also hold on with its feet, can spread its weight over more branches and so exploit that outer envelope of the tree's canopy. By the same token, using multiple supports makes it easier to cross into neighboring trees, although smaller ape species, as well as young orangutans, can move below branches and propel themselves with their arms to swing into the next tree.

This anatomical dedication to life in the trees has its price: orangutans are clumsy walkers on the ground. They waddle a bit, curling their feet and planting their hands on the last digits rather than on their knuckles, as gorillas and chimpanzees do. Most wild orangutans rarely come to the ground, although some Bornean adult males, especially older ones, do much of their long-distance travel on the ground.

Long big toes and thumbs would be in the way and might even break when an animal is trying to grab a branch. Hence, these digits have moved up toward a safer position; the big toes have become short and stubby, and in some individuals they are even reduced to little stumps without nails. Of course, having short thumbs and very long fingers exerts a toll: orangutans cannot easily grip small objects and manipulate them delicately.

Instead, orangutans have come up with an unusual solution—they can manipulate objects with their mouths. Orangutans have unusually "dexterous" mouths, an ability they use to good effect when making and using tools (see Chapter 6). Where chimpanzees hold tools in a precision grip between thumb and index finger, orangutans do equally precise manipulations while holding tools in the mouth.

In their movements, adult orangutans in particular seem to be very deliberate, even sluggish. Compared with the traveling style of the gibbons, the forest's trapeze artists, the red ape's progress seems decidedly labored and inelegant. There is a good reason for this. They are far too large to leap into the next tree. Boisterous juveniles or adolescents sometimes get away with it, perhaps pretending to be gibbons for a day, but we have seen them crash-land because they misjudged the strength of the branch they landed on. Any larger animal trying to jump would more often than not break through his support and plunge to the ground.

The much smaller white-handed gibbons can afford to make giant leaps through the air.

Orangutans have evolved a unique way of crossing small canopy gaps without ever letting go of the trees. They swing and bend a tree on one side of the gap and reach to grab a tree on the other, then let go, but in the meantime always hold on to at least one tree with some extremity, usually two. They usually test the next branch or liana by pulling or putting some weight on it before letting go of the previous support. Slow and steady wins the race!

In spite of all these precautions, the large adults still fall occasionally. Arno, one of the largest males at Suaq, broke through his support at least once a day. (He was usually able to escape serious injury, however, because he would grab on to some other support before he hit the ground.) But animals in a hurry, as when they are being pursued, risk smashing to the ground and breaking bones. Indeed, a survey of museum skeletons found twice as many healed fractures in orangutan long bones as in chimpanzee bones, and even three times as many as in gorilla bones, exactly the order in which the species rely on trees to get around.[19]

Orangutan								*almost all time in trees*	
Chimpanzee								*some time in trees*	
Gorilla								*almost no time in trees*	
10	20	30	40	50	60	70	80	90	

% long bone fractures

This leads to an obvious question: Why are orangutans (still) so strictly arboreal? Even apart from falling, climbing around in trees is costly: hoisting up one's own weight is heavy lifting, especially for larger animals. As a kid I used to climb trees like a monkey (or rather an ape), but I have somewhat more trouble now following my own kids up there. It is true that orangutan food is found only in the trees, but forest chimps and gorillas travel on the ground and climb only those trees that promise good food. This way, they can cover a lot more ground on any given day, and even visit a lot more fruit trees (or, in the case of chimpanzee males, find a lot more females), without necessarily spending any more energy. The orangutan must have compelling reasons to be so assiduously arboreal.

Ease of locomotion is not a good reason. Clumsy they may be on the ground, but they still find it easier to walk on the ground than to climb:

ex-captive rehabilitants prefer being on the ground, even when they have mastered climbing and balancing on branches. They have to be chased up the trees many times a day to kick the habit.

A better answer is that a terrestrial habit must be a pretty lethal one for orangutans: the forest floor is a dangerous place. Wild orangutans, especially Sumatrans, are very reluctant to come to the ground. When they do so, to drink water or to pick up a fruit, they repeatedly look around very carefully before they come down and will rush straight up again at the slightest disturbance. Whenever they detect a predator on the ground, say a tiger or a clouded leopard, they throw well-aimed branches at it. They also make loud noises—such as kiss-squeaks, or guttural grumphs when really scared—to advertise how upset they are and warn every other orangutan in the vicinity.

Perhaps the presence of predators is not the whole story, however. Chimpanzees and gorillas face terrestrial predators (lions and especially leopards), yet they travel on the ground. However, the African apes travel mostly in parties rather than alone.[20] The irony is that in the habitat where orangutans are most likely to form travel parties, the ground may be unpleasant or impossible to walk on. In the swamps, where we find the highest orangutan densities, the forest floor may be covered with dense pan-

Sumatran tiger

dans (palm-like trees with very spiny leaves) or horrible rattans, or it may be very muddy—or worse, it may not be there at all, in flooded areas.

This devotion to arboreality, in combination with limited sociality (and these two are related, as we shall see), has created an unforeseen advantage. Wild orangutans appear to be in robust health. African apes are often plagued by respiratory infections and have serious parasite loads, at least enough to make it possible to study medicinal plant use in visibly sick animals. But orangutans rarely look sick and listless or stay on their nest for long during the day, although they may occasionally have diarrhea during the rainy season. Sneezing and coughing are passing conditions. The comparative study of great ape skeletons I mentioned earlier noted that orangutans may break more long bones, but they suffer much less from caries and other tooth trouble, from a variety of infectious diseases that leave their mark on bones, and from trauma to the head as a result of violent altercations with their brethren.[21]

There may be simple socioecological explanations for these differences between the apes. Contamination with parasites may be less of a worry for the orangutan. Especially in Sumatra, where they stay away from the ground, they should pick up fewer parasites: many intestinal worms and protozoans are transmitted through contact with feces or feces-contaminated soil. In some zoos, chimps make a habit of hurling the stuff at visitors that annoy them. They also readily chew on their own and others' output, but captive orangutans never eat, or even play with, feces. Instead, orangutans, when they come in contact with feces (from a baby, for example), wipe it off immediately and sometimes use tools such as leaves or sticks to do so (as do chimps, sometimes). Contamination from fellow orangutans is also less likely because permanent groupings are absent. Several infectious diseases simply cannot be maintained in populations of low sociality and density. (The only exception to this rule is human-induced: animals may get sick when their ranges are compressed and degraded. More on that in the Epilogue.)

Orangutans may have fewer respiratory infections because they are better at staying dry during rain and thus avoiding heat loss. They like to cover their head during rain with large leaves or with the funnel-like tops of branches with whorls of leaves concentrated at the end. When on their nest, they can build a solid waterproof cover. When they re-emerge afterwards, they are perfectly dry. Chimps and gorillas, by contrast, just seem to

A leak-proof roof atop an orangutan nest.

accept the rain and sit shivering, looking miserable, perhaps catching colds in the process. Sneezing and runny noses are common in the rainy season (of course, the "cold" comes from their fellow chimps and not from the rain, but loss of thermal balance may make it easier for the infection to take hold). It remains puzzling to me why the African great apes never figured out how to protect themselves from rain.

This, then, is the introduction to our main character. The orangutan is not nearly as fanciful as the earliest descriptions suggested—in fact, there is nothing too outlandish in its morphology at all. The real surprise lies in its behavior! By having stuck to the canopy when the other great apes left it, the orangutan may provide us with the best picture we have of the common ancestor of humans and the living great apes. The combination of large body size and arboreality made great apes what they are: animals with slow life history and high intelligence who substitute mental agility for athletic ability.

ORANGUTAN HEAVEN

4

When we discovered Suaq Balimbing, in early 1992, it was entirely by accident. It had been our mission to find a large area of alluvial forest, because that was the habitat where we knew we would find high orangutan densities. The intention was to find a complement to Ketambe, home of one of the longest-running orangutan studies so far and located in the wondrously productive Alas valley. Ketambe was established in 1971 by Herman Rijksen. When I first arrived there, in 1976, Ketambe lay in a large forested landscape of flat alluvial terraces of various ages hemmed in by steep mountainsides. Over the years, however, we saw more and more of the nearby valley-bottom forest disappear, and by the 1990s Ketambe had become a small peninsula of lowland forest in a sea of cultivation, too small and isolated to help illuminate the orangutan's still elusive social organization. The main focal animals at Ketambe disappeared from the study area from time to time, and researchers had also noted seasonal influxes of others,[1] making it impossible to figure out their social organization. What we needed to solve this puzzle was a large study site with high orangutan density so we could find and follow animals and map all their social contacts.

I had earlier been to the pleasant riverine forests along the upper reaches of the Krueng Lembang, a tiny river that in a mere 25 kilometers or so goes from tiny, rocky stream to a murky and meandering river that can't seem to find its way to the sea. At the time, these forests seemed to me to be the ideal study area, but by 1992 they had already become too disturbed by illegal logging to serve as a secure basis for fieldwork.

The station at Suaq at dusk

Facing page:
The station at Ketambe from the high opposite bank of the Alas River

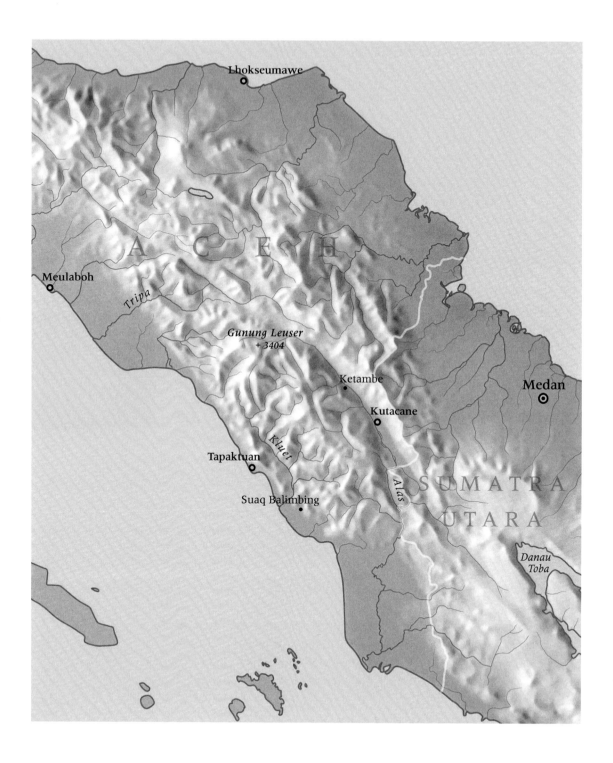

We were ready for the long and dreary march in the rain back to the coastal highway when Pak Amansurdin, the local head of the conservation service who accompanied us, had the idea to take us to Suaq. A few years before, he had built a simple guard post along the Lembang River, and he suggested that we spend the night there. It was getting dark, and we lost our way in the mud along the river, so we slept instead in a recently abandoned logging camp on the side of the river that was part of the logging concession (after removing

Our first trip to Suaq Balimbing: *(from left to right)* Thesi, Pak Amansurdin, Navi, Hasan Basri, Yus, Dolly Priatna, Azwar

a python lodging in the thatch above our heads). When we made our way to camp the next day, we were not pleased: the forest was extremely difficult to traverse. Just meters away from the dry riverbank, a backswamp began, where we had to find ways to get to the base of the next large tree or risk stepping into one of many treacherous channels, which were covered with a deceptively appealing green layer of a floating water plant. We hoped that the terrain would become drier inland, as it gradually gave way to the hills. No such luck, but we soon found that the swamp forest farther in from the river was not so bad to get through, and it had a relatively open canopy, giving us unimpeded views into the tree crowns. Best of all, we saw lots of nests. If we could find a way to get into it, this area would be a suitable study site. The concession road provided decent access, yet the study area was across the river and therefore inside the safety of the national park. Better still, the swamp seemed to stretch for kilometers toward the south and east, a large enough area to allow us to recognize communities if they existed.

We were of course not the first people to set foot there. Indeed, the site for the post, Suaq Balimbing, had been an overnight stop on the dugout trip from the coast to the upriver village of Pucuk Lembang, in the middle of one of the few extensive and reasonably fertile valleys in the region. In the Kluet language the word *Suaq* stands for oxbow lake, a good place to stop over and do some fishing for dinner. *Balimbing* refers to the small starfruit tree, no doubt planted here to provide refreshment to the weary traveler. We did not see any starfruit, but we did note a durian, the most highly prized fruit of Southeast Asia, and a kembodja, usually planted at gravesites. The guard post was not really used by the agency, but it provided wel-

A boardwalk through the backswamp

come shelter to a few hardy fishermen, for whom the swamp, the river, and the oxbows were a wonderful source of fish. Later, we got to know them much better, and some did odd jobs for us (and one of them became a valued field assistant). But at that time, all we knew of the fishermen were the messages they had scrawled onto the remaining walls. Some of the messages were astute local poetry ("a heartache is better than a tooth-ache"), but others suggested that the government take a hike and let the fishermen have a go at leveling the forest! This did not strike us as a very sustainable idea at the time, but the writing was on the wall. . . .

After we had made our decision to stay, Pak Poniran, then head of the Gunung Leuser National Park, proposed that we build a station on top of the small hill right next to the post. In February 1994 we proudly dedicated our little station in the swamp. My right-hand man, Yus, suggested that if we were to last more than a few months, we should build a few simple one-plank boardwalks through the backswamp. That turned out to be a stroke of genius, and we were able to establish a modest but adequate trail system. Observation conditions were ideal: the peat swamp forest is nice and open in most places.

With a few exceptions, the orangutans were easily habituated to our presence. No doubt the absence of hunting made our job easy. Most locals profess to be afraid of orangutans and to avoid them unless the apes raid their fruit trees. Adult males would come down, do a serious display, push over dead trees, throw down a branch or two, and then completely ignore us, unless we got too close to sexually attractive females, when they would chase us. Females would hide for a while, but when they noticed that nothing untoward happened to them, their anxiety would disappear. Sub-adult males, very brave when with females, would be skittish when alone, but even they gave up worrying about our presence. Generally, after a few days of following, we could begin data collection on any given individual. A large female without an infant, Afrika, was the exception. She would run for hours, making us criss-cross through the swamp and then run into the hills. We just gave up on her, but even she became less anxious as time went by and she noted that other orangutans were not nervous around us. In the end, we had named almost a hundred animals and had managed to collect decent focal data on 38 different individuals (not counting their de-pendents).

Our fieldwork consists of observations, nothing else. When we have found an animal, we follow it around and systematically record its activities, map its movements, and monitor all its associations and of course every social interaction it may have. This "focal animal" method, used widely by behavioral biologists,[2] allows for quantitative comparisons among individuals, among studies of the same species, and even among species.

Field primatologists face a conundrum. Legally, we are not allowed to conduct any experiments apart from simple ones that do not cause lasting aggravation to the subjects, such as playing back calls. Morally, most of us would not want to conduct experiments even if they were allowed. Still, as Yogi Berra once said, you can observe a lot just by watching—even when experiments are taboo, an entirely observational field study can still achieve much.

The individuals become so familiar they are like members of the family. In my dreams at night, I regularly had whole conversations with them, but during the day, in the field, we had to maintain our distance and tried not to interact. Sometimes that was hard. Young animals would try to involve us in their games or use us for target practice by dropping branches on us. The dense vegetation sometimes made it impossible for us to get out of the way, and then orangutans might pass within a few meters, generally ignoring us completely. Beth Fox, who spent two years at Suaq when she was a graduate student, once sat on a log, writing in her notebook, while following Arno. When she looked up, Arno towered right in front of her, studying the lines of her face, but he simply moved on when he had seen enough.

Arno

Of Apes and Fruits The love of forests is an acquired taste. We humans are savanna and seashore people, and most of us are uncomfortable when we find ourselves alone in a dense forest. Forests are indeed magical places, but for a biologist it is a good kind of magic. For those who grew up in northern temperate Europe, where the "forests" are structurally impoverished and contain a handful of tree species, the encounter with a tropical forest can be overwhelming. Many a levelheaded biologist is moved to lyricism upon first setting foot in a tropical forest.

Every field biologist gradually learns to recognize what makes a forest bountiful from the perspective of his or her favorite species. For the orangutan, perhaps surprisingly, it is not ease of travel. The cathedral-like dipterocarp forests that used to clothe Sundaland's hills have well-connected

canopies, yet orangutans are scarce there. On the other hand, some forests with very high densities have very irregular canopies, sewn together by lianas. Ketambe is such a place. These forests may look like a teenager's bedroom, but they have lots of food. In forests on dry land, the richer the soil and therefore the higher the forest's production of leaves, flowers, and fruit, the more irregular the canopy.[3] That is probably because trees on rich soils compete more for light than for nutrients and hence grow as fast as they can. What grows fast is not sturdy. Moreover, strangling figs tend to be most common on these rich soils as well. They start life up in the canopy, where there is plenty of light, but must send their roots down along the trunks of tall trees to reach water and nutrients. The richer the soil, the easier it is to develop a large spreading crown that deprives the host of light and smothers it. Such a parasitic relationship carries a price, however. Freestanding stranglers have broadly spreading crowns, and when a rainstorm catches them and they keel over, their fall creates big gaps in the canopy.

The messy canopy rule does not hold in swamps. At Suaq, the top canopy was rather flat, fairly open, and not too high; lianas were few. Peat swamps place upper bounds on how tall a tree can become without sagging. Yet, tree mortality rates in the swamp were rather low. When a tree started to topple, roots would not snap but move through the peat and stay attached, and if the tree got stuck somewhere, it would simply continue to grow.

Rather than structure, it is productivity that makes a good orangutan forest. We can recognize one by the never-ending drone of barbet calls, by the steamboat wing beats of hornbills, and by the whistled scales of the understory babblers. The noisier the forest, the better, unless the noise is the chirping of cicadas. Messy Ketambe and flat-canopied Suaq are noisy. We now know that the forest at Suaq is about as productive as that at Ketambe. Both are in the floodplain of a nutrient-rich river and are far

Opposite above:
An irregular forest canopy

Opposite below:
Strangling fig in dryland forest

Below:
The view across the flat-topped peat swamp, with the hills in the distance

Inside the transitional
peat swamp forest

more productive than most forests elsewhere. Suaq is in fact even better, because more of the production goes into fruit that birds and primates can eat: the kinds with soft, fleshy pulp, just like virtually all fruits domesticated by humans.

The main types of forest in the study area were riverine forest on the levee, the wet-and-dry backswamp forest behind it, the pleasant transitional swamp, which grades into peat swamp, and finally the hill forest. The transitional swamp was orangutan paradise, but each animal includes all forest types in its range.

What is so special about the transitional swamp? First of all, it is in the floodplain, and every flood brings in fresh nutrients. The Lembang, short as it is, comes from an area of mixed geology, including limestone peaks, and brings in more or less neutral water. By observing the swamp during floods, we could easily establish where the river influence stopped. Beyond that point, the understory is visibly different, several tree species drop out, and productivity declines.

Another feature that helps to make a forest productive for fruit-eating animals is lack of drastic seasonality in fruit abundance. Compared with the ubiquitous dryland forest surrounding them, swamps are much less seasonal. Virtually all trees in the swamp forest have bole climbers, flat vines seemingly glued to the trunk, a life form that is very sensitive to dry air. Humidity is high throughout the year, water is never limiting, and most months are pretty sunny. There is a steep rainfall gradient, with much more rain falling only a few kilometers farther inland where hillsides produce the rainfall that feeds the drier coastal plain.

We can add to this list the absence of mast fruiting—the synchronized fruiting of most trees in the forest once every few years. Masting is unique to Southeast Asia and is generally considered a result of the region's equitable climate: with trees producing a massive amount of fruit at the same time, the voracious seed predators are "swamped": so much fruit is produced in such a short period that the predators can't possibly eat them all, allowing some to escape and germinate. By its masting, the tree community creates starvation conditions for most of the time, and so keeps down the numbers of seed eaters. In more seasonal regions, the seed predators are kept in check by seasonal food scarcity. The masting strategy has important consequences: in the average Southeast Asian forest, fruit production is only about half what it is in tropical forests on the other continents,

Inside the hill forest

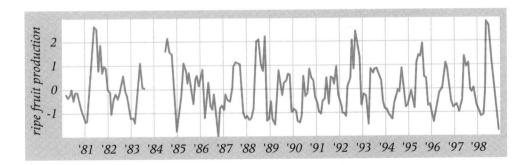

ripe fruit production

'81 '82 '83 '84 '85 '86 '87 '88 '89 '90 '91 '92 '93 '94 '95 '96 '97 '98

even though the production of foliage is pretty much the same. As a result of the years of bust, animal biomass in the region's forests is also far less than elsewhere. For primates, for instance, Southeast Asian forests have only about half the biomass found in African forests, where the primates are approximately the same size.[4] The good news for the orangutans is that in the swamp there is no need to swamp the seed predators on the forest floor: we did not succeed in catching any rats on the forest floor in the swamp, nor did we ever see any porcupines and even relatively few pigs (probably because of the difficulty of nesting).[5]

Incidentally, in habitats subject to masting, the occasional brief boom that punctures the long periods of scarcity is of course a bonanza for the consumers that do manage to hang in there. When a mast occurs, orangutans and other forest animals pig out, eating several times their regular amounts, and not surprisingly their reproduction is tied to masts in those habitats that are subject to masting.[6] Indeed, animals may come from far and wide; our swamp orangutans happily moved into the hills, where very few orangutans make their home, when the forests there exploded into a mast.

The most important factor for the high density of mawas at Suaq, perhaps, was chance: the high abundance of melaka.[7] Its fruit was by far the most common species in the orangutan's diet. Melaka was relatively common in the transitional swamp; most trees were quite large, and they could fruit at all times of the year. Most of the other trees also had edible parts, so virtually all the species provided something to the orangutans. That is rare. In a normal forest, species richness is much higher, but many species either do not contribute at all to the diet of orangutans, or do so once every few years.

A nineteen-year record of fruit production at Ketambe

The Swamp Ape In sum, the combination of high productivity, a large proportion of which is channeled into fruits eaten by orangutans, the reduced seasonality, and the absence of masting all conspire to make swamps premier orangutan habitat, richer than even the best dryland habitat. We found similar high orangutan densities in other swamps on Sumatra's west coast. These swamps and floodplain forests have the highest densities on record. Not all swamps are that rich, however. As the peat thickens, flooding is less likely to reach the active tree roots. In the end, the only source of new nutrients is rain, and the forest becomes less productive. On top of thick peat domes grows a pole forest—low, open, and full of pitcher plants. Even though some of the trees found there are the same as in the transitional swamp, they rarely fruit, and orangutan density goes down accordingly.

The map on page 47 shows the distribution of the orangutans in the Leuser region in northern Sumatra around 1992, before major changes in the land took place. The eastern boundaries of the distribution around Leuser are man-made, a product of poaching. The central empty areas are in the high-altitude zones, where productivity is too low to sustain more than wide-roaming stragglers. In addition to the swamps, there is one more region of extraordinarily high densities: the slopes of the Leuser massif, between the Alas River and the west coast. This may seem surprising, because elsewhere at these altitudes orangutans are very scarce, if they occur at all. The answer to the riddle is that the forests here have amazing densities of large strangling figs, the perfect staple food: bland, nontoxic, and abundant. The region to the east of the central rift valley, where the mountains are not as high and geologically different, is not as rich in food for orangutans. The lowlands and hills have more tall dipterocarp forests and fewer messy forests. North of Leuser, orangutans also do not reach into the highlands over 1,000 meters in altitude. The swamps, river valleys, and slopes of the Leuser massif, west of the central rift valley, are truly the world's best habitat for orangutans.

One striking aspect of orangutan ecology needs to be remarked upon. In each given type of habitat, Sumatran orangutans live at higher densities than Borneans. This contrast is probably not due to a difference between the orangutans. Again, productivity is the key. Botanically, Bornean forests are different in that dipterocarps—which are very interesting timber trees but, because they mast, not great staples—are much more common than in

Distribution of orangutans in the Leuser ecosystem, North Sumatra

Sumatra. Chemically, the leaves in these forests contain lower protein-to-fiber ratios, a good index of browse quality but also of productivity in general. These differences have their impact on the animals: Bornean gibbons eat more leaves and fewer insects and consistently less fruit than their Sumatran counterparts. Bornean macaques are also less insectivorous. On Sumatra primate biomass ranges from 700–1,000 kilograms per square kilometer in the lowlands of western Leuser to 200–400 kilograms per square kilometer in those of eastern Leuser. The values on Borneo tend

Rich volcanic soils support intensive agriculture in the Karo highlands near Lake Toba (North Sumatra).

to be at the lower end of this range. Orangutans, then, simply follow the general trend.

Humans, incidentally, are subject to the same differences. In 1980, rich, volcanic Java had a population density of 690 inhabitants per square kilometer, Sumatra had 59, and the Indonesian part of Borneo, Kalimantan, a mere 12.[8] According to the Soil Research Institute of Bogor, almost one-third of Borneo is unsuitable for agriculture, twice as much as in Sumatra.[9] These differences make one wonder what the orangutan density on Java was before humans settled the island.

If a species' density varies over a landscape, with some high-density zones acting as sources by exporting animals, and other marginal parts acting as sinks for these wanderers, we should look to the high-density areas to identify the key adaptations of that species. It is only a slight exaggeration to describe the orangutan as the swamp ape. During the Pleistocene glaciations, when most of the Sunda shelf was at or slightly above sea level, there must have been millions of hectares of various kinds of swamps. Perhaps there were areas like present-day Amazonian varzea: floodplain forests that were seasonally inundated. Perhaps there were peat swamps. Most orangutans must have lived in various swampy forests, and it is to such habitats that they are adapted. Under this scenario, the orangutan's extreme morphological adaptation to the trees becomes easier to understand: historically, most orangutans never had much dry land to walk on, even if they had wanted to.

I have dwelled on the productivity effect perhaps longer than most readers care, but productivity affects all aspects of orangutan intellectual and social life. As we shall see in the coming chapters, the richer the forest, the more exciting the orangutan social and cultural life.

ARBO-REALITY

To find mawas we slowly walk along the forest trails—which is easy at Suaq because fast travel is impossible in any event. At most intersections, we stop to catch our breath and to listen. One may think that we find them by looking for the stark red fur in the canopy. In fact, they hardly stand out against the sky: clumps of young leaves, big epiphytic ferns, and stout branches with reddish bark fool many a wanna-be orangutan observer. Instead we find most of our animals by listening carefully for the sounds that betray their presence—trees swishing back after an orangutan has let go of it, dead trunks being snapped to gain access to the termites, or, most commonly, fruit parts raining down when an animal is feasting up above.

Once an orangutan has been found, we follow it for as long as we can. That means getting up one or two hours before the crack of dawn the next day to make sure we get to the place where the animal made its nest the previous evening before it takes off. The trek to the nest in the dark is always the hardest part of the day, especially when there are wet tiger prints on the boardwalk. At that time the forest is still a hostile place, ruled by the creatures of the night, and we are reluctant to challenge their rule. Another unpleasant part of the day is the first plunge, when pristine socks and pants get their first baptism. The rest of the day, our feet alternate between dryish but burning, or wet but cool. (To combat the interesting variety of skin problems brought about by dampness we experimented with an equally diverse variety of treatments; most decided that petroleum jelly worked best, but some swore by gasoline.)

By the time our sweat has dried, we can enjoy the daily ritual of dawn. The first sounds will be those of the rhinoceros hornbill calling long-distance to its partner and of a white-handed gibbon starting up somewhere; then, slowly, some understory birds celebrate the victory over darkness. This is when we try to determine if the orangutan is still on its nest. Usually, at first light (in the canopy, on the forest floor it is still pretty dark), the animal will stir and sit up to relieve itself, aiming well so as to keep its nest clean. Active types will take off immediately and start to feed nearby. More lazy ones, especially flanged males, may doze off again for another hour or so. Sometimes, following orangutans is as exciting as watching paint dry.

Opposite:
Ripe figs are abundant and easy to process (*Ficus racemosa* at Ketambe)

Daily Life: All About Food The red apes spend the better part of their active day finding, processing, and eating food, so their daily routine is easily summarized: feed and travel, travel and feed. The details may seem arcane, even soporific, but the orangutan's exotic cuisine and its kitchen routines raise some very interesting questions. Consider Suaq's staple. If you spot an orangutan eating fruit in Suaq, chances are it is eating melaka: almost 40 percent of all time spent feeding on fruit is spent on this species. When the fruit is ripe—a pretty orange or red with a pleasant sweet-and-sour taste—everything is eaten. (Similarly, orangutans at Ketambe will simply pop ripe figs into their mouths and keep at it for hours, even days). But when the melaka fruit is half-ripe and yellow, it is cleanly separated into two halves and all the flesh is eaten and carefully scraped off the rind, which is then dropped. When the fruits are still green, they are taken in whole, chewed on for a while, and when the juice is sucked out the remainder is disgorged. One species of fruit, three ways of eating it.

Ripe melaka fruit

This example perfectly illustrates how orangutans exploit their environment. Unlike monkeys, orangutans, like people, lack anatomical specializations to deal with toxic or highly fibrous foods. The local people on both islands have noticed this, too, and turned it into a potentially life-saving rule: when you're in the forest and out of luck, you can always eat what an orangutan eats. The rule holds for no other species.

Unripe cemengang fruits are still closed *(above)*, but ripe ones open spontaneously *(center)*, exposing the seeds and the yellowish, razor-sharp whiskers in which they are embedded *(below)*.

Feeding should be a real challenge for great apes: there is plenty of toxic or fibrous plants that might be eaten, but very little of the highly digestible and chemically unadulterated food that great apes look for. How do they know what is edible, and how do they know how to process the food before it can safely or profitably be eaten? Orangutans are very versatile feeders who consume an enormous range of species, picking only the ripe fruit of one species but eating all stages of ripeness of another; ripping off the bark of one tree, nibbling on the leaves and shoots of this liana, and crunching the juicy storage bulbs of that epiphyte. Most animals rely on taste and consistency of food to determine what is edible, and many may also avoid foods that have made them sick on previous tastings. Such clues are not revealing enough, however, if an animal eats food that is hidden, such as seeds inside a fruit. Recognizing what is actually food is not that straightforward.

To illustrate the problem, consider cemengang (which is pronounced as "chimiŋùŋ"),[1] the tree with the large, woody capsules and the rich seeds we will see much more of in Chapter 8, on tool use. As the fruit ripens, the capsules split open along five preformed fissure lines to reveal brown arils. These seeds are not just edible; they are veritable calorie bombs containing almost 50 percent fat.[2] In this natural habitat without fast food, fat is a rare and eagerly harvested resource. Orangutans love these seeds—if they can get to them. The fat, of course, is intended to nourish the germinating seedling, helping it to get a head start on the competition. The tree is therefore not keen on having the seeds eaten and destroyed; the seeds are endowed with firm stalks and embedded in a mass of yellowish, razor-sharp hairs that easily, and en masse, pierce the skin of a nibbler upon contact. I learned this the hard way the first time I examined the fruit. I spent the rest of the afternoon removing the mass of broken hairs from my palms and fingers.

It took us a while to figure out who the invited diners are. These are hornbills, whose bills are obviously immune to the stinging hairs and who go for the small extra bags attached to the seeds toward the end of the season, when the cracks have widened and the seeds are clearly exposed. The bags contain a substance that tastes like pure cooking oil and is indeed nearly 90 percent fat. Although most of us do not fancy consuming this raw, hornbills have no problem doing so and ingest the seeds unharmed in the process, only to send them back to earth after an astonishingly fast throughput, on the order of 30 minutes. Orangutans love them, too.

Now imagine a naïve orangutan, ready to explore the world for its edible bounties. If her first attempt is an unpleasant experience, like mine was, she might avoid the tree forever after. And indeed, we know of several populations of orangutans where nobody ever so much as touches the cemengang fruits. But there are also places where some bold and brawny orangutans (mainly adult males) get access to the seeds by breaking off one valve and gingerly picking out one row of seeds. And then there are places, such as Suaq, where all local red apes feast for months because they do the same operation much more effectively by using tools (to be described in detail later). The moral of the story is that, since it is not always easy to know what can or cannot be eaten, the diets of different individuals or populations may vary.

Cemengang seeds, once fully ripe, have oily attachments.

There are many other examples of extractive foraging, prying edible items out of some matrix. Almost all of these items are not easily identified as food or, like the cemengang seeds, are protected from prying hands or beaks. To overcome plant defenses, orangutans have two major tactics at their disposal. The first is brute strength. As anybody who ever tried to hold on to an item that a small orangutan wanted knows, the red ape is as strong as a bear. And, much like bears, they get access to hidden foods by breaking away the casing around it: termite nests or the hives of stingless bees in tree trunks and branches. After the big branch is broken off, it is often dragged to a place where the animal can dismember the nest in comfort. Tearing the bark off tree limbs and carefully scraping off the wafer-thin layer of phloem, which may taste a bit like sweet coconut meat, may initially appear to be brute-force foraging in action. Yet, the bites are carefully placed to achieve the highest efficiency, and only a few tree species out of the many possible ones throughout the forest are selected for this treatment—raising the question how the mawas know which kinds of trees have the tasty inner bark.

A Bornean female orangutan debarks a pantung tree.

But as we saw with the cemengang fruits, brute strength may not be enough, at least not for the smaller members of the species. Where brawn fails, brains come to the rescue. For instance, detailed coordinated movements by both hands are needed to extricate heart of palms from the top of a small palm tree or the pith of palm fronds from another palm tree. More complicated separation procedures are also common. For instance, animals at Suaq, when eating kuli batu,[3] first separate the sap and flesh around the

Youngster picking some tidbit from her fur.

seeds and expectorate it out into the fur in a foamy mass, after which the seeds are crushed between the heavy molars and ingested. There must be something unappealing or downright poisonous about the flesh. The same technique is used on a range of other species at various field sites. Special tricks are also used to obtain insects. Ants either get sucked off the bark with the lips, scooped up in the fur and then picked off with the lips, or licked with the tongue. Sucking ants out of dead hollow branches is a common trick, but one female, Pelet, employed a variant where she blew on one side first to see if anybody was home.

Even in our swamp, fruit is not always abundant. The ability to solve technical challenges is especially useful when the easily harvested foods are scarce. When there is little to eat, orangutans often process consider-

Orangutans often chew on stems of vines, processing a few meters' worth at once, and then proceed to expectorate the chewed-up fibrous parts.

able amounts of fibrous green shoots of vines and creepers. They stuff meters of the stuff into their mouths until they are fully loaded up. Then they chew. And chew, and chew, until they have squeezed out all the juice and spit out the remainder, a so-called wadge. This is probably a smart way of dealing with so much indigestible fiber: get most of the edible material out of it and avoid having to carry around the ballast, so much dead weight taking up space for other foods.

A wadge

In all these cases, I can't help but wonder how the individual figured out these tricks. Some of it is learned socially, from mother or others, as we shall see in the next chapter, but clearly, even though it can sometimes be painful, exploration may also play a role: orangutans love to play with their food. The tendency to experiment with food to find ways of making it digestible comes naturally to them. Especially rehabilitants seem to be very methodical about these experiments: they may chew on some material for a long time, then push out the mash onto their protruding lower lip and peek at it with great interest. I suspect only orangutans can do this.

Rehabilitant orangutans are a great source of information on innovation. Rehabilitants are confiscated pets that are to be returned to the wild but are first quarantined and treated for possible diseases and then gradually re-acquainted with the forest. Here is what they do with mundane foods such as bananas: the mash of chewed up banana pulp is kept in the mouth for a long time and then regurgitated onto a nice flat surface, only to be slobbered up again, leaving the surface wet but totally clean. Some of them, when they are done with the banana pulp, will retrieve the peels that had been discarded earlier and go through the whole chew-and-look exercise again. The exact purposes of these routines remain opaque, but playing with food almost certainly leads to innovative ways of food processing. Remember that these rehabilitants are unlikely to have learned the techniques from anybody else: wild orangutans do not eat bananas, especially not the nice big ones produced by domestication and selection.

Most large animals are not feeding automata, programmed at birth to feed on a fixed set of foods that conform to a prescribed set of acceptable properties. Still, most of them have a limited bag of tricks. Even other primates tend to eat their food pretty much as they encounter it. Although they do extract—for instance, by unfurling curled-up leaves to find insects hiding there for the day—they do not really do much processing of their food before it is put into the mouth.

It is because of these striking differences that some theoreticians argue that orangutans and other great apes[4] use their considerable cognitive abilities to forage for foods that remain inaccessible to other species. Where the average consumer sees a homogeneous sea of inedible green, the discerning eye of the orangutan can recognize—and extricate—food. This tendency toward extractive foraging no doubt also has predisposed them to become tool users.[5]

Balancing Act Ripe fruits, when plentiful, make up the bulk of the orangutan's diet. They are usually good sources of energy but not of protein. Most primates find a way to balance their diet by adding young leaves or insects, both higher in proteins. But insects are small, and only smaller primates, usually well under 1 kilogram, tend to consume a large proportion of insects in their diet. Orangutans are a major exception, at least in Suaq: they spend some 15 percent of their daily feeding time feeding on insects, mainly ants and termites. The most plausible explanation for this anomaly is that insects are unusually abundant at Suaq and also occur in sizable accumulations, making harvesting relatively efficient. After all, there is no soil for social insects to nest in, leaving only the trees.

Most primates love to eat meat but rarely do because vertebrate animals are not easy to catch. Orangutans are no exception: they are too slow to hunt like chimps or baboons, but they can grab the unsuspecting slow loris that they chance upon while rummaging in liana tangles, the favorite diurnal hiding places of these small nocturnal primates. Snagging a loris is rare, occurring at only a few sites and among some individuals who seem to specialize in this tactic. At Ketambe, one female was responsible for most instances of slow loris feeding,[6] although several others also knew how to catch them. Such variability is the inevitable consequence of individuals having tastes acquired by experimentation and practice or by observing a small set of neighborly experts.

All these dietary elements need to be combined into a healthy and balanced diet, which implies some clever maneuvering. For instance, Arno

had a tendency during the cemengang season to spend a day or so eating cemengang in the deep swamp near the foot of the hill, and then to move back for one or two days to the transitional swamp, feasting on melaka and other fruits in season, only to return to cemengang feeding the next day. Females will spend some time searching for insects and eating some tender young foliage, no matter how much fruit there is.[7]

Suaq mawas rarely eat flowers.

Red Rovers: Dealing with Scarcity When a forest is more productive, the animals that live off that productivity can afford to be at higher density. Most of the time, these animals will also live in smaller ranges. It is one of those rules we take for granted, but it implies that the higher productivity is sufficiently regular in space and time that animals need to travel less far to find everything they need throughout the year. However, it need not be this way. Indeed, although the orangutans at Suaq lived at the highest known density, their home ranges were nevertheless much larger than any of the estimates on record. It is possible that the range sizes elsewhere are underestimated because animals may leave study areas unnoticed, but the difference is too large and consistent to be attributed entirely to artifact.

Why don't these orangutans follow the general rule? We discovered that all individuals at Suaq include pieces of all forest types within their ranges.[8] At Tanjung Puting on Borneo—likewise a patchwork of swamp and dryland forests—we see a similar pattern. Because so few tree species are found in this forest, most of which reach high density in only one or two of the many kinds of habitat we recognize, Suaq's mawas commute systematically among forest types depending on which major species is in fruiting season. Such movements are the first line of defense against local scarcity.

Most other study sites are on dry land, where the forests may not always be as productive but where tree diversity is very high and different forest types are close together. In the landscape typically inhabited by orangutans, streamside forest alternates with hills and ridges. That means that an animal seeking new foods outside its regular range is not very likely to find them. Of course, with so many species, all of them on slightly different schedules, chances are that something is fruiting nearby. The upshot is that individuals can get by in smaller areas. Given the lower productivity of the forest, those individuals would have to compete more if they all stayed in the same area, so they space out more and favor home ranges that overlap less than at Suaq. As a result, they run into fewer of their neighbors during the course of a year.

The wanderlust of Suaq mawas is not limited to the swamps. The hills are used very little in normal times. Their vegetation is luxuriant but fruit is scarce, and they have either a very low density of residents or no permanent residents at all. But when the hills come alive during a mast year, our orangutans are drawn to the slopes for a celebration of fruits they have not tasted for years. They even eat the fruits of dipterocarps in long sessions, usually followed by a drink of water; apparently, the turpentine that drips down their chins (and can be smelled on the forest floor forty meters below) makes them very thirsty. With the food supply guaranteed, swamp orangutans become adventurous and go deeper into the hills, keeping to ridges to avoid getting lost and behaving rather sheepishly when running into strangers, local residents or commuters like them, but from the swamps on the other side of the hills.[9]

A similar pattern is found at Ketambe, where some animals follow the predictable timing of fruit abundance from the river valley up the mountain slopes in an unvarying annual cycle. But, as in the swamp, there is some asymmetry in directions taken: the lowland residents tend to stay put, whereas the highlanders dare to come down in the time of fruit abundance, knowing they are more likely to be tolerated by well-fed locals.

Moving away does not help an orangutan when food is scarce throughout its range, so it must find other ways of dealing with scarcity. In most other areas, without access to a quilt of forest types nearby to maintain the food supply, the point of having to find other options is reached earlier. The best way to cope with scarcity in these areas is by staying put and making do with the so-called fallback foods.

Hungry orangutans turn to vegetables. They will endlessly chew on the fibrous tips of long, pandan-like lianas (known as *rotan tikus*), discarding

The two forms of keladi: thorny but edible *(left)*, and aromatic but inedible *(right)*

the wads of chewed-up fiber. There are also herbs, locally known as *keladi,* giant relatives of the jack-in-the-pulpit and closely related to the cultivated *talas.*[10] Of the two varieties at Suaq, the orangutans pick the tasty one, carefully eating around its thorny defenses, but eschew the one fortified with a strong, aromatic taste like sweet flag *(calamus).* Then there are palm hearts, the pith of rattans, and a large variety of young leaves and liana shoots.

A last resort is to feed on the thin, nutritious layer of phloem and cambium right under the outer bark of trees and lianas, through which sugars pass. It is hard work for a marginal gain. At many sites in Borneo, bark stripping is the major response to scarcity, but the mawas at Suaq rarely turn to this drastic alternative. When they do, paradoxically, one of the favorite trees is mempalam,[11] a member of the infamous Rengas family, whose sticky sap can cause skin rashes and swellings in people. Orangutans don't seem to have such sensitivities. The most commonly used tree for bark stripping is basung,[12] which has copious white latex and is a close relative of the undisputed favorite in much of Borneo.[13] Fig trees also secrete large amounts of white or yellow latex and are singled out where they are common (note, however, that it is the phloem and not the latex that the orangutans go for). Miraculously, the trees seem to withstand these onslaughts and soon cover the wounds with new bark.

Much lean-season food is not exactly nutritious, and animals visibly lose condition in such times. Babies whine, sometimes incessantly, perhaps reflecting natural selection's way of coaxing mothers to produce more milk. Yet these conditions are characteristically rare at Suaq. Compared with other study sites, the local mawas eat fewer vegetables and "bark." That is because they consume more fruit and especially far more insects; these insects are so rich in protein or fat that they are eaten all the time rather than just as a fallback food. Suaq orangutans are also more likely to chew leaves or shoots into a fibrous wad that is spat out later, rather than swallow the whole lot and have it occupy valuable gut space. The use of tools also guarantees that they eat more honey. And they do all this despite their higher density.

The data so far indicate that the orangutans on the two islands differ in diet. The Borneans eat somewhat less fruit overall and turn more to vegetable foods and tree sap, whereas the Sumatrans eat more insects. Other primates show very similar differences, which we think reflect differences in productivity. In environments with higher productivity, in other words, it is easier to maintain a mixed package of fruit, insects, and some foliage.

In the face of lower average productivity, Bornean orangutans may have evolved more thrifty genotypes, such that they respond to periods of high food abundance with more storage of energy in the form of fat than their Sumatran brethren. Cheryl Knott has shown that Bornean orangutans mobilize their reserves during the lean period that predictably follows in the wake of a masting event, by demonstrating the telltale signs of ketone bodies in their urine.[14] So far, Serge Wich failed to find the same phenomenon at Ketambe, in Sumatra. More so than other great apes, orangutans have a tendency to become obese in captivity, as noted by everyone who has ever tried to buy postcards of orangutans. It is a distinct possibility that Bornean populations, exposed to lower productivity, have a higher proportion of thrifty genotypes. Systematic comparisons are needed to test this idea.[15]

Till the Morning Comes After a hard day's work, the weary forager rests in a comfortable place: the nest. Great apes are the only animals that sleep in a bed that is made anew every day. In fact, they may make more than one nest a day. Especially mothers with young infants like to rest several times a day on a fresh nest; and kids make play nests when they are together. The big adult males often rest without bothering to make a nest; they just lay down on a big bough. But day nests are kid's play in comparison with the serious business of making a sturdy night nest.

That serious business starts with the selection of a proper location. Not all tree species have equal chances of having the dubious honor of being selected for nest building. The most preferred trees have a special architecture, with multiple horizontal branches coming off the main trunk and large, soft leaves. Other structural positions are also acceptable but less preferred. Also, orangutans like their nests to have a bit of a view, so it has to be near the top of the tree, but they also prefer to have some taller trees nearby to avoid getting too cold at night. And to top it off, it is nice if the tree has soft leaves that are not too big and has no nasty ants living in it.

The nest itself is supported by a few strong branches that are broken and then folded backward to create the basic platform. Shorter branches are then pushed into the platform or artfully woven into it. Finally, leafy twigs are added to make a soft mattress. This last phase is fun to watch, as

A treetop view of a freshly made nest.

it involves elegant wrist flicks, of which there may be several local variants, as we will see in Chapter 7. If rain threatens or has already begun, a detachable roof is added. When the nest is finished, the contented builder collapses onto it like a bag of potatoes, forward or backward. The owner usually ends up lying on its back, staring into space, but almost always holding onto a branch with one hand. Great apes really sleep on their nests; superior snoring often emanates from the treetops.

Night nests may take up to ten minutes to construct. Needless to say, they are amazingly sturdy. We have never seen a nest keel over or fall apart after an animal lies down in it (as can happen with the much flimsier day nests). The better-made nests can last for months, or well over a year where the wood is dense. It almost seems they are over-designed, because almost all of them are used only once, unless there is no other choice—probably an excellent way to avoid ectoparasites and the diseases they carry.

It must be a reassuring skill to have. All great apes possess it, and our remote ancestors must have made good use of it as well. When we are on expedition in some remote forest region, my companions build a camp every

night by cutting down some pole-sized trees and creating an open shelter. This may seem wasteful to those with temperate-zone temperaments, but in the tropical jungles these camps disappear fast. The orangutans are equally oblivious of any damage they might cause. Highly suitable nest trees that happen to grow near favorite fruit trees look decidedly tattered after orangutans have been camping out for a week or so.

Why is it that orangutans and other great apes build these sleeping plat-forms, whereas other primates don't? (Many prosimian primates, having retained many of the original characteristics shown by the early primates, build nests, but never on a daily basis. Their nests are of a different shape, more cave-like as opposed to the orangutan's platform.) Great apes lack the pieces of callus on their behinds that make it easy for monkeys and gibbons to sit down. Perhaps their short legs make it hard for them to sit upright, but because gibbons have short legs too, body size may be the determining factor. It may be hard to find a good place to sit down when you're as big as a human being. It is much more comfortable to take to one's bed.

When all is quiet, we mark the place with a removable flag. If we are lucky, there is still light left, but the Sumatran mawas tend to work harder than the Bornean ones and retire after dusk. (When animals eat lots of leaves and other fibrous materials, they may simply have filled their intestinal tracts to capacity and then must take a break.) We find our way to the nearest trail, leaving some flags in the dark to mark the route for the next morning. From there we head for the nearest boardwalk, our home away from home. It is just as dark as it was in the morning, but now the forest is ours, and we slug along without a care in the world, on our way to a bath and a meal.

The trek home gives us time to ponder our findings. We have seen that feeding is not just a matter of opening one's mouth at the right place and time. Some species may feed in this manner, perhaps rabbits and possums (although we may not do these critters full justice and underestimate their daily foraging challenges). Still, browsers and grazers can pretty much see all their food in front of them and rely on some simple rules to evaluate if their food is edible, and their young quickly forage as effectively as adults. Even omnivorous monkeys, although they do some extractive foraging, pretty much see all their food in front of them and need not rely on clues to find hidden food items. Moreover, their fruit is almost always directly eaten, not processed in various ways before the edible parts can be eaten. We will see in Chapter 7 that it takes orangutan youngsters many years to learn to forage properly.

It is probably not really surprising that there is a correlation between a species' intelligence and the complexity of its feeding niche. But what is more difficult to demonstrate is that the process of finding and processing food actually drove the evolution of intelligence, that feeding challenges were its evolutionary pacemakers. In Chapter 8 we will look elsewhere for the evolutionary drivers of intelligence, but our observations at Suaq point to the critical importance of intelligent foraging for the survival of wild orangutans.

PARTY ON (AND OFF)

6

Walk into your average Bornean rain forest. The orangutans you find there are reclusive, spending at most some 5 percent of their time in association with others. Interactions are usually for such short periods that some researchers felt the need to test whether these contacts reflected tendencies to come together or were what might be expected when animals roam around randomly and bump into each other.[1] The term *solitary* is fitting.

Now move to Ketambe, in Sumatra's rift valley under the shadow of the Leuser massif. Here we see a lot more grouping, but we must be careful with our interpretation. It is possible that orangutans in Ketambe are simply brought together by the abundance of massive strangling figs, in which they may spend days eating: "groups" here may be like meetings in a massive student cafeteria—just because you eat at the same table does not mean you're friends. More convincing evidence for grouping are the travel bands, animals that travel through the forest together from fruit tree to fruit tree. These require active coordination, an active desire to stay in contact.[2]

Finally, visit Suaq Balimbing, in the coastal swamps of northwest Sumatra. Suaq mawas love company. Their parties do not happen by accident. Feeding time per tree is low, so association is not likely to come about passively by meeting in the same fruit tree. Instead, animals travel together between food patches, in various combinations, coordinating their movements so as to stay together. Their time spent in company is about the same as it is in Ketambe, but party sizes are bigger. On average, a Suaq orangutan is in the company of one other independent individual. Not surprisingly,

Two females with infants share a tasty termite branch.

the animals are friendlier: they spend far more time together (within a distance of ten meters) and can often be seen to share food, something you would have to wait a long time to see elsewhere.[3]

These vignettes illustrate that orangutans vary quite a bit in how solitary they are. Borneans are on the whole much more solitary and much less gregarious than their Sumatran counterparts. But the opposite of *solitary* is *gregarious* (group-living), not *social*. The Bornean animals are every bit as social: active avoidance is also social behavior. For even at the sites where animals are the most solitary, association patterns are far from random: flanged males will never associate peacefully whereas newly independent youngsters at the same site seek out parties whenever they can.[4] What is different between the sites, and perhaps the islands in general, is the ease with which animals can mingle. And where animals can spend much time together, they are definitely more *sociable* (i.e., socially tolerant and inclined to share food), even if they are not necessarily more *social*.

This kind of flexible grouping system is known in the trade as fission-fusion sociality: rather than staying together in the same group all the time, animals come together and go separate ways on a regular basis. In other primate species, the animals engaging in similar ever-changing associations are organized in distinct communities. The members of such a community are rarely seen all together, and in fact some may never show up in the same party, but their network of social contacts is clearly distinct from other networks. Whether communities characterize fission-fusion sociality among orangutans is one of the questions we aim to answer in this chapter. But first, we must turn to more immediate questions raised by our comparison of behavior across the orangutan's range. First, how do we explain the variation between sites; and second, why do orangutans travel together in the first place?

The answer to the first question is not very romantic: food. The orangutan is the largest arboreal mammal; it blows lots of calories simply by climbing around in the trees. This bulky animal with its expensive life style needs a lot of food, yet it is not a bulk feeder like the zebra. Instead, it needs fine foods that are thinly distributed or have to be obtained through hard work. We should therefore expect a clear relationship between the abundance of readily available calories—ripe fruit—and party sizes in orangutans. If animals strive for a particular net intake, they can afford to spend more energy on a given day when food is abundant and crude energy intake can easily be increased. If this is what they do, the higher association levels at the Sumatran sites should reflect higher food abundance, and therefore lower feeding competition. There is also some effect of food abundance within a site over time, but perhaps less than expected. We will examine why this is so after considering the next question.

Vertical climbing is hard work.

If this reasoning is too prosaic, consider rehabilitant juvenile orangutans in forest conditions. They are well fed, of course, and frolic in the forest all the time, playing or just hanging out together. The rule underlying their behavior is simple: play all the time, unless you are really hungry and need to find food. This is an example of an adaptive scarcity rule. Their forest brethren follow it too, except that they need to go after food and can't afford to play most of the time. The rule is adaptive, because it allows the animal to get enough of a scarce but critical resource. In many places, meeting suitable playmates when you're not busy looking for food is so rare that if it happens, you go for it. (It is exactly the kind of scarcity rule that

gets us humans into trouble: sugar, fat, salt all used to be encountered so rarely that they might well limit growth and reproduction.)[5] As the rehabilitants become adolescents, the rule still applies, except that sex replaces play.

Turning to the second question, we must ask what the animals get out of getting together. Generally speaking, among primates active during the day and large enough to evade their predators, grouping provides benefits against the threat posed by predators. They reduce the risk of capture by sharing the demands of vigilance and by communicating rapidly through alarm calls; if necessary, they may employ some form of communal defense or mobbing, usually led by the more daring adult males. Living in areas with many potential predators, then, favors living in groups. But group living comes at a price. Transmission of parasites and disease is easier, and living together inevitably forces animals into direct or indirect competition over food. Hence, the poorer the habitat, the smaller the groups. An animal can compensate behaviorally for living in a small group, and so keep its predation risk low, but it must accept lower food intake as part of the bargain. If productivity gets even lower, group-living species won't be able to live at the site.

Orangutans, provided they stay in the trees, have few natural predators. Youngsters are vulnerable. At Ketambe, some ex-captive orphans were lost to tigers, because they have a tendency to play around on the ground, and some fell prey to the clouded leopard, an agile, medium-sized canopy cat.[6] Mothers take no chances, though. Clouded leopards hunt especially at night (in Southeast Asia, the smaller the cat, the more it concentrates its activity during the night).[7] Females with infants tend to build their night nests farther away from the last fruit tree they ate in that day than do other classes of orangutans.[8] We suspect that the clouded leopards concentrate their prey search at the hot spots of nightlife, and in the forest those are trees with an attractive fruit crop. Mothers do not want a clouded leopard to come across their nest at night and so build their nests in more quiet places. The bottom line is that orangutans do not need to form groups just to stay alive, as other primates must.

So why do they still get together? Obviously, the most compelling reason for committed loners to become intimate is to mate. But we also see another major context for party formation, which can be summed up as the crèche. We will examine these contexts in turn, but we could determine the likely benefits by checking out patterns in party composition. We were lucky that in the main study area at Suaq Balimbing, the females were ready to conceive again more or less at the same time. That means we witnessed about one-and-a-half years of sex, detailed below, followed by a few quiet years when mothers took care of new babies. The main association patterns switched from being mainly sexual to being mainly maternal (many of the sexually active males had gone off to greener pastures by then).[9]

Party Schools Mothers with babies are generally of no interest to males hell-bent on mating. In most places in Borneo, a mother's life is lonely. With food on her mind, mom is in no mood to socialize, except when the tedium is punctuated by the rare mast fruiting. At that time, though, she's got both food and sex on her mind, and socialization is largely of the mating variety. In Borneo, births tend to follow masts,[10] although in richer Sumatra this trend is not found.

When enough food is available, as at Suaq, mothers too will gather. Their children will play together. Indeed, when mothers meet, it is the youngsters who show the greatest interest in making contact, running ahead. When the mothers are not real friends and at least one of them is nervous about the contact, it is the kids who force the issue. The females may sit tens of meters apart, casting the famous sideways glance,[11] while the kids are wrestling somewhere in the middle. When the going is good, though, many Suaq females gladly hang out together, creating a play school for their children.

Social play shows interesting sex differences. Male immatures play more roughly than females, preferring chasing and wrestling. Female play is far less intense: they get entangled as much as the males do but do not go in for the serious wrestling and mock biting, and they rarely if ever chase. Females therefore often try to disengage themselves from playing with males or avoid them altogether. The most successful mixed-sex play pairs are those where the female is a lot bigger than the male.

Playing is serious fun, not entirely devoid of risk. The partners hang upside down, and sometimes one of them holds on to nothing but a playmate, dangling in midair—not the position an orangutan usually considers ideal. It is of course much safer to play on a nest. Sometimes youngsters build nests when they meet just to play on them.

Another favorite activity by youngsters in parties is peering. Youngsters creep up to adults who do what they consider interesting things, usually some kind of foraging, and often end up cheek-to-cheek with the forager. The remarkable thing is how tolerant the older animals are of this uninvited intimacy, even those that we think are not all that familiar with the little voyeurs.

Perhaps these opportunities for watching what new skills others may have picked up also explain why adolescents spend so much time in association: as we shall see in Chapter 9, they are sponges soaking up others' knowledge. That the chance of learning novel skills underlies the friendly camaraderie displayed at Suaq is supported by observations of unkind reactions. Sometimes, older females do chase adolescents: they have little to learn from these greenhorns.

Females without babies may join play-school parties for the same reason. Even they might learn a trick or two from others. One day, Tevi and Ani were foraging together in the hills next to the swamp. Tevi had been watching Ani extract the pith of a thorny ground palm, which is a pretty complex activity, but initially seemed to have no interest in eating any of it herself. It became clear she was very interested in it when, once Ani had procured a nice piece, she tried to scrounge it, and Ani immediately let her have some (even though Ani was dominant to Tevi). In other words, Tevi did not know how to extract the pith, perhaps because she rarely came into the hills and even more rarely came so close to the ground.

A juvenile male orangutan peers at a subadult male extracting ants from hollow twigs.

Orangutan Romance No other word conjures up such a mix of horror and ecstasy as the short and simple *sex*. Humans have a very schizophrenic attitude toward it, but animals, being amoral, are not supposed to. Among orangutans, sex is more complicated than the frenzied, brief coupling seen in many animals. True, they are no bonobos, the African apes that seem so obsessed with sex that it permeates their whole social life.[12] Still, orangutans put on a nice show: females tend to get pregnant after half a year, but usually a lot longer, of frequent mating.

Our friend Daniel Saputra recalls that in the puritanical Islamic society

A two-year-old infant orangutan stimulates herself on her mother's head *(above)*; an ex-captive female uses a dildo to do the same *(below)*.

of Tapaktuan, on Sumatra's west coast, the town's local youngsters received from a couple of young captive orangutans what their schoolteachers did not give them: sex education. Sexual interest awakens early in orangutans. We have seen small infants engage in genital stimulation on their mother's heads and older male infants practice the art of intercourse on their mothers, who seem to be only mildly annoyed. Adolescent rehabilitant apes explore their sexuality with abandon, finding numerous ways, including the use of tools, to satisfy their urges single-handedly.[13]

In the wild, sex among adults is not so wild, but it is still unusual enough to warrant detailed examination. It certainly is a protracted process. Females even continue to mate while pregnant, until the signs of pregnancy, swollen labia, begin to show. Adolescent females do a lot of cavorting with very young, not so young, and no longer young subadult males, and perhaps the occasional low-ranking flanged male. Parous females (those who have given birth before) attract more interest from subadult males as their babies get older and more independent, with a rather dramatic increase when the infant is around 6 years old. We suspect this is because their ovaries are gradually waking up and estrogens begin to circulate, making them smell better to males, who come to visit and literally sniff out the females. But then something unexpected happens. When the females seem to get really interested in sex, instead of waiting for males to come and find them, they become restless, traveling more widely, and look to hook up with the locally dominant flanged male. In Suaq this is Arno. Arno regularly announces his whereabouts, and his travel direction, with the loud booming vocalizations known as long calls.

Arno and other dominant males have a habit of long calling when they run into a female who looks, or perhaps smells, attractive. If it is his lucky day, she will come running to him. Once associated, the estrous females actively maintain their association with the dominant male. He charges around, going after each long call that is deemed too close and chasing each subadult male not keeping a respectful distance. The females appear to love it.

The interest he takes in mating with a female varies with her age. If a young female who has never given birth yet wants to mate with the irresistibly attractive big, flanged dominant male, she's got some convincing to do. Indeed, she's got work to do: approach the bored-looking male and mount him while he is leaning back, achieve intromission, and thrust hard on him to get him to ejaculate. On the other hand, Arno would be very interested in an older, more experienced female. With her he would gladly mate, quite literally bubbling with excitement (i.e., rhythmically produce the bubble portion of his long call). This indifference to young females, however mysterious to the casual human observer, may in fact be adaptive: these females go through a period of at least two years when they are sexually active but unlikely to conceive, and the male probably does best by playing coy until they show clear signs of ovarian activity. But when a fully mature female is interested, the male means business. Such matings have a good chance of resulting in fertilization.

The strong preference for mating with the locally dominant male is accompanied by antipathy to mating with others. Preferences and antipathies are two sides of the same coin. Preferentially mating with the dominant means avoidance of the other males, mainly the nimbler subadult males. Harassment by males is found in many Old World primate species (being rare to absent in the other major primate lineages: New World monkeys and prosimians),[14] but it is not common in the majority of species. The most extreme form of harassment is probably suffered by female orangutans: at some sites, the lion's share of copulations is forced.

It would not be a forced mating if the female did not put up resistance. In fact, this resistance can be fierce. Sometimes the grappling and the biting and tugging goes on for half an hour, but almost always when the male is bigger and stronger he perseveres by biting her to keep her still in place. The female's previous offspring, usually fairly large by the time the males become interested in their mothers, try to do their bit by getting in the way and trying to push the male away when they are nearby (this happens about one in every six male attempts at forcing themselves on the female). But the male can usu-

Mating among adolescents tends to be a relaxed affair.

ally shove the infant aside, if need be after hitting or biting it. Nonetheless, some attempts do not quite succeed, sometimes because the female's screaming and grunting attracts help in the form of an adult male, because the female struggles free and takes off, or because the rapist is less adept and his ejaculation misses the target. In Sumatra, the culprits are mainly subadult males, but in Borneo, fully flanged adult males also force mating quite commonly.[15] The thing all of these males have in common is that none of them is the dominant male in the area.

The higher incidence of forced matings in Borneo is almost certainly due to the short duration of voluntary consortships with the local dominant male in Borneo. The duration of such consortships is usually measured in hours. In Sumatra, where associations are more easily maintained, they can last for weeks. During that time, there is only very limited opportunity for the nonpreferred males to barge in, and females engage mainly in voluntary matings.[16] Hence, when all is tallied, the percentage of forced matings in Sumatra is less than half of what it is in Borneo.[17]

For those forced to watch the events from the ground, it is very difficult to avoid the loaded term *rape* for what they see and not to stand in judgment on the males. I remember following a subadult male who was traveling alone after he had given up shadowing a party of subadults that followed a consorting adult male and a young female. He knew something I did not, because not long after I heard the unmistakable pig-grunts of a female being "raped" by another male. He hurried over to the scene and chased the rapist away. Before long his true motive became apparent and I dispelled all notions of gallant knights and damsels in distress: he repeated the act. Animals have no moral qualms about their behavior, as far as we can tell.

That females really mean it when they announce their displeasure at mating with these local punks was brought home to us when we followed Ani, around the time she was just beginning to become attractive to males (her infant was about six years old at the time). The most unpopular subadult male in the neighborhood, Dio, began to stalk her, and there was no escaping him. It was not that Ani did not try, but whenever she tried to run away from him, he would cut off her escape route. After a few hours of frustration, Ani built a nest in the top of a tree and lay down on it. For some strange reason, Dio could do nothing about that and could not forcefully mate her on the nest: the nest became her social refuge (a strategy also observed in chimpanzees). He just sat there, making a whimper face, stretching out his hand to her in a begging gesture whenever she happened to glance in his direction. Ani just turned her head and continued to lie on her nest for over two long days. Dio tenaciously hovered around, nibbling on this and feeding on that, eating stuff we never saw orangutans eat before or since, but never letting her out of his sight. Once we heard a long call not too far away. Ani shot up and tore off in its direction, but Dio intercepted her and Ani hurried back to the relative safety of her nest. We do not know how this story ended, because when we came back to the nest early the third morning, they were both gone. We like to think that Ani had successfully sneaked away in the heat of the night, because when we found her again a few days later she was alone.

Ani rests safely on her nest.

At Suaq, where long consortships with the local dominant are common, all manner of males are attracted and aggregate around the paired female and flanged male. And when more than one female is ready to mate with the boss, they all converge on him. The bizarre party travels through the forest together, with the dominant flanged male in the lead, going after long calls by real or imaginary rivals. Arno simply will not tolerate any other long-calling males in the vicinity. The hapless male that happens to be caught by Arno will drop out of the tree and run away on the ground in blind panic. Indeed, the other flanged males pretty much avoid the general area where the dominant male is.

The females follow close behind, because they would otherwise be intercepted by a horde of eager subadult males making up the rear. These males can afford to stay in the race because they can flee faster through the trees than the heavy flanged male can chase them.

During the height of the period of debauchery, we had a large party of about 15 animals (counting several infants who were all at the age that they travel independently). Its composition varied somewhat over time, but it cruised in and out of the study area over a period that lasted some three weeks.

Toward the evening, without fail the same bizarre spectacle would unfold. The subadult males who had hung back all day would become increasingly reckless in attempts to satisfy their desires. Perhaps they were frustrated that yet another day went by without any action, perhaps they sensed that the old man was getting tired, or perhaps they simply felt that the nighttime is the right time. Whatever the reason, the females now had to stay really close to the adult male if they did not want to get attacked and raped. The boss, in the meantime, remained alert. When in consort with a single female he would invariably wait to build his nest until after the female was well on her way to build hers. Moreover, he would always build it right below hers, to make sure none of the upstart suitors found his way to her nest in the dark. In the larger groups, we could not figure out exactly who built their nests where because, unfortunately, all the excitement would keep everybody awake until well after dark. We would see only black shapes in dark, waving tree crowns. We don't know much about what happened at night after they finally bedded down, but we have seen moving shadows and heard the accompanying noises indicating coupling, so we suspect the action lasted deep into the night.

Making Sense of Orangutan Sex How are we to make sense of these bizarre behaviors? The root cause, obviously, is the female preference for mating with the local dominant. Female mating preferences are almost universal among animals. Being the slower-breeding sex, females do not improve their fitness by mating with more mates, but instead may get the most out of each reproductive event by maximizing the quality of their mate. Red ape females put only a few infants into this world over a lifetime and should, of course, try to give those precious few the best possible endowment. The female's benefit to careful mate choice might therefore be genetic. She should above all avoid mating with male relatives because the resulting offspring, being more homozygous, is much more likely to die or to remain stunted. In orangutans, however, as in most other mammals, the risk of inbreeding is low because males tend to move away from their natal area and will rarely encounter their female relatives once they are sexually mature.

Males may also vary in their genetic quality in a more general sense, in that they vary in the number of genes conveying resistance against currently prevalent diseases or increasing growth on local diets, and so on. These males will be healthier, bigger, and stronger for their age, and therefore they are likely to end up as the dominant males in the population. In turn, females will usually acquire the best genes for their progeny by preferentially mating with dominant males. This argument would explain the preference for flanged adult males, who have all passed some test, but it does not explain why flanged males have to resort to forced matings when

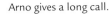
Arno gives a long call.

they are not the local dominant. Nor does it explain the striking observation at Ketambe that the females immediately switched allegiance to the challenger when he defeated the resident flanged male, who had been dominant for many years.[18] Before the takeover, only females with weaned infants associated with the male who would soon challenge; after the takeover all sexually active females associated with him. Not only was the losing male shunned by the females, he also pretty much stopped his long calling.

Other known benefits from mate choice are more direct. For instance, a female may acquire access to scarce resources controlled by the male, or the male may provide assistance in raising the young. But these kinds of advantages do not apply among orangutans, where males are not territorial and don't participate at all in infant care. The only other plausible gain to females is protection. Beth Fox has shown at Suaq that females consorting with the dominant male were less likely to be raped, although the attention bestowed on her by other males is certainly not less.[19] Not that the dominant male worked up a sweat to protect the female—it happens entirely by default, because he keeps the other males away or attacks them when they are trying to force themselves upon the female. Nonetheless, a female is better off when in his presence, if we may assume that associating with him does not cost her too much in reduced food intake.

The problem with this explanation is that it is circular: the females need this protection exactly because they resist the subadult suitors. Why not let them mate? The risk of injury may be small, but it would be smaller if she just gave in without a fight. Moreover, it is energetically costly: her regular activity schedule is thoroughly disrupted by the constant nagging of the unwelcome suitor. Ani's three-day ordeal shows that females are serious about their aversion to mating with nondominant local males. They must be gaining something critical from consorting exclusively with dominant males.

The critical benefit may well be protection from infanticide. Because the argument is complex and for orangutans as yet incomplete, let us first explore the argument in detail for primates in general. In many primate species, males protect infants they may have sired. Primate females, along with those of a few other mammalian lineages, are uniquely vulnerable to a particularly nasty form of male harassment: infanticide. In these lineages, a baby has a very long period of utter dependence, and during this time the mother cannot conceive again.[20] However, females will return to estrus quickly if they have lost their dependent young (something also known to happen in orangutans).[21] They return to estrus whether the infant's death is accidental or not.

Suppose a male stranger encounters a female whom he has never had a chance to mate with (and therefore is certainly not her baby's father). If he manages to kill her child, she soon would become ready to conceive again. If the killer can then sire the next child, by the cruel but elegant logic of natural selection, he gains in fitness (unless the act of killing is dangerous for him), and any genes that increase the likelihood of such acts in the proper circumstances will spread. We are not assuming that males are aware of these benefits, but simply that they have evolved tendencies to attack infants in a very restricted set of circumstances. By the same cruel logic, incidentally, there is no reason for the female to be vengeful and refuse to mate with him. And these males turn out to be very protective of their own children, an indication that infanticide is not the act only of aberrant individuals. Indeed, observations on scores of primate species—and a few carnivores, such as lions, some dolphins, and a few rodents—have provided abundant support for this seemingly brutal argument.[22]

Females may be vulnerable, but that does not mean that they lose most of their babies to infanticide. They have their countermeasures. A major defense is social. We now think that the typical primate tendency to live in groups in which both males and females live together year-round—uncommon among mammals generally—is a response to this vulnerability.[23] Mothers have an interest in seeing their child survive, but so do fathers. Males that were successful at mating may do best to stick around so as to be able to protect the infants in case of attacks by new males. In orangutans, permanent association is not possible, but we will see that there is nonetheless some evidence of protective association.

A second countermeasure involves sex. Here is the female's problem. Males should never kill their own infants. If a female can mate with a male, he is unlikely to attack any infant born some time after their intercourse. Even if he is not quite sure, it turns out that he is better off (in terms of fitness) leaving the kid alone.[24] But not all males would be equally menacing: most dangerous are the ones who stand to gain from killing the infant. And those are the ones who will gain some degree of exclusive sexual access to the female following the infanticide.

There are two main classes of dangerous males when it comes to infanticide. First, new males may show up out of nowhere and claim the dominant's throne: they are a real threat, because the option of preventive sex was not available to the females. To deal with them, females need to rely on the protective services of their offspring's likely sire. Hence, where dominant strangers occasionally show up, it is imperative to mate with the strongest local male and to mate with him often enough to make him willing to take risks in defense of the offspring.[25] Even if the new male can defeat the old dominant, the latter is usually still powerful enough to discourage the new leader from attacking the infants: infanticide is most likely when the old dominant has disappeared or is disabled.[26]

Unfamiliar flanged males are one class of dangerous males.

The second class of dangerous males are those younger local males that have grown strong enough to challenge the local dominant in the period between mating and the weaning of the infant. It is important for a female to recognize these future winners. If possible, she should also mate with them. There is no real need to mate with any of the other males.

Of course, all of this is more easily said than done. The female must somehow make sure the dominant male is willing to defend the baby, while at the same time making sure the possible future dominants will not harm it when they become dominant. The female must work hard to mate with the males in the right mix; when she fails, infanticide is more likely.[27] This problem is exacerbated because the dominant male's optimum paternity chances differ from the female's optimum. For him it is best to be certain that he has sired an infant, whereas the female should prefer to reserve some likelihood for the promising up-and-coming males.[28] By this reasoning, females should engage in highly visible couplings with dominants, but try to escape his coercive mate guarding to engage in secret trysts with chosen subordinates. This argument would suggest that there is much more to sex than mere reproduction, although, as with the infanticidal male, we do not need to assume any conscious deliberation on the part of the scheming female.

Does this general idea, which applies to many primate species, also work for orangutans? Several pieces of the puzzle fit. The potential for infanticide exists because infants are dependent for a very long time (see Chapter 7), and males who succeed in beating the local dominant do settle and so reliably encounter females in their new dominions. So, despite the absence of direct observations of infanticide by orangutan males, the potential is there. Do we see the expected female responses?

We will review the social organization of orangutans below, but we have learned that females maintain some loose association with the local dominants through their long calls and can therefore turn to him in moments of danger. There is also more direct evidence. Playback experiments by Roberto Delgado suggest that females with infants who hear the long calls of strange males get very upset. Their babies, when they are away from mom, run back in panic. Sometimes, mothers with babies clinging to them take flight in the opposite direction from where the calls emanated. By the way, when they hear a long call by a local resident male, they hardly bat an eyelid. Why be afraid of a strange male if he may carry superb genes?

Infanticide avoidance may even explain why orangutan females are so concerned to avoid mating with the nondominant males. In most primate species, the dominant male tries to monopolize matings with receptive females. Those females, however, actively seek out copulations with many males.[29] But what looks like a mating orgy may not be random: the female mainly targets males that may become dominant in the near future. There is nothing to be gained from mating with those too young to become dominant during the coming baby's dependency period or too old to still harbor such aspirations. Indeed, there is a potential risk attached to mating with these males, and this risk is all the more serious in a dispersed society like that of the orangutan. The female may need the protective services of the local dominant, and if he senses that she has mated with too many other males, he may not feel compelled to offer any protection. Thus, in orangutans, because males live for decades and turnover of dominants is bound to be low, only some males may have a chance of beating the dominant.

Females should resist matings by all those unlikely to become dominant in the near future, but not by those few who might break through to "flangehood" and local dominance in the coming years. The observations we have are not inconsistent with this interpretation. At Suaq, some of the largest subadult males could mate without meeting resistance (although it might be that the females gave up before trying). More strikingly, at Ketambe, some infants were conceived in consorts with local subadult males who later did become flanged.[30]

The same argument would also make sense of a particularly puzzling aspect of the forced matings. Why, in a semi-solitary species, would female resistance be so tumultuous, if it were not to attract others to the scene, or at least to inform these others that she is not mating voluntarily? Even if she cannot prevent the mating, the dominant male may be alerted and she may be able to initiate a lengthy consortship with him. At the very least, he may come and reassure himself that the female's ovarian state was not that exciting after all, suggesting no threat to his paternity. This sounds as though there is some Machiavellian element to the female's emotional outpouring, but it is very unlikely that the female is consciously aware of it.

Until we see infanticide by strange males in the wild, this account of orangutan sexual behavior remains conjecture. Speculation it may be but it is the only story so far that makes some sense of our observations and would simultaneously fit neatly in the overall primate framework.

Sarah Hrdy has called this situation we researchers find ourselves in the White Knight problem, after the strange horseman in *Alice in Wonderland* who wears sharp anklets to keep sharks from attacking. When Alice questions him about their function, the knight points out that they must be very effective because there have never been any shark attacks on his horse. Our arguments may seem like that of the White Knight to outsiders, and unfortunately there is no easy answer to such objections. The selective advantages that come from performing a particular behavior pattern in its proper context are often hard to spot, especially when they were designed to keep something from happening, as in the case of infanticide. Hence, we will have to live with having to provide the most plausible scenario, and wait for that rare moment when the system fails, unless of course we can do elegant and convincing experiments (not so easy in the case of infanticide). This does not mean we can't do science. We just keep adding predictions, and if they hold up, the story is increasingly likely to be correct, and alternatives increasingly less likely to be right. We must therefore keep making new predictions, especially ones that don't make sense except in light of the infanticide threat.

Apes, Sex, and People King Kong, the overgrown gorilla in the movie, is not only really strong, he is also lascivious. The most memorable scene in the film (after the view of the ape atop the Empire State Building) is the one in which he carries off the nubile blonde star. If this fictitious ape were simply the product of artistic license, the lasting appeal of the sexual male ape would be hard to explain. Do male great apes have such sex appeal, or do they instill fear of being raped into women? Why should human women fear or be attracted to great ape males?

These questions may not be as strange as they seem. The woodcut reproduced here shows a raid on a village by lecherous ape monsters, who kill the men but abduct the women. Apparently, stories about sexually hungry apes fell on fertile ground even in areas where they have been extinct since prehistory! It is perhaps worth noting that these associations were also not far from the mind of the earliest anatomists and taxonomists studying great apes when the first specimens arrived in Europe. Why is the orangutan's original name *Simia satyrus?* (My *American Heritage Dictionary* defines a satyr as a woodland creature with pointed ears and the short horns of a goat and also a fondness for unrestrained revelry; or, in its derived sense, a licentious man.)

How realistic are these depictions of the ape libido? A persistent story on both Sumatra and Borneo is that orangutan males rape human females when they can. Odoardo Beccari already mentioned it more than a century ago: "the Dayaks tell many a tale about women being carried off by orangutans."[31] Although legends are hard to verify, no less an authority than Biruté Galdikas reports that her cook at Camp Leakey was forcefully mated by an orangutan male.[32] Now that we know more about the sexual habits of male orangutans, it is not so hard to understand that ex-captives may take an active interest in human females, especially since many of them are likely to suffer a species-identity problem. Since the human females, like their orangutan sisters, do not take an active interest in these males, they resort to the only tactic they know to get what they want.

A more general question also emerges from these depictions of oversexed apes. Why are humans so obsessed by sex? Now that we know more about bonobos, and I dare say about orangutans, it may not be much of an exaggeration to say that all great apes (including humans, but with the exception of the gorilla, King Kong notwithstanding) are obsessed by sex. The main reason is probably that ovarian cycles in all but the gorilla are so vaguely delineated, with the timing of ovulation so unpredictable that very lengthy periods of mating are the rule. Females are of course active players: we saw young female orangutans masturbate with sticks and will encounter in Chapter 9 females at Ketambe who practice genital rubbing together (seen only once at Suaq). It is reasonable to assume that infanticide avoidance has instilled a strong and suitably diverse sexual appetite in primate females, including those of the great apes.[33] Needless to say, males have responded to the situation by having become positively lecherous.

So how different are we humans? We are sort of different in that we live in pairs. Nonetheless, in comparison with other pair-living species, we are surprisingly interested in mating, particularly when we are well nourished, healthy, and not distracted by other problems. Given the human ovarian cycle, with its highly unpredictable ovulation, frequent copulation is necessary for fertilization or rather to ensure paternity when mating is not entirely exclusive. It would be unnecessary if the pair bonds were exclusive and monogamous, but they are neither. Although pair bonds exist, neither the history of our species nor comparative ethnography indicates that pair bonds remain monogamous. Hence, although the duration of our mating periods is on the long side, we do not radically deviate from the other great apes in most of our sexual behavior.

I stressed "in most," because what is radically different about our sex is that we couple in private—a human universal.[34] Not much thought has gone into explaining the origins of this trait, even though it is incredibly important for us culturally. One does not need an overly fertile imagination to picture the scenes on our streets had we lacked this tendency. One possible explanation is that it is in the interest of both partners. Dominant male primates tend to get offended when a lower-ranking male copulates right in front of them with a sexually attractive female: they may be enticed to attack the male, and separate him from his partner. Rank-related sexual access has largely disappeared in humans, apart from the occasional religious sect, probably largely because pair bonds have evolved. Main-

Above:
The ape myth: A party of apes brutally kill men and children and carry off women (note that they are also efficient weapons users).

Below:
Humans differ from orangutans, chimpanzees, and bonobos in having strong bonds.

taining these more or less exclusive pair bonds, however, requires mating in private. First of all, it keeps the peace among the male allies; the male alliance may be critical to the success of the group in many human groups, where hostility with neighboring tribes can be serious. Second, it may serve to keep the pair bond more or less intact—an essential condition if the male is to provide some investment in the woman and her children. Finally, there is a benefit to the woman (and her male friend): sex in private allows her discreet opportunities for extra-pair matings without her primary partner knowing about it. As we saw, trysts of that kind are common in many primate species, but they tend to be accompanied by much aggression. Human males are every bit as jealous as those of other species, but our biology has made it harder for men to obtain proof of betrayal.

Orangutan Society The great majority of primates live in stable groups. It is easy to recognize such groups, because animals are together and membership is stable. These groups are not observational artifacts, convenient labels for researchers. They are equally real to the animals themselves: groups rarely mix amicably, and once separated, they revert to their original composition. Immigration and emigration events, the only punctuations of compositional stability, are often associated with substantial social upheaval.

Unfortunately, orangutans belong to a class of species whose social units, if there are any, are not so easily recognized. The difficulty is largely due to their solitary life style.

Even if they lack discrete societies, however, individuals must at least selectively avoid or repel one another. Still, in most solitary species, it is pretty meaningless to ask what social unit they live in: the individual itself or the mother-offspring combination is the social unit. If you want to be generous, you can call the neighborhood the social unit, because neighbors know each other well and tend to have social arrangements in that they have peaceful means to keep themselves apart. Rather than fight each time they meet or come near, they use signals to regulate their relationship. It is quite possible that this is also the best way to describe the orangutan's social unit.

If that were so, though, it would be noteworthy, for there is not a single "higher" (anthropoid) primate that lives in neighborhoods. All live in clearly defined social units in which members spend their time physically and socially together. Even chimpanzees, in which the females are about as solitary as the most gregarious orangutans, live in well-defined communities. You will never find all community members together, but if you carefully map where they go and whom they spend time with, it becomes clear that they share a common home range and interact in a friendly way only with community members.[35] Hostility at the boundaries between communities makes it easier to identify the fundamental units of social organization, even to the animals themselves.[36]

Yet, there is some social structure among orangutans. The goings-on among males are most predictable. Utter intolerance is the simplest way to summarize the social relationships among adult males. Whenever two happen upon each other, there is a rumble in the jungle, with one chasing the other (see photo on next page), except for one unusual observation we had of a standoff. A subordinate adult male caught unawares will run away on the ground. And he'd better, or else he'll be mutilated: many adult males have lost pieces of fingers or have chunks missing from their flanges, silent witnesses of past fighting.[37]

Normally, the local dominant will approach any long calls he hears nearby and give chase if the caller does not retreat. It is a bit of a puzzle why the subordinate adult males keep on calling, because it may get them into serious trouble. The only reasonable interpretation is that the primary function of these long calls is to attract females; the fact that they also attract local dominants may merely be a painful side effect. How else to explain that males rarely make calls once they are in consort with a female, and perhaps mainly in response to other long calls[38] (if they failed to respond to those, the female might decide he is not so cool after all)? Repelling adult male rivals might be a plausible function if males had territories, but they don't. And if defending their turf is the primary function, males should perhaps call more when fertile females are around, but they don't. However, long calls clearly attract females (at least those of the dominant male do), so there is not much else these subordinate males can do to gain access to them—their only reason for living. And they do minimize the chances of being caught: at Suaq, we noted a very distinct pattern in adult male presence. Whenever Arno was away, pursuing consort activity in the south or in the northeast, these lesser males would show up, pretending to be the local dominant and looking for the odd female that would be sexually attractive.[39]

David glances fearfully to his left, seconds before hurtling to the ground, chased by Olly.

Subadult males, while not exactly chummy among one another, tend to be much less intolerant, except in the presence of attractive females. The younger ones, however, will travel around together, even playing with each other and with the young females with whom they like to cavort.

It is among females that we see signs of some real bonding. Females, once mature, tend to settle near their mothers and sisters and so form clusters of relatives. Cluster members preferentially associate and are visibly more relaxed when they get together in crèches with their own than when they associate with females from other clusters. Their home ranges overlap to the point that they practically coincide.[40] They also tend to move with the food in the same way, and as a result they tend to be on the same reproductive schedule, sharing the same dominant male when they are ready to conceive again.[41] These female clusters form the core of orangutan society.[42]

In solitary species without territories, any higher social order that exists must emerge from the interactions and relationships between the sexes. Among orangutans there is some evidence for a male-female component, giving rise to what might even be called a form of diffuse society.

Because females prefer to mate with the same dominant male, they also orient toward that same male. Flanged males regularly emit long calls. There is enough variation in these calls to make it possible for a listener to tell different callers apart, and there is evidence that orangutans actually do so.[43] Tatang Mitra Setia has shown at Ketambe that females tend to stay away from the calls of subordinate males, whereas they approach those of dominant males, and so coordinate their movements with him.[44] Roberto Delgado's experiments nicely verified these descriptive findings.

Females are able to coordinate their movement because of the special way in which the long calls are made. When flanged males make a long call they face in a particular direction, and after the call they are likely to travel in that same direction. The grotesque contraptions that are the orangutan's cheek pads have often been interpreted as a means of making the animal look bigger and hence more intimidating to rivals. That is the kind of deceptive signal that should not fly in a world ruled by natural selection, unless it is backed up by true grit. Yet, many of the long-calling flanged males are small or old, unlikely to follow up on intimidating threats issued to rivals. The pads have also been thought of as fat stores.[45]

The straightforward interpretation is that the flanges serve as a bullhorn, channeling the energy in the direction the male is facing when he is giving the long call and creating a very uneven sound shadow: long in front of him and short to the back. This allows the calls to serve as mobile beacons, telling the rest of the local community where the caller is and, indirectly, where he is headed. If the caller faced away from the recipient during the call, he would seem farther away than if he faced toward them. By traveling in the direction he calls, he gives anyone who is listening in an oppor-

Olly interrupts his pursuit of David to rattle the forest, vigorously shaking the vines he holds.

tunity to move closer to the call before he moves out of audio range. And indeed, when Roberto played back long calls, females did exactly that: those hearing the long calls tended to move toward them during the next hours and so to remain in vocal contact.[46]

Why would females prefer to stay within earshot of the local dominant male? The infanticide-avoidance hypothesis requires it. In the unlikely event that a new and scary stranger shows up, they need to be able to run in the direction of the familiar long calls and seek shelter with the preferred flanged male. We saw earlier that mothers and infants clearly considered the playbacks of the unfamiliar calls very threatening. There is no obvious alternative explanation for the tendency of females to coordinate their range use with that of the local dominant male.

More work, both descriptive and experimental, is needed, but it seems that the structure of orangutan society, just like that of other primates, is best understood as a product of both ecological and social pressures. The main difference is that these lumbering arboreal giants cannot afford to live close together. Nonetheless, the work at Suaq shows in rich detail that, more or less solitary they may be, orangutans form loose societies.

It is fair to say, however, that these societies are not very complex, certainly not so much more complex than that of monkeys that invoking it will explain their high intelligence. And because we have already seen that their foraging is clearly very demanding, it is reasonable to look to these habits for clues about the pacemakers of cognitive evolution. That turns out to be a good guess (see Chapter 8), but there is an interesting twist in this story. Life history plays an unexpectedly major role in shaping orangutan intelligence. We will therefore turn to a consideration of this issue next.

LIFE IN SLOW MOTION

7

Not only do orangutans move like molasses, they also grow and breed in slow motion. Indeed, orangutans live their lives more slowly than any other mammal, even elephants and whales. Infants are not weaned until they are some seven years of age, and after that the young tend to stay near their mother for another two years or so. Adolescence also takes several years, and most females are about 15 years old when they finally give birth to their first baby.[1] Our field studies have not yet been long enough to get a decent estimate of their longevity in the wild, but the highest recorded age in zoos was for a male who died at the ripe old age of 58, and we are beginning to suspect that some wild ones live at least that long.[2] Take one of the better-known females at Ketambe, named Yet. When Herman Rijksen got to know her in the early 1970s, she was a dashing adolescent female, perhaps 12 years old. Almost 30 years later, Yet is still going strong, raising offspring, and looking mature, but not at all as though she were approaching senescence. Similarly, O.J., or Old Jon, the flanged male who took over the dominant position at Ketambe in 1972, when he must have been at least 25 years old (though probably more like 35), was still around in the mid-1990s. While not looking fresh and sprightly, he still cut an impressive figure, at an estimated age somewhere between 45 and 60. Compare this to our closest living relatives, the chimpanzees—who begin to look visibly aged after age 35.[3]

In economics, time is money; in biology, time is fitness. If you wait to grow up, you may die before you become adult. Moreover, individuals who mature faster than you do will tend to pass on their genes much

The slow pace of senescence in orangutans: Yet *(above)* as an adolescent female in 1973, as a young adult in 1977, and as a mature female in 2001;

Jon *(below)* in 1973, 1981, and 1995.

sooner and, by the rules of compound interest, their progeny will crowd out yours. Slow-paced life history has another price. It makes a species very vulnerable to extinction by new predators and possibly new diseases, if they are virulent enough. All other things being equal, therefore, those who live in the slow lane will lose out.

Orangutans as Prey The first human inhabitants moved into Southeast Asia around 40,000 years ago.[4] It is believed that these hunter-gatherers settled mainly along the coast and in relatively open forests, drifting toward the more seasonal eastern parts of the archipelago. Nonetheless, those that made it to the denser forests soon found that they loved orangutans—as food, that is. Some of these early colonists lived in Niah cave, in coastal Sarawak (northwestern Borneo), and littered the floor of the caves with their leftovers. Pig teeth were most common but, astonishingly, orangutan remains came in second, despite the fact that orangutans are never more common than monkeys or even deer.[5] Being so sluggish, they are a lot easier to catch than almost any other animal their size or smaller. Just like so many other large, slow-breeding mammals and birds, they almost certainly showed no fear of humans in the beginning. And like so many other large, slow-breeding Pleistocene megafauna, they were wiped out from large areas before they could adapt to humans.

Gradually, the evidence of the so-called Pleistocene Overkill is becoming so overwhelming that alternative interpretations for the major wave of extinctions during the late Pleistocene (between 50,000 and 10,000 years ago) are looking less and less likely.[6] The blame is still often put on changing climates, but extinction waves happened at different times in different places, and they consistently happened to follow some time after humans colonized the area. Some oceanic islands first colonized in recent history, such as Madagascar and New Zealand, still had a wonderfully diverse large-animal fauna when humans arrived. The only exception is Africa, where most large mammals survived, perhaps because this was where man the hunter evolved, giving animals time to adapt to the new predator. Moreover, it was always the largest animals in any region that went extinct, because they faced the double whammy of being the slowest breeders and the most attractive meat on the hoof (or claw or hand).

Most people are loath to accept this idea, but it really looks as though our ancestors caused a massive extinction wave, compared to which our cur-

People prefer fertile river valleys for their fields.

rent impact looks rather insignificant. And it is not too fanciful to argue that our banishment from paradise was simply due to the fact that we ran out of large and naïve, and therefore easily killed, prey animals.[7]

Much more recently, around 5,000 years ago, other people began to move into Southeast Asia, most likely from Taiwan and through the Philippines.[8] These "Austronesians" reached Borneo roughly 4,500 years ago, then made their way to Java, and only gradually moved back north into Sumatra. They were farmers who grew rice and millet and brought dogs, domesticated pigs, and chickens—as well as rather fancy technology—along with them. Their main impact was the clearing of forests. Orangutans may be the "people of the forest," but the human people now living in and around these forests have a love-hate relationship with them. Both agree on what is the best fruit to eat and what is the best real estate, and as a result they have been in conflict ever since agriculture came to the region. The farming newcomers also shared a taste for orangutans with the earlier foragers that they largely replaced. Early ethnographers noted that monkeys and apes were favorite prey of hunters.

It is a miracle that orangutans survived these successive onslaughts. The orangutan is the slowest-breeding mammal among those alive today, although it is a safe bet that the species that went extinct in the wake of human colonization took every bit as long, or even longer, to mature. Slow life history makes a creature extremely vulnerable to exploitation. It only takes a modest harvest rate to cause inexorable population decline among slow breeders: they just can't make up the numbers lost.[9] Pigs tend to do much better in hunted areas than primates; with their litters of up to a dozen piglets every year, they have no trouble rebounding rapidly after a population crash, or simply compensating for the numbers lost to human consumption.

Perhaps the orangutan survived because its strongholds are in remote and virtually inaccessible swamps. Malaria-infested, these swamps were very lightly inhabited by people.

So, it is not surprising that the distribution of orangutans is the mirror image of the density of orangutan hunters. In Borneo, most of the people that live inland have settled along the numerous rivers. Most of the many different Dayak tribes hunt orangutans when they can, and orangutans are either extinct or so rare that they are sporadically encountered. Where hunting orangutans is taboo for religious reasons, they may still (or perhaps again) be found. In present-day Sumatra, mawas thrive only where the local inhabitants do not hunt them because of religious prohibitions. From north to south along the West Coast, the orangutans begin to disappear where the crescents and sickles of mosques begin to give way to the crosses of churches.

Given the evolutionary disadvantages of life in slow motion, why have any species evolved to have such extremely prolonged development? There must be some hidden advantage. The standard answer is that prolonged immaturity means more development: the animal grows larger and eventually produces more or better offspring, offsetting the cost attached to the higher risk of dying before reproducing (and reproduction is still the best ticket to genetic immortality). But orangutans grow very slowly: by the age of 15, females still weigh in at no more than about 35 kilos. Almost inevitably, extremely slow growth implies that the benefit of prolonged immaturity is not simply large size. Many scholars have long suspected that it has something to do with experience. To see if this idea holds water, we must examine how orangutans are reared.

Mother-and-Child Union There is no bond like the one between mother and child. These words will make most readers think of humans, but they apply even more strongly to orangutans. Their mother-and-child union arguably is the longest and most intense among mammals. The average interval between two births is around eight years, and, despite the orangutan's solitary tendencies, the older sibling is not completely independent even after the new baby is born: it will travel through the forest as if tied to mom by an invisible rubber band, out of sight most of the time but hovering nearby. A female can expect to give birth to at most five young during her whole life, so every individual represents a precious investment to be cherished, loved, and pampered. Not surprisingly, then, orangutan females make perfect mothers, with the attentiveness of a private nurse and the patience of an angel, responding to every whimper with a simple but efficient solution to any problem.

Coordination between mother and infant is so smooth that they look to us like a couple of veteran dancers, with the mother in the leading role, anticipating the infant's moves and responding to the slightest signal by the baby. For instance, when a small infant after nursing on one side has trouble reaching the other nipple, mother shifts the baby while continuing to pick or process her food, seemingly without even looking. Moms will also hold on to one leg or arm if a small infant does something dangerous. It looks as if mothers have insight into their infant's abilities and needs. This is hard to demonstrate in the field, and it could merely be an ability to make predictions based on detailed associations between context and outcome. But we have seen mothers bend the tree in which they were feeding, of course without interrupting their own feeding, to allow an exploring youngster who has wandered off into a neighboring tree to return by the shortest route, even before the infant itself seems to be aware of the looming problem. Mothers will also visit trees in which they would not normally feed to allow the kid to feed on flowers, probably the first solid food many infants will eat.

Mothers hold their kids so dear that they will defend them against threats, if necessary to the death. Poachers know this. It may be possible to harass a macaque mother to the point that she is in such a blind panic that she leaves her infant behind when fleeing, but the only way to capture the commercially valuable orangutan infant is by killing the mother. It is impossible not to be struck by how human it all seems, and yet, orangutan mothers are perhaps closer than human mothers to the Platonic ideal of perfect motherhood. As Sarah Hrdy has argued persuasively, such unconditional maternal love does not characterize the human species because a human mother, unlike her orangutan counterpart, is critically dependent on support by others and natural selection has equipped the human female with psychological distancing mechanisms in the absence of any prospects for support.[10]

Small is beautiful. In nature small is also vulnerable. With their spindly arms and legs, newborn orangutans are pretty helpless, but by about a month they are good at one thing: holding on to mom. For the first few weeks after birth, new mothers when they move often support their babies

with one arm. Their dislike of this tiresome form of travel shows in their spending more time on their nests. Mothers also change their nesting behavior: they build their night nest farther away from big fruit trees, probably to avoid predators searching where prey predictably accumulate.[11]

It takes almost half a year before the baby starts to explore the forest on her own, initially mainly when mom is resting, especially when she is on a nest.[12] The youngster climbs up and dangles over mom's head but gradually starts to move farther away, spinning around or clambering around in short circles, not going anywhere in particular, just practicing the basics of canopy navigation. Over time, the kid moves off the mother more often, especially when clinging to her would hamper mom's movements, such as during feeding and especially during nest building. Nonetheless, for the first two years, pretty much all travel is "safe ride" style for the infant, hopping on the canopy express as soon as mother decides to travel. Most of the time, the infant knows when mother wants to leave, but occasionally it is so busy clambering around or studying the leaves that mother starts off before the infant has hopped on. Ever alert, mom has usually foreseen the problem and slowed down, but the infant, all of a sudden finding itself alone, will rush toward mom in near panic, sometimes crying. These whimpers sound much like those of human babies, and the mother's response is the same as those of any human mother: she comes back to fetch her child or at least waits. By the time her infant is around five years old, however, a mother gradually begins to ignore whimpers and whines. She probably reckons the youngster no longer needs her help to solve these problems.

After about two years, the infant has the hang of arboreal locomotion and moves alone much of the time, but it is still so small that it has trouble crossing canopy gaps. This is because its own body is not heavy enough to make the tree tops bend over so the animal can grab on to the neighboring tree. Mother then starts to show a peculiar behavior unique to apes, called bridging, where she positions herself so her little one can move from one tree to the next using her as a bridge. The fact that infants so rarely seem to have to ask for help is another indication that orangutan mothers have insight into the abilities of their children and can estimate beforehand when their bridging service will be required.

At least up to age three, orangutan kids, once they are off the mother, spend about half their time playing in slow-motion cavort, exploring the

natural world, practicing their aim by throwing down branches, and whenever possible by playing with their peers. At places like Suaq they can play in groups on many days, but elsewhere opportunities for such social contact may be less abundant.

Youngsters are not always in a hurry to cross the bridge made by their mother.

The Ape Apprentice Ever so gradually, the infant starts to take care of itself. By age three, the young ones have learned how to build a proper nest. They may build nests during the day, and even for the night, but they almost always end up in mom's nest to sleep. They tend to do that until they are weaned, around age seven.

Very young babies already show great interest in what mom does. They grope at her food—all the while flopping and bobbing around like a drunkard—perhaps learning the properties of what mother considers food at an early age. By the time they are a year old, they may appear to be feeding quite a bit, but when we watch more closely it is clear they are largely "mouthing" the food items, rather than actually eating them, probably learning the food's properties in the process. In general, the youngsters are

not adventurous feeders, sticking pretty closely to what mother shows is edible and good by her example. Real feeding starts as "shadow-feeding": eating exactly what mother eats but only doing so after mom has started, suggesting that it is safe to eat this particular food. Kids of all ages are immensely curious about what everybody else is eating. They will crane their neck to examine a food item closely whenever they get half a chance and try to grab hold and sample it. From an early age, they will also take food directly out of their mother's hands or pull their mother's face toward them and suck food out of her mouth. As with nest building, by age three infants are fairly independent in their feeding, although they are still nursed every day.

In this gradual, supervised learning process, orangutans resemble us: human children who find something come to their adult caretaker, show it, and will only eat it after the adult has indicated that it is all right to do so.

The orangutan's feeding niche is skill-intensive: many foods need some form of handling or processing before they can be eaten. Such techniques are unlikely to come naturally, in the sense that they simply appear during development, because orangutans in different areas face a bewildering array of different food species and have various techniques for eating them. All youngsters must learn by observing and copying their elders and by practicing their skills. Most challenging, perhaps, is learning tool-using skills. Early attempts are gradual, tentative, and mostly silly. As in so many behaviors, the components are all present well before they are functionally integrated into effective combinations that get the job done. Yet by age seven, the kids are able to use tools for food preparation and, to our eyes at least, are doing so effectively. At that age, too, the mother is generally getting pregnant again, and the drawn-out weaning process will be completed.

By the time they are fully weaned, immature orangutans know what to eat and how to eat it, but apparently they are not yet capable of designing adequate exploitation schedules: they do not know when to move or where to go to make full use of the forest's hidden bounties. Indeed, it is remarkable how long these apes take to reach the last stage of independence. After weaning, the juveniles hang around their mother for another one or two years, frequently associating with her and traveling together. Even when they are not in the same party as their mother, they are usually not far away and may hook up with her several times a day. This is also the period when the juveniles interact a lot with their new sibling, gently playing with the new baby and later even occasionally bridging between trees for them.

That only changes when they are about age 10 or 11, when they may be gone for days or weeks without meeting up with mother. This is the period when kids of both sexes start to roam more widely, looking for interesting company and perhaps places to settle. At this time, they may also run into novel foods and observe new techniques, and they use this time of intense social contact to pick up a few more skills. We suspect that soon after that the boys wander off, greatly expanding their range. Experience at Ketambe suggests that they may still occasionally return for years. Indeed, we cannot even be sure that their natal home range becomes fully excluded from their new range, although that is very likely.

Why Live in the Slow Lane? As we have seen, it takes a decade or more for an immature orangutan to reach true independence. Why does it take an orangutan so long to grow up? There are two possible answers to this question, but they may end up being essentially the same.

The answer from life history theory is that species with low adult mortality and hence long adult life spans, such as orangutans and other great apes, have long periods of immaturity precisely *because* they have low adult mortality.[13] This theory claims that the average rate of mortality among adults selects the optimum age at maturity, leaving nothing to explain about the duration of the period of immaturity: it is simply the time needed to reach the optimum moment at which to start breeding. This explanation is perfectly sound and reflects a broad biological pattern, but it leaves unexplained why great apes, and chimps and orangutans in particular, have such excruciatingly slow growth rates.

The other, complementary explanation stresses the importance of slow development in animals with very long adult life expectancies. To fulfill the potential of a long adult life, all the essential pieces that make it possible must be carefully and slowly assembled: large brains, large immune systems, and the kits to repair molecular damage by free radicals and other harmful chemicals. Putting together a large brain takes a long time, and during this period the growing animal is not capable of adult-level performance, no matter how simple or complex its feeding niche or its social life. Although this simple version is probably close to the truth, less parsimonious versions of this other approach are around, perhaps the most popular still being that these animals have much to learn before they can be effective adults.

These general theories explain why great apes are slow developers, but they cannot tell us why orangutans are even slower than the rest. We are beginning to believe that it is a result of life in the high lane.[14] The difference in weaning age between orangutans and chimpanzees is telling. Females of the two species are about the same size, and growth in captivity at least is pretty similar. Still, orangutan infants are about two years older when they are fully weaned than their chimp counterparts, and intervals between births (assuming the infant lives) are also about two years longer in orangutans. Why this difference? Chimpanzee juveniles, though weaned, nonetheless continue to associate very closely with the mother for many years. They eventually leave her side when they are about age 11 or so, probably spurred by the first stirrings of interest in the opposite sex caused by surges in the sex steroids. It is quite common, then, to see a chimp mother accompanied by a few of her offspring of different ages, much like a human family taking a Sunday stroll through the park (with the notable difference that the father is not in the picture). In orangutans, such continuous association is not possible ecologically; even at Suaq, mothers occasionally chase their juvenile offspring out of fruit trees when their new infants are one or two years old and they need the calories to satisfy their demand for milk. But any mother sending her immature scion into the wilderness would have wasted years of investment if it were unable to look after itself properly. Hence the two-year delay: Mother Nature produced a prolonged period of tolerance for nurturing offspring on the part of the mother so that she would let them go only when they are prepared to sustain themselves.

We more or less understand why orangutans mature slowly, but some puzzle remains. Was the acquisition of numerous complex skills simply made possible by the long developmental period that accompanies slow life history ("so much time so let's use it to learn"), or was the need to learn these skills so important that that need led to selection on slower

Does this youngster need a decade of learning to become a competent forager?

development ("so much to learn and so little time")? The jury is still out on which of these two variants best captures life history variation in primates. New fieldwork on orangutans will have to establish whether they mature before or after all the essential skills are in place, so we can at least evaluate the idea that dependence lasts so long because there is so much to learn.

The resolution of this debate is not merely of academic interest. It will help us interpret the remarkable changes in human life history that evolved during the 6–7 million years since we parted company with the other great apes. One major idea is that there is nothing to explain: humans have evolved even longer adult life expectancies and therefore also have a drawn-out development.[15] But a fascinating alternative was recently proposed. Dubbed "embedded capital," it proposes that learning skills is so difficult in humans that maturing children remain in negative energy balance well into their reproductive years.[16] Middle-aged and older adults, the ultimate skillful foragers, subsidize their developing children for much longer than in any other known species. If the orangutan data also show that critical foraging skills reach peak levels late, around or even after sexual maturation, then that controversial theory for human life history evolution would gain much credibility.

Career Choices Zookeepers around the world tell one version or another of the following anecdote. Mr. X was a scrawny young male that did not seem to want to grow up, languishing despite excellent feeding and perfect care. Then, one year, the keeper retired, and within half a year reedy Mr. X had become a fully flanged and impressively filled-out adult male. Anecdotal? Absolutely. But these kinds of stories abound, although it is sometimes the keeper and sometimes an adult male cage mate who plays the suppressing role. And in descriptive studies, it is tempting to believe that the plural of anecdote is data.

Boris was a good-looking and fairly robust subadult male at Ketambe in the early 1970s, and he remained a good-looking and fairly robust subadult male for the next 25 years! Skeptical? So was I, suspecting mistaken identity, until DNA analysis by Suci Utami and her colleagues showed unambiguously that the Boris of the early 1970s and the Boris of the mid-1990s were indeed one and the same.[17] A few more such examples suggest that the subadult males at Ketambe may reach flanged-male status only when they are 35 years or over.[18] Maturation does not get much slower.

The anecdotes are slowly adding up to data, especially since museum collections tell a similar story. Researchers had been puzzled before by skulls displaying mixed signals regarding age. Tooth eruption follows a fairly rigid sequence on a strict time schedule, so the presence of all the completely erupted permanent cheek teeth indicated that these males were fully adult. Yet the skulls did not have the crest at the top characteristic for the flanged males; these crests are where the muscles attach that keep flanges in place and pull the heavy jaws. If there were one or two, these skulls could simply represent individuals in transition, but there were a lot, suggesting a pattern of developmental arrest.

Some developmental arrest is not that uncommon among animals: individuals vary in how fast they pass through the stages to reach fully adult size and shape, and some of that variation is linked to their social situation. Such delays have even been noted among humans; for example, a serious delay in the growth of children in one orphanage in postwar Germany was linked to the presence of Fraulein Schwartz, a particularly overbearing mother superior.[19] But it seems that these discrepancies are a bit more extreme in orangutans, at least in the males (nothing like this arrest is seen in females).

Waiting for his chance to grow flanges.

This type of developmental arrest is not explained by a simple "time is fitness" story. These subadult males are sexually mature and can sire offspring just fine. Why, then, are they spending so much time in the waiting room?

We saw earlier that females who are likely to conceive seek the company of the dominant adult male, who is likely to do well reproductively. Subadult males have to nag females, follow them around like stalkers, and force themselves on them if they can. Perhaps surprisingly, the data from various field sites show that theirs is not such a bad strategy: subadult males do score some paternities, especially if they were lucky enough to engage in a longer consortship with the female and there was no adult male around to interfere. (Females will consort with a subadult if he is larger than her and there are no flanged males around.) Missing so far is the third class of players: the other adult males. In fact, they were missing from our data, too: for years, we never saw a mating by a nondominant adult male. They only showed up as mates in our regular study area, when Arno began to spend more and more time to the south of it because the females there were becoming ready to conceive again. Nondominant flanged males may only be attractive to females when dominants are off to greener pastures. Normally, subordinate males are not reproductively active: they cannot pursue a female over long distances the way subadults can because females can outrun them.

A subadult, then, faces an important decision. If he just keeps maturing he will be a fully flanged male, but the payoff of maturity in terms of matings may well be far less than his current siring rate as a subadult male, unless he succeeds in becoming the local bigwig. However, in any given place there can be only one such big male. Subadults should break their developmental arrest when they have a good shot at becoming the local dominant male. It is a mystery to me how they make the decision to go for it. I do not for a minute think there is any conscious decision making involved, but exactly how the possible social clues, based on assessment of the local social scene, get translated into physiological triggers is not known. What is known is that it is not simply social stress that keeps the males from growing flanges. Work in zoos showed that the actively growing males had the highest cortisol levels[20]—a good index of chronic activation of the stress system—rather than, as one would perhaps expect, the arrested males.

This scenario is of course still speculative, but the number of examples begin to add up. Moreover, one would predict that where locally dominant males do not have an effective monopoly on sex with the females, the reason for arrest becomes a lot less compelling. In most of Borneo, as we saw in the previous chapter, adult males cannot keep consortships going for long, and subordinate adult males see a lot more action with the females. Indeed, they feature heavily as rapists. It is perhaps no coincidence that for every adult male in Sumatra, we see 1.8 subadult males in the study sites, whereas in Borneo we see about two adult males for every subadult. The latter number is close to what you would expect if there were no developmental arrest and each male simply spends a similar number of years in the developmental waiting room we call subadulthood.[21]

Boris was in the waiting room for at least a quarter-century. Only in a species with radically long life spans can males afford this strategy. If we wanted to find similar developmental arrest stories, we should look to similarly long-lived species in which only the top adult males get matings.

Elephants, of course, avoid this problem by continuing to grow throughout life. Older males are bigger than their younger rivals, making up what they lack in agility by sheer strength. Smaller males can challenge this domination by older males only by entering the mysterious period of musth, in which they are so pumped up that they dare take on bigger males. Orangutans have solved this problem in a different way, through their self-imposed developmental arrest, probably because unlike male elephants, they can have some reproductive success as a smaller male.

In this chapter we have documented the phenomenal slowness of orangutan life, and their remarkable life spans. We also noted that animals with such slow life histories are generally large-brained and intelligent. The red apes fit that pattern: we saw that they used remarkably complex foraging techniques on a daily basis to get by. In the next chapter we will examine the clearest benchmark of such intelligent foraging: the use of tools. After that, we will see how intelligence and slow life history conspire to make culture possible.

THE DAWN OF TECHNOLOGY

8

For a long time, we used to think that only human beings were capable of using tools. That notion, based on poor natural history, went the way of the dodo when it became clear, a few decades ago, that various animals, including of course great apes, used tools in the wild.[1] Especially the discovery of chimpanzee tool use had a major impact on our self-image of being the toolmaker, *Homo faber*. Why should this be the case, when tool use has been observed in assassin bugs, spiders, hermit crabs, archerfishes, vultures, woodpecker finches, crows, sea otters, monkeys, dolphins, elephants, to name only the most obvious species?[2]

A distinction is often made between inflexible and flexible tool use, the latter involving intelligence.[3] Suppose we see an animal do the same task over and over again in a very stereotypic way and can easily fool it into making mistakes (for instance, by providing it with a new tool too big to fit into the hole in which the old tool used to fit). We might then be justified in calling the tool-using pattern "instinctive" and assume it is based on some rapid learning process that is very goal-directed (psychologists call it prepared learning). The key issue is that in such cases we do not think that the animal has developed any real understanding of the task. It is as if it just knows which buttons to push, but not how the tool actually works (a bit like the way most of us use computers).

If, on the other hand, the animal uses the tool flexibly—or, better still, *makes* the tool itself, tailoring it to the task at hand by making it bigger or smaller, thinner or thicker, depending on the need—then we have some grounds for calling it intelligent tool use. The animal apparently under-

The dadap tree *(Erythrina subumbrans)* has spiny branches but edible leaves, prompting some orangutans to make leaf-gloves.

stands what it is doing, perhaps by having some mental representation of the whole task.

If we don't know the details, it is safest to assume that tool use is not intelligent; this is the principle of parsimony, Occam's razor, or Morgan's canon, stating that we should only invoke the simplest cognitive abilities needed to perform a task. But wild chimpanzees use different kinds of tools for different tasks, up to seven or eight tool types in some sites.[4] One or perhaps a few of such skills could be based on trial-and-error learning of the use of tools in the first place, and then of the functionally appropriate dimensions of each tool to boot. But there comes a point where Occam's razor cuts the other way, and it becomes more parsimonious to argue that the animal uses its insight into the nature of the tasks to produce a great variety of tools, each fine-tuned to the one at hand. By this reasoning we say that chimpanzee tool use is intelligent. And such intelligent tool use is clearly an antecedent to the stone-working technology that arose during human evolution.

But before we claim that flexible tool use is unique to our own lineage, consider New Caledonian crows.[5] They show intelligent tool use by these criteria, and they are good at making their tools, too, so perhaps nonprimate species may be credited with intelligent tool use as well. And it is conceivable that more careful study of elephants and dolphins will reveal that these species too show intelligent tool use. However, we can grant these cases without losing sight of the special nature of intelligent tool use: it strongly suggests that some species in some lineages evolved the capacity to represent problems in their minds in such a way that allowed them to use a modified external object to fashion a solution—for example, to get at food that would otherwise be out of reach (or not even be recognizable as such).

Most primate species are not terribly good at using tools. In zoos primates use tools if we provide them with ample spare time, opportunities, and incentives. In the wild, however, tool use is quite rare and incidental, with the remarkable exception of semi-freeranging capuchin monkeys using stones to smash nuts,[6] a case of apparent convergent evolution that was not entirely unexpected[7] but that needs to be examined more closely for parallels with great ape tool use. On the other hand, we have known for almost 40 years that wild chimpanzees make and use tools in flexible ways, and more recently we have also learned the same of orangutans.

Captive orangutans are avid tool users; indeed, they are notorious among zookeepers for being able to break out of pretty much any cage. Yet, in the wild, tool use is rare. In fact, until recently, none of the half-dozen or so populations in which animals had been studied in detail had yielded evidence for routine tool use. This is the orangutan paradox, and if we can solve it we will gain major insight into the evolution of technology.

Some mundane tool use is found in all orangutans: nest building, branch throwing, snag crashing. All orangutans, indeed all great apes, build nests: simple ones during the day, more elaborate ones for the night. The basic design, as simple as it is effective, comes in a few varieties. The most common recipe is as follows. Look for a tree that grows nicely horizontal branches; break two that come out next to each other and fold them back to cross over each other to form a roughly triangular platform. Add additional branches, some simply bent into place and some gathered from nearby, and keep them in place by latching them behind some protuberance. Then add soft, leafy twigs, as many as needed to make the bed soft and comfy. A variant is to select a fork in the tree and build the platform right above it. When these easy options are not available, look for a sizable horizontal bough and build the nest where it sprouts some branches. If there are no large trees at all, tie two small ones together and hope you won't fall through.

An impromptu nest

All orangutans break dead branches and toss them at predators on the ground. Juveniles in particular are fond of playfully harassing observers. In any good forest, there is a lot of dead wood up in the canopy, stuck in lianas or balanced on a live branch. We always counsel newcomers not to stand directly underneath an orangutan. Beth Fox was well aware of this advice, but she was busy catching Ani's pee for hormone assay and did not pay attention to Ani's daughter Andai, then about six or seven years old. Andai simply lifted a liana with one finger and unleashed a stout limb that produced a direct hit! Fortunately, Beth walked away with nothing more than a slight concussion and renewed respect for Andai's aim.

The bigger males push over large dead standing trees, or snags, toward annoying predators or observers. They do this with amazing accuracy, as can be attested by several photographers and filmmakers who have lost expensive equipment in order not to lose life and limb: orangutans do not like big eyes staring at them.

These habits are examples of tool use, of course, but virtually all tree-living primates drop down branches, and many small primates share with great apes the habit of building nests,[8] although perhaps they need to practice less than orangutans do before they can build proper nests. Hence, none of these behaviors is necessarily convincing evidence for the flexible or intelligent use of tools that we are looking for here.

A subadult male orangutan in a dry-land forest tries to bite his way into a nest of stingless bees . . .

Tool Use at Suaq Tool use may be rare in the wild, but the orangutans at Suaq are the exception. They are very diligent insect foragers who spend more time than orangutans in any other population going after insects, such as ants or termites, chitin-covered packets of protein and fat. Sometimes, all that an individual needs to do is to lure the insects to step on to the furry back of its hand and then carefully pick them off with the lips, making soft popping sounds. To obtain mouthfuls rather than single insects, though, an orangutan must usually become destructive. In Suaq, many termites nest in dead branches, and the orangutans will bite away all the soft dead wood on the outside to get to the inner chambers brimming with larvae, pupae, and adults. Some of these nests are in the rotten interiors of otherwise healthy trunks or branches, and then the only way to reach them is through a hole, if there is one. A stick tool will help to knock loose chunks of nest that can then be grabbed and devoured.

Ant nests in trees are always hidden well inside, and their entrances are mere cracks or tiny holes. A stick poked inside will stir up the ants, which will angrily stream out, only to be picked up by the eager forager.

These forms of tool use are relatively less common than the one used to obtain the best food inside tree holes: honey from the soft nests of small stingless bees. Orangutans often cast discerning glances at tree trunks, spying for air traffic in and out of small tree holes. Once discovered, these nests are subject to careful visual and then manual inspection by a poking and picking finger. Almost inevitably, the finger is not long enough and a stick tool has to be prepared. Carefully inserting the tool, the orangutan moves it back and forth and then withdraws it, licks it off, and sticks it back in, repeating the process.

All this tool use occurs up in the trees and, perhaps surprisingly, most of it is accomplished with the mouth. Of course, making tools is handiwork, but once tools are made, most of their use (terms such as *handling* or *manipulating* will not do here!) is with the lips and teeth. Orangutans have very agile lips, and they clench tools like cigars between their teeth. The bigger ones can turn tools front-to-end

. . . whereas a female orangutan at Suaq solves this problem by using a tool, held in her mouth, to penetrate the bees' nest *(see lower right).*

without ever using their hands, as some people can do with a burning cigarette. Not surprisingly, hands are used with larger tools, but the great majority of cases involve the mouth. This odd pattern has now been confirmed in captivity.[9] There is irony in this observation: the hands of orangutans are such that if similar ones were found as fossilized remains, many physical anthropologists would deem the species unable to make and use tools. This may (or may not) be true for stone tools, but technology is not limited to stone.

The second and very different context in which the Suaq orangutans use tools is the extraction of seeds of the cemengang fruit.[10] Cemengang trees grow in the wetter parts of the swamp, usually near flowing water, hence near the river or the hillsides. The fruits are large, five-angled woody capsules up to 10 inches long and some 4 inches wide, which contain brown seeds the size of lima beans. The tree protects its seeds against seed predators by growing a very tough, woody husk. When the seeds are ripe, however, the husk begins to crack open, and neat rows of seeds become ex-

After feasting on cemengang *(left and right)*, animals quench their thirst by visiting tree holes that have collected water *(far right)*.

posed. The cracks gradually widen, exposing the seeds, which have grown nice red attachments (arils). But the fat and thus irresistibly scrumptious seeds and arils are embedded in a mass of razor-sharp needles. The orangutans at Suaq have solved this problem by using a tool to remove the seeds. The tools are short, straight sticks with the bark stripped off. The animals hold the tool in the mouth, insert it into the cracks between two valves, and then strongly move it up and down inside the crack, thus detaching the seeds from their stalk. In the process, they also dislodge numerous hairs, which fall like snow to the ground (at the end of days spent observing this procedure we were itchy all over), and they often wipe off the accumulated hairs with the back of a finger. After this, they push the seeds toward the open top of the fruit and scoop them out with one finger or the (hand-held) tool, or, most commonly, they drop the seeds straight into the mouth. Then, the seed coats are removed and spat out. Late in the season, the orangutans eat only the red arils.

Animals often make the tool before they enter the tree, and sometimes use the same tool on many fruits. Commonly they will pick several fruits and carry them in hand or foot or mouth to find a comfortable spot, where they will work away for hours at a time. Once the fruits are open, they are the ape's mainstay until the very last ones have disappeared several months later. Feeding on these fatty foods makes the orangutans unusually thirsty. At the end of cemengang days, the animals will often drink water from tree holes or directly from groundwater in parts of the swamp that have a clear water flow.

The craving for cemengang seeds and arils makes perfect sense; they are easily the most nutritious food items on the orangutan's menu. During the months that they devote the majority of their waking hours to feeding on the seeds or arils, we see the animals visibly fatten.

In Gunung Palung on Borneo, the animals break open the fruits to get to the seeds.[11] It is a true spectacle to see, and especially to hear, them do it:

Cemengang fruits broken open by an adult male orangutan.

the animal hangs by one arm and uses the other arm and both its feet to tear a valve off the fruit, which is held tight between its clenched jaws. Then, with a loud bang, the valve breaks off, and the seeds are there for the picking. Spectacular it may be, but easy it is not, and of course any animal not strong enough to perform this tour de force is excluded. At Suaq, tool use makes it possible for all to gain access to this delicacy,[12] and to obtain a season-long intake of calories that exceeds the one at Gunung Palung many-fold. What better evidence does one need to argue that the possession of technology enhances fitness?

Both main forms of tool use are customary—that is, all able-bodied adults and adolescents perform the trick, although individuals vary tremendously in the rate at which they use tree-hole tools. We shall see in the next chapter that tool use occasionally crops up at other sites, too, and that the big difference between Suaq and all other sites is its unusual social situation. But first I must convince you that this tool use is intelligent.

Tools for Fools, or Signs of Intelligence? The tools themselves seem ridiculously simple: just short, straight sticks, usually peeled. The sticks are simply made from branches snatched off the nearest tree, and preparing them rarely takes more than 30 seconds. Yet, this simplicity is deceptive. It takes youngsters several years to develop the proper skills, and some adults seem to be clearly less capable when it comes to tree-hole tool use. We are not sure whether the difficulty lies in the actual handling of the tools, as seems to be the case in chimpanzees,[13] or in recognizing the details of the setting in which a tool can be used with a successful outcome.

There is only so much we can learn from watching, because the orangutans have a habit of turning their backs on us when they are tooling around up in the trees, leaving us with a perfect view of their lower backside but not much else. Moving to a better spot takes so long in the soggy muck that by the time we get there, either the show is over or the animal has turned again. But we have learned a lot from examining the discarded tools, and this study has convinced us that making and using tools is pushing the cognitive envelope.

The first thing we learned from our measurements is that tree-hole tools and fruit tools differed clearly in their dimensions; in each cemengang crop we examined, fruit tools were shorter and thinner, and also more com-

Tools are tailor-made for the task at hand.

monly peeled, than tree-hole tools. Among the tree-hole tools, those used on termite nests were the largest and thickest and least likely to be peeled, whereas those used for honey were the most delicate. The removal of bark turns out to follow a rather simple rule: the smaller the tool, the more likely the bark is peeled off. Is this a sign of laziness, ðr is it linked to use of the mouth? We don't know yet. But other differences are not so simple. For instance, longer tools tend to be thicker, but at any given length, tree-hole tools are thicker than fruit tools. A closer look at variation in tools is in order.

More detailed analyses have shown that the apes make on-the-spot decisions about the dimensions of their tools. Take cemengang tools, for instance. Early in the season, when the cracks in the fruits are thin slits, the tools are thin, but as the season progresses and the cracks widen, thicker tools are used. Thicker, but not longer: the fruits do not become bigger, they merely open more and more. We saw the same pattern in three different cemengang seasons. We discovered variation in length by checking another swamp (see below for more details), where the fruits were much

The tools Andai used to extract the cemengang seeds *(above)* are shorter than those she used at tree holes *(below)* (scale is in cm).

The tools used by Ani *(right)* at different tree holes for honey extraction tend to differ in size, presumably because the holes themselves varied in internal dimensions.

smaller, at least in that year's crop. As expected, the tools were shorter there!

We would like to go back and study in more detail the nature of the decisions going into tool making, but now we must rely mainly on analysis of the videos taken by Michelle Merrill. The mawas have a tendency to make the tools a bit too long: we often saw them trim a stick by biting off a piece after using it a bit (not such a bad habit, since the opposite tactic would require a lot more work). They also discard some tools soon after putting them to use. But once a tool was exactly the right length, it could be used on several fruits and even carried to the next tree. Occasionally, we'd see orangutans carefully stash a cemengang fruit in a tree fork that they had selected earlier, only to return to it half an hour or so later. We found this puzzling at the time, but now we think the orangutans use one tool for fruits with particular crack sizes and store fruits of other sizes for consumption later, when they have a tool of the right thickness.

This flexibility suggests a careful functional fit between tool dimensions (length, width) and tool efficiency. Tools may be made a bit too long, then trimmed to the right length, but those that prove too short are discarded. A particular tool, given its immutable length, can be used on fruits with a particular range of crack widths. If a fruit is picked with the wrong crack width, it is set aside for later, when the right tool is around.

Lest you get nervous that we may be overinterpreting the orangutans' insight into the functional use of their tools, let us take a closer look at the tools used at the tree holes. Each tree hole is of course unique, with internal dimensions that can only be estimated, especially by us, down on the ground, but probably also by the orangutan peering into it. To eliminate possible variation among individuals in tool decisions, we focused on the tools made by a single female, Ani, on a single task (obtaining honey). She worked on a wide variety of tree holes but showed remarkable consistency among tools used on any particular tree hole. Perhaps she decided the dimensions of the needed tool upon inspection of the tree hole, before making the tool. Although it often goes unnoticed when we just watch in the field, the videos show that there is quite a bit of tool trimming going on. As with the cemengang tools, the tactic seems to be to make the tool on the long side first because it is easier to trim than to make a new tool.

Planning is also part of the package: when animals are on their way to a cemengang tree, they often make their tools during the approach. Nut-cracking chimpanzees likewise often schlep their hammers over hundreds of meters because suitable tools are rare.

The behaviors we have observed suggest that our mawas first have to make up their mind whether a tool-using opportunity presents itself (trivial in the cemengang tree, not so simple in tree holes). After that, they have to make up their mind how big a tool is needed, and this determines how thick the branch is that they end up using for the tool. The length is guessed, and if the tool is too long, it is trimmed. Intelligent tool use, all right!

The Philosopher Ape Intelligent tool use in wild orangutans may not have been seen before our study, it nevertheless comes as no real surprise. There is no doubt about it: orangutans are smart, regardless of exactly how you define that term. Whether intelligence is defined as creative problem solving, uncanny memory, or thinking (mental simulation), orangutans get high marks. Their intellectual prowess is on display in the wild, in captivity, and in the laboratory.

Wild orangutans surprise us pretty much every day with their insight. When rain threatens, they may make a rain hat, usually by selecting a species of leaf that is especially suitable to keep their heads dry. In Suaq, for instance, this is the gersang[14] tree, and when an animal is near this tree, it is likely to make a short detour to get its hat. Similarly, when a hard rain is going to fall, an orangutan may make an elaborate nest, if it is close to bedtime, and add a carefully woven cover onto it. These covers are so good that we have seen orangutans emerge gloriously dry from under them after a serious downpour. In some places, orangutans even build a nest over the nest to keep out the rain.

Intelligence is also on display during travel, so much so that some scientists have speculated that the need to somehow navigate in the three-dimensional canopy with a body as heavy as that of an adult orangutan has been a major pacemaker for the evolution of this species' intellectual abilities.[15] To get into an adjacent tree, orangutans cross the gap by bending the vegetation in the right direction and then grabbing on to the next tree,

pulling it in until enough of a toe- or finger-hold is obtained and then letting go of the previous tree, which sweeps back. The favorite technique of the heavy and lazy is tree swaying. By subtly shifting their weight, orangutans make trees sway back and forth and then give an extra push whenever it sways in the direction they want to go. They create a controlled fall, almost always reaching their destination before the tree breaks. Each movement an orangutan makes through the trees presents a unique problem requiring a different sequence of moves; there is no standard way to get into the next tree. And the price of failure is high: misjudge one element and you may crash to the ground.

It could of course be argued that navigating around the canopy is simply conditioned behavior. Perhaps much of it is. But the reactions of orangutans to unusual events suggest that conditioning cannot be the whole story. When the canopy gap is too wide to be crossed by tree swaying, animals may break off branches and use them as hooks to rake in the tree on the other side.[16] Once, after a long and frustrating struggle to get across a gap, a female bit off a liana and used it to swing across, Tarzan-style. And, as we noted in Chapter 5, intelligence also helps during foraging.

Orangutans in zoos have the reputation of being devilishly smart, as do the ex-captive youngsters held in "rehabilitation" centers. Every zookeeper and rehab center staff member has a favorite orangutan story.[17] I myself have seen some impressive exploits in the 1970s, when Ketambe was still a rehabilitation center. Calina was a rather worldly rehab who had lived in a bar and knew how to smoke cigarettes. She disdained the forest and instead hung around camp to see what she could scrounge there. One day, I accidentally noticed from a distance that she was trying to gain entrance to the shed that held the bananas. I snuck up and observed her from behind a tree. There was a little slit between the boards and the roof, and she had decided this was going to be her point of entry. After checking out the place, she seemed to leave, but actually she moved resolutely to a thin post a few meters away. She pulled the post out of the ground (I had never even noticed its presence before) and then proceeded to use it as a crowbar, trying to wedge it between the boards and the beam of the roof. Her efforts were to no avail: the construction was too sturdy, and she broke the post. She then searched for something else, and after some roaming she found a metal chain. She tried to pry a board loose by trying to get the chain behind its edge. She worked very hard at it—a sweet irony, because Calina was never much of a worker. Again she failed, but I was duly impressed with her intelligence and determination.

To place such anecdotes into a comparative perspective, let me repeat the favorite story of Ben Beck, a renowned student of tool use. If you happen to forget a screwdriver in the gorilla cage, the animals will hesitantly approach it, briefly sniff it, and subsequently ignore it. Leave it in a chimp cage, and it will be used in vigorous display, thrown about, and forgotten. But if you leave it in the orangutan cage, one of the animals will unobtrusively pick it up, hide it, and use it to let itself out when you've left for the day.

Now, it could be argued that these are mere anecdotes and not the product of rigorous scientific experimentation. True enough, although the sheer volume of accounts is certainly suggestive. And there are good reasons why psychologists tend not to take anecdotes too seriously. First, some animals are incredibly smart in one domain but not at all in others. This modularity problem is potentially lethal to claims about animal intelligence. For instance, seed-caching birds may have amazing spatial memory, easily beating ours, but they have no special abilities when it comes to the social realm.[18] Vervet monkeys have great social smarts—they remember the dominance relations among all others in their social group, for instance—but do not seem to realize that clear tracks leading to a bush suggest that a hungry python lurks within.[19] Second, it may be easiest to recognize intelligent behavior in animals that are similar to us. Such anthropomorphism may lead us to conclude that great apes are smarter than sharks because we would not readily recognize a particularly intelligent (or stupid) move on the shark's part.

In an attempt to minimize this risk and not fool ourselves into thinking that apes are smart simply because they are like humans, we also constructed formal comparisons of a large number of species whose cognitive abilities had been assessed in objective experiments. Rob Deaner and I, supported by statistician Val Johnson,[20] compiled all studies of cognitive tests that involved more than one primate species in a way that allowed direct comparisons. Over the last century, comparative psychologists have performed thousands of experiments on animal learning and memory; library shelves groan under the weight of their reports. Unfortunately, these experts often used different experimental procedures, selected animals in different ways, and so on, making it hard to make direct comparisons. But

The mean intelligence scores of different primate genera, resulting from a meta-analysis of numerous experimental tests of primate cognitive abilities

	Genus	intelligence score
PROSIMIANS	Brown Lemur	
	Bush Baby	
	Mouse Lemur	
	Slow Loris	
	Ringtailed Lemur	
	Fork-marked Lemur	
	Ruffed Lemur	
NEW WORLD MONKEYS	Night Monkey	
	Spider Monkey	
	Marmoset	
	Capuchin	
	Woolly Monkey	
	Squirrel Monkey	
OLD WORLD MONKEYS	Mangabey	
	Guenon	
	Macaque	
	Mandrill	
	Talapoin Monkey	
	Baboon	
	Langur	
	Gibbon	
GREAT APES	Gorilla	
	Chimpanzee	
	Orangutan	

intelligence score: -2   -1   0   1   2

among this enormous number of experiments, some were designed to generate directly comparable data. We brought together all snippets we could find. Val, a statistical wizard with a special interest in Bayesian methods (where rather than testing the fit of data to a preexisting model we estimate directly the most plausible relationships among variables), had developed a technique to bring together a number of incomplete comparisons in a single scale (and made the data tell him whether using a single scale was justified). The results we found were startling.

The first result was that all primates could be ranked efficiently along a single dimension; there was no need to postulate separate and independent cognitive adaptations to different problems (the modularity problem noted above was not in fact a problem). When we examined the ranking, it looked as though we had set the clock back half a century or more: great apes emerged as smarter than monkeys, who in turn outperformed lemurs and lorises (prosimians). What professional psychologists had spent decades denouncing as preconceived notions based on a deeply ingrained cultural bias known as the *Scala Naturae* or the Great Chain of Being emerges vindicated. We found there is no reason to yank at the great chain: those species more closely related to humans were indeed smarter than more distantly related species. And, by the way, on top of the list sat the orangutan.

The *Scala Naturae* was Aristotle's ladder of similarity to humans in the hierarchy of life. In the Christian era, this age-old notion was modified into the Great Chain of Being, the notion that the Creator made beings closer and closer to His own image, until He finally created humans, His crowning achievement. We are not reinventing the *Scala Naturae* with our results: the resemblance to the phylogenetic tree is merely fortuitous. True, the sequence in primates does resemble their phylogenetic similarity to us, but when other mammals and especially birds begin to appear in the ladder, the neat array obviously breaks down. Clearly, it is not similarity to us that counts in this cognitive ranking, but something else.

We should not be surprised that among primates, similarity to humans and greater intelligence are related. Great apes show many other signs of cognitive excellence not linked to any of the tests used to generate the ranking shown here. Mirror self-recognition, some language abilities, the ability to count and to form categories, learning by insight, tactical deception, perhaps the ability to read the knowledge or beliefs of other individuals: among primates, all of them are unique to great apes.[21] As you might expect, some other animals (dolphins, elephants, parrots, ravens) also seem to be able to achieve some or all of these feats, whereas numerous attempts to demonstrate any of them in monkeys so far have failed.[22]

These abilities are all close to what we define as intelligent, but it is also absolutely true that our definition may be anthropomorphic: we define as intelligent those behaviors that we humans can imagine, can conceive of as intelligent. Indeed, we might not even recognize intelligent behavior that is sufficiently different from ours, especially if it involves senses we do not possess, such as acute smell. However, there is a problem with this objection: it does not explain how we can recognize parrots, crows, dolphins, and elephants as intelligent. Obviously, these species evolved abilities and insights that we identify as intelligent independently from us, in a striking case of convergent evolution. So, although we may miss certain forms of intelligence, behaviors that we can recognize as intelligent allow us to put a select array of species from a variety of lineages in the "smart" category.

Regardless of how we classify the behavior of the nonprimate species, our results demonstrate that the mind of a great ape (and perhaps some other animals) works in many respects in the same way as ours. Of course, we are not the first researchers to make such a claim, and philosophers are still busy sorting out the implications of this conclusion, including those with respect to animal rights. To the extent that dolphins, elephants, parrots, and the others on that elite list show the same cognitive features, however, it can be argued that evolution has found multiple occasions for great minds to think alike.

The Evolution of Great Ape Intelligence Why did Mother Nature make orangutans and the other great apes so smart, relative to other primates? Was intelligence perhaps a byproduct of some other development, such as the evolution of large body size? Although large animals tend to be smart, this idea in itself does not explain much. Brain tissue is costly to build, requiring special building blocks, and energetically very costly to maintain.[23] It would not be there unless it was absolutely critical for survival and reproduction.

Was the evolution of intelligence perhaps related to the demands of social life? This idea, popularly known as Machiavellian intelligence, has recently become very popular among cognitive scientists.[24] On the face of it, the hypothesis has a lot going for it. Primates live in permanent social groups that contain both males and females. In these groups, dominance hierarchies form in which individuals know their own rank relative to those of all others and in some species even how third parties rank among themselves. They form coalitions, and the choice whether to join or not, and whom to support, may require complex and above all quick mental gymnastics. In a few species, males are known to manipulate the opportunities of possible rivals to build bonds that could lead to an alliance that would threaten their dominance in the future; they do so by selectively intervening whenever potential rivals show signs of getting together.[25]

Especially Old World primates also clean each other's backsides and use

Old World primates use grooming as a form of social currency: long-tailed macaques at Ketambe.

this service as a social currency: they trade grooming given not only for grooming received but also for tolerance or even support in conflicts. Some versions of the hypothesis place the emphasis on the ability to cheat or, perhaps more realistically, to detect cheating, in potentially endless series of giving and taking services (reciprocity). An individual without social "smarts" is a sucker, taken advantage of by everyone, but an intelligent animal may be able to cooperate with others to mutual and lasting benefit. Finally, the Machiavellian hypothesis can account for the remarkable ability of a few primates (probably only great apes) to take the perspective of other animals and act as if they know what it is that these other individuals know.[26]

When it comes to Machiavellian intelligence, the orangutan is a serious fly in the ointment. Orangutans have no permanent groups, although neighbors establish long-lasting dominance relationships (similar to pretty much every other solitary mammal), and no one has ever seen a coalition in the wild among independent animals (they are sporadically seen among rehabilitants, but such coalitions always involve humans).[27] No matter how one stretches the argument, it is hard to maintain that the smartest of all nonhuman primates owes its brain power to the need for social maneuvering. The orangutan is not an isolated case: societies of many monkey species are at least as complex as ape societies, yet monkeys are not nearly as intelligent.[28]

Is foraging the answer, then? Indeed, we saw that the orangutan's amazing mental abilities do come to the fore during foraging. It is true that among primates more generally, opportunistic foragers—animals that make food available where most others do not know it exists (this includes, but is not limited to, extractive foraging)—tend to outsmart others. Even the least intelligent great ape, the gorilla, uses delicate manipulation to prepare its food.[29]

Foraging seems a viable candidate, but other ecological demands may also have acted as an evolutionary pacemaker. A wide-ranging, fruit-eating ape may need to remember the location and the approximate ripening schedules of numerous tree species and even individual trees, along with their location.[30] Orangutan watchers have all seen straight-line travel over long distances, for up to 2 kilometers, through seemingly featureless forests straight to a prized fruit tree, such as durian. Of course, it is hard to exclude the role of cues, such as the presence of other animals, or simply visual cues visible from the top of the canopy. Moreover, a lot of other fruit-eating animals would benefit from this ability but lack it.

The relative merits of these ideas are hotly debated. They are often treated as alternatives, although they almost certainly are not. For instance, the selective advantages of social ("Machiavellian") intelligence may be important in primates in general, and monkeys in particular, but the demands of extractive foraging may have been important pacemakers for apes. And, given that the all-purpose computer that is the brain can handle problems in multiple domains, these advantages may all select for the same thing at the same time.

Something is missing from the debate, however: an appreciation of the costs of mental agility. Brains are expensive. This might help us to answer the most obvious objection to all the theorizing discussed above: if intelligence is so good, why are not all animals intelligent? Social intelligence, proficiency at finding, remembering, and processing food, etc.— they should all be really useful to their owner, whether that owner is a shrimp or a chimp. We believe the answer to the question is that most simply cannot afford it, in that intelligence is incompatible with their life history. Primates are among the mammals with the slowest life histories. In Chapter 7, we noted that great apes are among the primates with the slowest life histories. What makes for slow life history? Being large helps, as does being arboreal: both help to reduce unavoidable mortality, the ultimate engine of the pace of life history. Great apes, of course, are the largest primates and are descended from strictly arboreal ancestors.[31]

Why would life history affect intelligence? First, investing in structures such as brains that will only begin to yield benefits after a considerable delay makes no sense unless there is a reasonable life expectancy at the time the investment is made. Second, cognitive abilities are adaptations, which means that they should improve survival and so indirectly select for slower life histories. Finally, because growing brains are critically sensitive to nutrient shortages, growing a large brain is risky; the production of unfit morons is best avoided by keeping the brain on a very conservative growth trajectory. That takes lots of time, and only organisms that tend toward slow development in the first place have that kind of time. For all these reasons, we expect that cognition and life history will evolve in lockstep. Indeed, there is evidence for such correlated evolution among a wide array of mammals—and, importantly, among primates as well.[32]

Slow life history, then, is a precondition for cognitive evolution. Numerous are the pressures that would favor improvements in cognition, but in animals with hurried life histories these pressures simply cannot produce the enlargement in brain size needed to support the improvements in cognitive skills. All the warm-blooded vertebrates that we know to be intelligent are animals with long life spans. The life-history perspective does not tell us which pressures get translated into enhanced cognition. In fact, all known pressures may apply to some extent, but with different weight in different species, and we may not yet have identified them all, although I believe the demands of foraging play an important role in great apes. But the life-history angle does tell us why there are no cunning cuscus or shrewd shrews.

THE CULTURE CLUB

Tool use offers a wonderful window on ape acumen, but intelligence alone does not explain the odd distribution of tool use among great apes, or for that matter the orangutan paradox. After all, all orangutans should be born about equally smart, so how come most wild orangutans don't use tools? Consideration of chimpanzees invites the same conclusion: some populations seem to use tools in many different ways, but quite a few show only very modest evidence of tool use, even after years of careful study. This leaves only one reasonable conclusion: intelligence is a necessary condition for sophisticated tool use, but it is not a sufficient one. So what are we missing?

Perhaps this technological variation is simply due to variation in ecological opportunities. After all, the swamp is an unusual habitat, with lots of insects above ground level: termites, ants, and stingless bees of numerous varieties all nest in the trees. The Malayan sun bear is also very common in swamps, and, like the orangutan, it eats these insects, but it needs no tools to do so. It simply uses its strong claws to pull a tree trunk apart until it breaks open with a loud bang. (These are the moments when bears give away their presence and one can sneak up on them without being noticed. The other way to see sun bears is to bump into them; they don't pay much attention when traveling and may blunder right into us, so we fieldworkers usually let them know we are near, lest they try sharpening their claws on us.) It is therefore quite possible that the swamp environment offers special opportunities for tool use to its smartest denizens.

Tempting as it sounds, this idea does not explain the absence of tool use

A sun bear ripped the hole in this tree to find the insect nest inside.

Opposite:
Tevi (*left*) shares the fruits of Ani's labor (palm pith).

in populations that have the cemengang tree and eat the seeds but do so without tools. These animals end up eating much less of the nutritious seeds than they could have with tools. Nor does it explain the fact that the Suaq orangutans, when they enter the hills, use tools to exploit the contents of tree holes. The hill habitat is (or at least was) a dime a dozen throughout the orangutan's geographic range, so if tools can be used in the hills above Suaq, they should come in handy anywhere.

Another plausible idea, captured in the old adage that necessity is the mother of invention, is that the Suaq animals have a harder time making ends meet and so need tools to balance their budget. Perhaps the high population density leads to much competition; another reason could be that the short time per visit to fruit trees makes it harder for dominants to monopolize food, forcing animals into scramble competition and making life equally miserable for all. Orangutan density is high at Suaq, but so is productivity, and the birth rate is not any lower than at Ketambe, nor do Suaq infants seem to develop more slowly. But the strongest argument against this idea is that the kinds of food made accessible by tool use are very high on the preference list and should therefore be liked by all orangutans. Red apes everywhere are willing to be stung many times by honey bees to get at their honey; and the calorie bombs that are cemengang seeds or arils would make orangutan mouths anywhere water. So, the idea of necessity as cause also does not have much explanatory power.

It was only after I had convinced myself that these plausible ecological explanations did not work that I began to think seriously about how animals pick up the habit of tool use. Are the orangutans at Suaq and the neighboring coastal swamps intrinsically smarter than all the other orangutans elsewhere? Unlikely. Are they just lucky to live in a very large population, where they have drawn the winning ticket in the invention lottery? Possibly. But the differences are so black-and-white that another process is also likely to be at work.

Please board this train of thought. All individuals other than babies at Suaq use two kinds of tools—to extract cemengang seeds or honey and insects from tree holes—whereas not a single individual at Ketambe does. Apparently, the complex skills demonstrated at Suaq are at the very edge of what a wild orangutan can figure out on its own. Does it make sense, then, to assume that each and every individual at Suaq invented tool-using behavior independently, when not a single one did so anywhere else?

Once the problem is represented like this, the conclusion seems inevitable: the skills are learned through some form of socially biased learning during the individual's development. Or to put it differently: these tool-use patterns are traditions, or incipient cultures!

The Trouble with Culture For decades now, anthropologists have considered culture, along with language, humanity's Rubicon, a divide that even the behavior of great apes could not bridge. Yet, culture is a slippery customer. The founder of anthropology, Edward Tylor, defined it in 1871 as "that complex whole which includes knowledge, belief, art, morals, law, customs, and any other capabilities and habits acquired by man as a member of society."[1] In the century that followed, scores of attempts have produced a wealth of definitions of culture.[2] But for us, Russ Tuttle[3] recently put it most succinctly: culture is a "symbolically mediated, shared system of meaning."

The emphasis is on the symbolic nature of culture: behaviors and artifacts have arbitrary, and therefore geographically varying, meaning—a meaning that is shared by all members of the tribe or region but not by outsiders. This definition makes symbolic signaling the hallmark of culture. Little wonder, then, that many definitions also contain reference to that ultimate symbolic communication system: language.

How are we supposed to ever find culture among animals? The anthropological definitions emphasize the underlying beliefs and values of culture bearers, but these are mental constructs that may remain utterly inaccessible to the student of animal behavior. The Japanese primatologist Kinji Imanishi was perhaps the first, in 1952, to have pointed out that at its core, culture is socially transmitted innovation: culture is simply innovation followed by diffusion.[4] This biological (as opposed to anthropological) definition leads to an operational emphasis on observable behaviors or artifacts, things we can actually see in animals, rather than beliefs or values, which we cannot. It also explains the key property of culture in humans: geographic variation. Useful or popular innovations spread until they hit some barrier, producing geographic differentiation. So, if we see geographic variation in behaviors that we know reflect innovation and are transmitted through some socially mediated learning process, then we have animal culture (and we can worry about how symbolic any of it is later on).

Orphan orangutans peer at their role models, who are engaged in food processing.

Imanishi's lucid explication of the culture concept should have led to an avalanche of studies, but for decades only a small trickle followed. The rub is to prove that an animal that cannot be followed all the time, for which our observations constitute at most a few slivers of its lifeline, invented some new trick and did not simply use a well-remembered but rarely practiced near-instinctive behavior. It is equally impossible to prove to everyone's satisfaction that she learned a new skill from another group member who already had it rather than figured it out all by herself. Socially mediated learning can only be proven in the laboratory, where the experimenter exposes a naïve animal to a knowledgeable conspecific (the "model") and can subsequently establish whether or not the naïve animal adopts the skill. Such experiments have been done with chimpanzees and more recently with orangutans, and to good effect.[5] Less controlled studies of spontaneous imitation had already made the presence of these abilities more than a mere possibility: Anne Russon and Biruté Galdikas documented, in glorious detail, the imitative abilities shown by the rehabilitant orangutans at Tanjung Puting.[6] These rehabilitants not only washed clothes in the river, scrubbing and rinsing, but they would try to make fire and siphon gasoline from tanks using hoses. And the wild ones seem to use their observational skills all the time: at our field site, we have seen numerous instances of younger animals edging closer and closer to adults engaged in some intriguing activity, studying their every move with great alacrity.

But studies of imitation can only demonstrate the potential for culture: they cannot tell us about culture in nature, neither what it is generally about nor how much of it is there ("content and extent"). Cultural potential is a necessary but not sufficient condition for culture. Hence, there is no substitute for field studies, and no alternative but to design new methods to infer the existence of culture, the process, from the patterns it produces. All we can do, of course, is to show that these patterns are consistent with those produced by culture. But if we can do this repeatedly, and in species with a demonstrated capacity for advanced forms of observational learning, there must come a point where concluding that culture underlies a particular geographic pattern is just more parsimonious than inventing special and increasingly convoluted ecological explanations for each geographic variant. For this analysis, we could do worse than to pick tool use.

Orangutan Tool Use Is Cultural We have adopted a three-step procedure for compiling evidence that makes it increasingly likely that a certain pattern of behaviors is cultural, despite our inability to really prove it.

The first step is to demonstrate the basic conditions for the existence of culture: the behavior varies geographically, and where it occurs, the variant is customary and persistent. The tool-using behaviors of orangutans clearly pass this first test, because the two forms of tool use are geographically restricted. At Suaq they are ubiquitous: all known individuals exhibited the behavior or, if not, had been followed for rather short periods of time. At all other sites, however, not a single animal has ever been observed using tools as they are used at Suaq. The variants are persistent as well: the tool-using behaviors were observed throughout our years at Suaq, and we saw several youngsters beginning to use tools and becoming more proficient.

The second step is to eliminate simpler explanations. We have already excluded developmental versions of ecological explanations. To the extent that the incidence of these skills can be ascribed to genetic factors, we can also exclude simple genetic explanations. Using tools is not an innate behavior, but animals might differ in the spontaneous invention of these skills if certain morphological features—for instance, the form of the hands or particular behavioral tendencies—predispose them to it. Genetically based differences are of course expected at the level of species, or perhaps subspecies, but we have observed the presence and absence of particular skills within the same rather small region (northern Sumatra) among populations of the same subspecies. Of course, the ecological conditions have to be suitable for tool use (for instance, it is impossible to see cemengang tool use in the absence of cemengang), and the animals must be genetically capable of developing the skills, but these factors do not explain the geographic pattern of tool use.

Finally, we must be able to find patterns that are consistent with culture, and not easily explained any other way. One of these is the disappearance of the skill on the far side of a dispersal barrier. The geographic distribution of cemengang gave us decisive clues.

Impassable rivers may have halted
the spread of cemengang tool use
into smaller swamps *(map)*.

Tripa

Kluet

Batu Batu

Singkil

tool use present   no tools found

The nice thing about cemengang tool use is that it can be demonstrated without a single orangutan making an appearance: the tools themselves are the evidence, for they are discarded under trees, usually still inside the fruits, or on the forest floor. We are not likely to mistake these clean, straight sticks, with the bark peeled off, for fallen twigs. Suaq is part of the Kluet swamp, and everywhere you go in there, discarded tools may be found under cemengang trees.

In order to gather this evidence the site must harbor orangutans and cemengang trees, and it must have a fruit season in progress or just past. During the second half of the 1990s we made many a visit to other swamps on Sumatra's west coast, hoping to hit upon the right combination of factors. These swamps were being targeted for their lumber at the time, and cemengang was among the most popular timbers.

Some 15 kilometers southeast of Kluet is the large Singkil swamp, formed when the Alas River transported an enormous amount of sediment following the eruption of the Toba volcano, one of the largest known in the history of Earth. The Singkil swamp, all 100,000 hectares of it, juts out from the straight coastline and contains one of the largest single population of orangutans anywhere in the world. We found stick tools under cemengang trees some 15 kilometers south of the old port of Trumon (a town with a proud history and a fort going back to the pepper trade of the sixteenth century). In fact, we even saw the animals eating in the cemengang trees right on the beach! Because the Singkil swamp is not too far from Kluet, it stands to reason that dispersing animals could have brought the skill from one swamp to the other.

We also looked for, and found, the tools near the mouth of the Tripa, another large swamp area formed by volcanic action. After several unsuccessful visits, which failed in part because we could find no more cemengang trees, we hit pay dirt in August 1999 by befriending the illegal logging gangs and asking them to show us the remaining trees. This is especially exciting because the distance to the Kluet swamp is well over 125 kilometers, too far for even the most adventurous orangutan to cover. (Such long treks have been observed only through areas containing no conspecifics; but here, all the area in between is inhabited by red apes.) That means that the inhabitants in this swamp have independently discovered, and maintained, the technique of extracting cemengang seeds with stick tools.

The wildcat loggers in the Tripa swamp took us to the last few cemengang trees, where we also found tools jammed into the fruits *(inset)*.

So, in the two other major coastal swamps besides Suaq we could demonstrate the presence of Cemengang tool use. But, and this is the critical result, we also found a place without any tools: in the Batu-Batu swamp, across the Alas River from the Singkil swamp (see map). Cemengang trees occur, orangutans occur, and they also clearly ate the fruit, as evidenced by nests next to cemengang trees and the presence of fruits on the ground with torn stalks. Proving the absence of something is always difficult. Yet, from data collected at Suaq, we could estimate what proportion of fruits on the ground should have tools sticking out. After the inspection of numerous fruits, all without tools, we could reject the hypothesis that tools were just as common in Batu-

Batu as in the other swamps. It is possible, of course, that a few individuals there did use tools, but there was nothing on the ground even remotely similar to tools.

However, we also produced more positive evidence. Many fruits from Batu-Batu had valves missing. At Suaq, orangutans break open only those fruits that have not yet opened spontaneously, yet here they broke valves off fruits that had dehisced naturally. The abundance of these broken fruits (and their absence at other sites with tool use) allowed us to conclude definitively that the orangutans at Batu-Batu ate cemengang in very much the same way as their colleagues did in distant Borneo (Gunung Palung), but completely differently from the way their colleagues did right across the river.[7]

Batu-Batu is a small swamp area, and as it does not contain much of the best swamp forest, it supports a lower orangutan density. It is possible that tool use there was never invented, or that it could not be maintained in the population. We can be sure that migrants from across the river never brought it in because the Alas is so wide there that it is absolutely impassable for an orangutan. Genetically, the two populations are connected indirectly; farther upriver the occasional animal must have crossed over until very recently. Genes, then, could have wandered upriver, crossed it, and gradually wandered down again, over generations reaching the swamp on the opposite bank of their point of origin. Populations on opposite banks of major rivers can therefore be genetically rather similar. Individuals could not make this up-and-down journey in a single lifetime, of course, so the skills that were useful in the swamp of origin would be long gone by the time the genes had diffused back down to the opposite bank. Populations on opposite banks of major rivers can therefore be drastically different culturally while being fairly similar genetically. Only the cultural interpretation can explain the unexpected juxtaposition of knowledgeable tool users and brute-force foragers living only a few kilometers from each other.

How Much More Orangutan Behavior Is Cultural? The orangutan, that proverbial outsider, has now joined the culture club. Membership so far is pretty exclusive: apart from humans, only the chimpanzee has been admitted, although people studying other primates and other mammals or birds are busily filling out the application forms. We are now ready to ask the question: how much more of orangutan behavior is cultural? This question is important because a better feel for the natural content of culture might yield hints as to the evolution of the cultural ability. A few years ago, Andy Whiten, Christophe Boesch, and colleagues completed a comparison among half a dozen active chimpanzee field sites and noted many apparent differences in behaviors. Several of these differences concern tool use, but many others are about behavioral signals animals exchange, such as tearing up small leaves to catch the attention of another chimp, or styles of grooming: regular or with the partners clasping hands overhead.[8]

The study sites involved in the comparative study of orangutan culture.

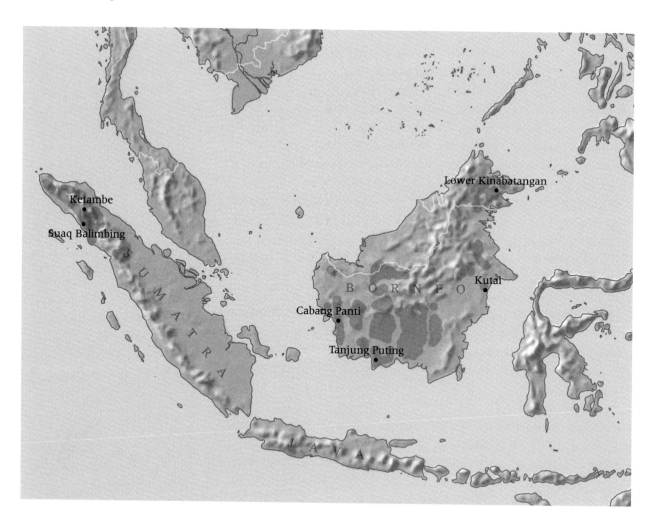

The basic procedure of the chimp researchers recognized cultural variants as those that show all-or-nothing geographic variation that cannot be attributed to ecological or genetic differences. We also had six study sites, two on Sumatra and four on Borneo. These were the sites with the best long-term data. Our enterprise was of course a collaborative effort involving many colleagues, who in most cases represented multiple observers contributing data. We sat down in the quiet of a former monastery, compared field descriptions, and watched each other's videotapes.[9] In the end, well over 150,000 hours of observation were condensed in a single table.[10]

To organize the data, we considered skills separately from variant communication signals. Skills come in two distinct types: those that improve the intake of food and those that make life more comfortable in other ways. Subsistence-related skills we found to be geographically variable were:

- using a handful of leaves as a napkin to wipe the copiously flowing latex oozing from otherwise edible fruit off one's chin
- using a leafy branch as a swatter to ward off angry bees (the reason for the attack usually being that the orangutan is busy raiding their nest!)
- using a bundle of leaves as gloves, to handle spiny fruits or spiny branches, or as cushions, to sit on these branches
- using tailor-made stick tools to poke around in tree holes and extract honey from stingless bees or larvae and pupae from termites or ants
- using customized stick tools to extract the seeds from the cemengang fruit
- using a leafy branch to scoop water from deep tree holes, out of arm's reach
- grabbing a cluster of leaves inhabited by weaver ants and picking off the (biting) ants with the lips
- rummaging through decaying orangutan nests to find ants and other insects in them
- sucking on dead, hollow twigs to draw the ants that live in them into the mouth
- searching for sleeping lorises in dense tangles of vines and hanging roots of strangling figs, grabbing them with a quick, decisive move, and biting them in the head (and then of course devouring them!)

Other variants were modest inventions that served to make life a little bit more comfortable:

- building a nest not far above the nest just finished to serve as a roof
- making a cover on the nest during midday resting (very much like the rain covers made at all sites, but made during the heat of the day)
- hiding under a nest: sheltering from heavy rain underneath a nest, especially one constructed for the purpose
- using a stick to scratch one's back
- using a stick to masturbate

The remaining variants were mainly communication signals that varied from place to place:

- snag crashing, the nearly ubiquitous habit of flanged males when they are exercised about something; they push over large standing dead trees ("snags"), sometimes aimed with amazing precision at a target on the ground
- snag riding, a rare variant on this theme, where the male rides on the snag he just pushed over, jumping off just in time by grabbing on to vegetation

- kiss squeaks, the vocalizations an orangutan gives when annoyed at someone (a predator, a noisy human, an unpleasant male); these are normally just loud kissing sounds made with pursed lips, but there are a few variants in some places:
  - the kiss is planted on a leaf
  - the kiss is planted on the back of the hand or into a fist, with the hand acting a bit like a trumpet
  - the kiss squeak is of the standard kind, but in addition the animal grabs a handful of leaves, squashes them, wipes its face with them, and then with an exaggerated move drops the leaves

- building a nest just to play on with one's peers (only done by immatures in the presence of peers)

The three last variants are probably communicative as well, but we do not know what meaning, if any, they convey:

- raspberry sounds, produced in the context of nest building

- a symmetric scratch with both arms moving at the same time in wide circles, scratching the sides of the body on the way up
- during the final stages of nest building, while lining the nest with finer twigs, passing these twigs by the mouth after they have been picked, as if to bite them (and occasionally biting them), often more or less coincident with making the raspberry sounds

Quite a few of these behaviors we have already encountered at Suaq, but many are not found there. In all, this list contains 24 likely cultural variants. We need to qualify them as likely because we do not have the detailed information—such as absence across a dispersal barrier or a documented origin and subsequent spread—that would make the cultural interpretation truly compelling for the great majority of these variants. But all the variants are unlikely to be instinctive or near-instinctive behaviors that simply reflect some ecological or even genetic difference. Almost certainly a lot more than these are cultural: this list of 24 may be the tip of the iceberg, but it is a respectable start.

Every site has a unique signature of likely cultures. Add a new site to the list, and you'll find new variants: Beth Fox and Ibrahim bin'Mohammad, for instance, found that the orangutans they observed in Agusan, upriver from Ketambe, used branches trimmed to have a hook at the end to latch onto trees that were out of reach.[11]

The cultural variants are those innovations that have become very common at a site. But every cultural variant starts life as an innovation. Some of these innovations may have been made decades or even centuries ago. We suspect that to be true for some of the important skills, such as tool use for obtaining food. Indeed, there is archeological evidence that nut cracking with stone tools by the Taï chimpanzees is at least several centuries old. But many variants may have a shorter life span; some may even be fashions, especially those that may work well because they are new and then lose their effectiveness as their novelty value disappears. This may be true for some of the communication variants.

A cross-sectional survey of variants should therefore catch these innovations as rare variants. We found 12 variants that were never common enough at any site to qualify as cultural. Interestingly, at least half of these can be called comfort-enhancing innovations. New tricks need not always induce an urge to copy in others, even if they are observed. Examples are using a leaf to clean the body, making a leaf bundle that might act as a doll while bedding down, or embellishing the nest with a row of neatly arranged twigs.

As one would expect, most of the noncultural variants are rather private, or actions that are rarely performed even if they have become a routine part of an individual's repertoire, such as biting through a vine to cross a gap that was too wide to cross any other way or neatly scooping water out of a tree hole with a vessel-shaped leaf. Hence, these actions are not easily spread. A good example of that was a solid subsistence skill practiced by an old adult male at Ketambe who was well known to researchers there for about 30 years, O.J. or Jon. In his later years O.J. adopted the habit of chiseling with a firm stick into termite-infested logs on the forest floor. This new trick would be a hard act to follow because old males are real loners, and even if others were in the neighborhood they would not come close enough to study the behavior because they stay away from the ground.

And again as expected, only one of the rare variants was a communication signal—such signals work only if other individuals interpret them correctly and will therefore generally also use them. This case was a branch-dragging display, more or less like a bonobo display,[12] by an adult male in Kinabatangan, Sabah (East Malaysia).

After all was said and done, the results of this orangutan comparison were remarkably similar to those found for the chimpanzee, suggesting a strongly convergent cultural tendency, even down to the proportion of variants that were subsistence skills, comfort variants, and communication signals. In all, then, we now seemed to have two species that show near-human levels of cultural variation.

Beyond All Reasonable Doubt But can we really be sure that this geographic method allows us to identify orangutan culture? The approach has been criticized as producing artifacts because it is overly generous in attributing culture where none exists. After all, it is possible, and some might say more *parsimonious,* to assume that geographic variants reflect differences in individual learning or even that they are instinctual.[13] The opposite is possible, too, of course: the geographic method might be too conservative,[14] but since we are trying to convince ourselves that the variation we see is cultural that kind of criticism is methodologically irrelevant here, even if potentially right on the money!

To eliminate this nagging doubt, we decided to subject this orangutan data set, and where possible also the chimpanzee data published earlier, to three additional tests. First, we examined the pattern of variants among sites: If innovations diffuse until stopped by a dispersal barrier, and if many innovations crop up randomly, nearby sites should be more similar culturally and more distant sites less similar. The data agreed with expectation: as geographic distance between a pair of sites increases, so do their cultural distance. Moreover, distance had no effect when we examined the similarity among sites in the rare behavioral variants—i.e., those innovations that did not spread to others to become cultural. This finding confirmed that the distance effect on cultural similarity was not some kind of artifact.

Second, we examined the effect of habitat. If sites with similar habitats are very similar in culture, this is consistent with the idea that similar ecological conditions induce individuals to learn particular variants independently because of their exposure to similar opportunities. Habitat did not play a major role: different sites in coastal swamps were not more similar culturally with each other than with the mixed alluvial-upland sites, and vice versa. In humans, likewise, as noted by Felix Keesing in 1958, "the habitat, both limiting and stimulating as it is, cannot be counted as the sole, or even the prime, creative factor in cultural development."[15] This was reassuring.

Finally, we examined the size of the cultural repertoire at a site. The number of local cultural variants should be linked to some measure of opportunities for social learning, hence some measure of association. In both orangutans and chimpanzees, we could confirm that sites in which individuals spend more time in association with others have greater cultural repertoires. This effect was strongest for food-related variants (shown here); it makes sense

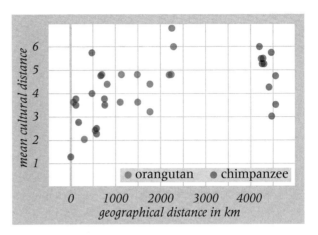

Geographical distance affects cultural similarity.

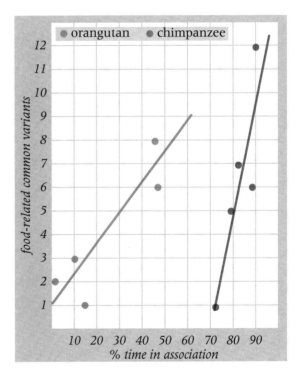

Association with others increases cultural repertoires.

to expect that acquiring feeding skills from another orangutan may require more close-range observation than picking up a conspicuous communication signal. In other words, those orangutans that did not get exposed to the refined knowledge of sophisticated and educated individuals had the smallest repertoires of cultural variants; they might be described as the country bumpkins of the forest.

Data for orangutans and chimps have different slopes in this graph, but that is almost certainly an artifact. Because most members of a community learn most of their cultural variants as they mature, mothers are the natural focus for this kind of analysis. We had to use community-wide association data. If we had data on adult females, the mothers, the curves would have come much closer. In chimps, adult males are the most gregarious, whereas in orangutans they are the least. As a result, relatively higher association values were found among chimps.

Michelle Merrill and I now have also shown the association effect on repertoire size in a more detailed comparison between the two Sumatran sites.[16] The animals at Suaq spent more time together, indeed more than any other orangutans, and were more friendly, feeding at close distances, even sharing food, and allowing each other to watch very closely. Apes in general are tolerant (see Chapter 10), and a minimum level of social tolerance is necessary to make social learning possible. Being together is necessary but not sufficient: for animals that must always be alert to avert attacks by hostile neighbors (or predators), it is difficult to concentrate for long on any task. And if the expert does not allow the learner to come close enough to carefully observe its skills, social transmission of skills easily invented by each individual will occur only if the right combination of instinctive actions and objects is created by social attraction. Consequently, tolerant sociality may favor the transmission of cognitively more challenging skills in those species capable of learning them. Suaq orangutans had the larger cultural repertoires.

The richer educational opportunities at Suaq may even explain variation within the study population.[17] The home ranges of the northern females at Suaq contained much less melaka, and these females were much less sociable than those in the central and southern ranges. The northern females were much less prone to use tree-hole tools, even though they searched for insects about as much as the others, and even in parts of the area where others used tools a lot. Somehow, they were less able to recognize the tree holes that provided opportunities for successful tool use (we can't tell whether they were less successful at the tool use itself, although that is conceivable). The most plausible interpretation is that they had had less schooling: they were able to watch fewer others, and for less time, while growing up.

The data we compiled on "culture" among the great apes therefore passed these three additional tests with flying colors, corroborating the conclusion reached for individual variants that were studied in detail: Orangutan and chimpanzee geographic variation is entirely consistent with the notion of culture and therefore almost certainly *reflects* culture.

Bridging the Rubicon, or at Least Building a Ferry We are now ready to return to the question of the gap between hominoid and human culture. Great apes have culture—great! But, by the definition we have employed so far, so may lots of other animals. Birds have local dialects that are learned by the young as they listen to adult singers. Rats in Israeli pine plantations have figured out a way to eat pine seeds by removing the scales from the cones. Clever experiments have shown that naïve rats do not know how to do this, and in fact they never even try, whereas those born to mothers who know the trick pick it up too.[18] If these lovely rodents have a cultural variant, then what is the big deal? Wasn't human culture supposed to be our most important distinguishing feature, setting us apart even from similar animals, such as great apes and dolphins?

At this point we must return to the notion of culture as a system of shared symbolic meaning. Clearly, not all cultures are equal. We must somehow dissect culture into components, so we can make more detailed comparisons of the cultures of different species and explore the evolutionary relationships among these components (for instance, maybe the presence of one acts as a precondition for the evolutionary emergence of another). The challenge, of course, is to identify components that make this exercise a productive one, and we have only just begun this kind of work. One approach is to classify variants on the basis of how difficult it is to invent them and how difficult it is to pick them up from the example of others. We also expect that these two kinds of difficulties are correlated, given how our brains work (more on that later), which means that we should be able to rank them.

Here is a first, preliminary categorization I have come up with in order

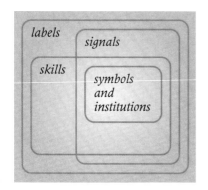

The components of culture

of increasing difficulty: labels, signal variants, skill variants, symbols, and institutions. I will present them in a slightly different order because signals, symbols, and institutions belong together, as explained in the accompanying figure.

Labels are the simplest kinds of culture. Labels allow an animal to recognize food or enemies. The process involved is probably a very direct triggering by sensing that another, usually reliable conspecific considers some species edible or dangerous. For example, young rabbits or rats learn what is edible from the chemicals in mother's milk and from odors on the breath of their mother or other adults.[19] Primates learn about the edibility of species simply by observing that a reliable conspecific is eating it[20] or by smelling the food on its breath. I suspect that almost all birds and mammals that are not committed hermits will have this basic form of culture.[21]

Things get really interesting with skills, variants invented to improve subsistence and often involving tools. These variants are true innovations, and the ones that are interesting from a cultural perspective are not easily invented. Widespread presence in a community implies that they are maintained by social learning. We should expect that only more intelligent species can make worthwhile inventions and at the same time will be able to pick up inventions from others. These cultural elements are at the edge of the cognitive reach of the species, and learning the skills requires much more than just being notified that something can be done.

Skill cultures are much less common among animals. Perhaps they are even limited mostly to great apes, a few birds, and some cetaceans, but a lot more thorough comparative fieldwork needs to be done before we can be confident about this conclusion. They are interesting from an evolutionary perspective because skill variants may well have been driving the push beyond labels, the basic cultural foundation shared by many species. More than signal variants, new skills can improve fitness. Signal variants probably represent mere byproducts of a capacity to experiment and to copy put in place by selection for the skills they produced.

The demonstration of the existence of skill cultures in orangutans pushes back the origin of the foundation for material culture to the time when Asian great apes split off from the African lineage. The capacity for material culture is therefore a universal feature of great apes, not a feature limited to hominins (a taxonomic term for all the human-like species that ever lived, a term that excludes the apes). The implications of this conclusion will be examined in more detail in the next chapter.

The critical reader may well object to this as an over-generalization, because gorillas and bonobos are not known to have extensive cultures. This argument can be countered, however. How much do we really know about these two species? We have one long-term field study in meticulous detail for gorillas, and some shorter studies for bonobos, but we lack accurate studies at multiple sites needed for a thorough comparison.[22] The feeding techniques of mountain gorillas are so complex that they almost inevitably contain cultural elements. The jury, then, is still out, but my prediction is that we will find fairly rich cultures in these two species as well, even if tool use remains rare among them.

Signal variants come in various guises, but the basic idea is that a regular social signal has different forms in different places. Signal variants may be rare among mammals, but they are quite common among song birds, whose dialects are a dime a dozen. Many people suspect, however, that there is something special about bird song, owing to the presence of dedicated brain modules for vocal learning, because those same species show very little evidence of other skills that might be cultural,[23] at least for now. But let's return to mammals. Signal variants are of special interest, because a newly coined variation on an existing communication signal has to be understood by others to be effective in the first place. In other words, its meaning has to be shared. Most of the time this is not a big deal because the meaning is the same throughout the species in spite of minor variations in the signal. Local uniformity and geographic variation may simply be the result of drift.

But more interesting scenarios are possible, too. It could be that local uniformity indicates that individuals *prefer* their local variant to the one used elsewhere, as if to say: we do things this way here! Another, perhaps less fanciful possibility is that animals prefer to do things in the same way as the most influential or dominant animal in the neighborhood (the "cool" factor in human decisions to adopt a cultural variant). Finally, as a killjoy alternative, the local signal variant may simply be the most efficient way to get the signal across in the local habitat. I am raising these possibilities to show how much there is still to learn about animal cultures, not to make higher claims. But if a preference for the local variants exists, independent of ecological efficiency, signal variants approach our notion of what symbols are.

To date, the evidence for the use of symbols among great apes is thin. For now, this may be a clear demarcation criterion: Animals may have labels, skill variants, and signal variants, but they do not have symbols and institutions. Symbols, remember, are signals whose meaning is arbitrary, not shared throughout the species but merely shared locally or regionally. Just think of flags and all that goes on around them: hoisting and greeting it; flying it half-mast; burning it; kissing it; draping oneself in it and running around a stadium. And, please, make sure you pick the correct flag to burn or drape around you lest you be tarred and feathered! Does any animal have the equivalent of these ultimate arbitrary symbols? And how about our institutions, such as marriage, or rites of passage?

Before rejecting the existence of symbols among animals, let us examine the great ape record again. Signal variants probably are not symbols, but there is one highly suggestive case: the grooming handclasp in chimpanzees. Bill McGrew and Linda Marchant describe how young females that moved from one community to another changed their handclasp style to match the one used in the new community.[24]

The plot thickens, however, when we see that the same signal has different meanings in different places, which must imply arbitrary meaning. Christophe Boesch raised the possibility of arbitrary signal meaning in chimpanzees.[25] He noted that the same signal, leaf clipping, means invitation to play in one place, an invitation to have sex in another. In our own orangutans, we have the tantalizing case of the raspberry sounds an animal makes when finishing a nest and just before bedding down. Why do all orangutans make the sound at exactly that time? Do the *prt-prt* sounds mean that the sender is saying good night to others nearby? But why should it mean that? At first the sound may have been completely meaningless to the local mawas and later acquired its meaning through the forming of an association. If orangutans at Suaq show clear signs of understanding the meaning of the sound, for instance by being more likely to make their own nest after hearing the raspberry, whereas those elsewhere do not "understand" them in the same way, then the *prt-prt* may qualify as a symbol. If a particular signal variant means different things at different sites (e.g., leaf clipping), or is used at only a single site with a seemingly arbitrary meaning (e.g., the nest-time raspberries), that comes perilously close to symbolic use.

Humans have institutions that lean heavily on symbols. Apes do not have such things as marriage rules or rites of passage. Or do they? Consider the grooming handclasp again: Michio Nakamura describes how adolescent males in one community in the Mahale Mountains in Tanzania try to perform the handclasp with adult males, who in turn usually ignore them.[26] Nakamura concludes: "it is possible that there is some kind of consensus that this is a behaviour of adults."

The Rise of Symbolism It is not known in which hominin species symbols first became an important component of the human cultural repertoire, but their prominence in human culture is a fundamental departure from the repertoire of the great apes. We noted that great apes show some trend toward the use of symbols and speculated that future work may yield more evidence of it. But what caused the major increase in the use of cultural symbols?

The key difference between a cultural symbol and a mere cultural signal is that the meaning of a symbol is clearly locally distinct. What was initially an arbitrary distinction has become highly meaningful, perhaps even to the point of reaching moral status within the community. It is clearly important for members of the same community to advertise their shared membership. As human bands grew in size and individuals spent less time together, it may have been difficult for all members to recognize each other. Membership badges can be linguistic or behavioral and can involve customs, dress, and appearance. Much of human symbol use, such as headdress or use of colors, can be recognized at a distance, suggesting that perhaps not making your membership clear is particularly dangerous.

Advertising one's membership may have become very pressing among early humans because relationships with other communities had turned increasingly hostile. With the rise of *Homo erectus,* hominins had become effective carnivores: long-distance hunters or scavengers who roamed over far larger home ranges than their ancestors had. Between-group hostility is the hallmark of carnivores, and among nonhuman primates it is most pronounced among chimps. When a group of lions, wolves, or chimps come across a solitary animal from the other community, they will attack and kill it. In a species that can kill at a distance, it is better for an individual to advertise before that happens that you are a member of the same social unit (band or tribe).

If this speculation can be supported by new information and analyses, it suggests that between-group hostility, by favoring symbolic cultures, helped to lay the foundation for human language. One essential feature of language is that it manipulates symbols. Hence, the ability to manipulate symbols was perhaps honed by cultural evolution, perhaps especially by our xenophobia.

The examples noted above of the use of signals with arbitrary meaning by great apes—such as the grooming handclasp or raspberry sounds during nest-building—should alert us to the possibility that symbol use and even symbol-based institutions are found in great apes. Obviously, we must design clever field protocols and experiments to put this interpretation to the test before we can declare victory for the notion of cultural continuity between great apes and humans. One thing is certain, however: signal variants are a necessary precondition for the evolution of symbols, and symbol use is a necessary precondition for the establishment of institutions. Even if they are not symbol users in the wild, the great apes have at least passed the entry exam for the symbol club. Thus, even though we should not deny the massive differences in culture between humans and great apes, these differences seem increasingly quantitative rather than qualitative. We will, of course, return to this most interesting question, but first we will pause to explain, at long last, the orangutan paradox: the near-absence of tool use in most wild populations and its rich presence in most zoos and the occasional wild population.

The Orangutan Paradox Resolved We set out to solve the orangutan paradox: the incongruent juxtaposition of zoo genius and forest bumpkin. We found that the bumpkin was not the isolated idiot he was made out to be, but in the process we also learned that the explanation presented as an alternative—that we humans "enculturate" orangutans into intelligence by exposing them to numerous opportunities for socially biased learning—is actually part of the main story. Intelligence is very useful in the wild, for solving social and especially ecological problems, but it develops slowly and through extensive social inputs from the mother, other adults, and peers.

Field studies of orangutan tool use and culture may hold further clues about the nature of intelligence. Because intelligence is about finding novel solutions to problems, in some sense intelligent animals are necessarily born as blank slates. Obviously, it is risky for evolution to rely on such an unpredictable process to bring about skills that are critical for fitness. After all, innovated skills themselves are not heritable; the only heritable property is the *capacity* to invent them. When the inventor dies, her offspring will have to start from square one. The best way to ensure the development of a vital skill is for natural selection to strengthen any and all tendencies that make a maturing individual more likely to perform the behavior (i.e., to make the behavior nearly instinctive). That kind of behavior may look intelligent, but it is not, at least not in the conventional sense of the term. Lots of behavior by animals is of this kind: take dam building in beavers, tool use in Galápagos finches, or extractive foraging in capuchin monkeys.

The fitness value of the ability to innovate is limited because the innovations are not passed on. However, the capacity to innovate will be favored by natural selection if it is accompanied by the ability to learn socially. Social learning may occur through an indirect social process, making an individual more tenacious in exploration when others seem to find rewards around particular objects or in a particular microhabitat, or through a more direct observational process, such as imitation of actions or goals. If innovators and bystanders are kin, both benefit and selection will improve both components of the cultural process. If they are not, selection can still improve social learning processes if the bystanders already happen to be there and do not need to be brought in for the purpose. In that way, learning from the innovator is not costly to the innovator. Hence, some level of social tolerance is a precondition.

In terms of mechanisms, perhaps the best way to assure the combined presence of innovation and social learning capabilities is to build brain structures that are good at both. In fact, it is almost inevitable for the system to be designed this way: the separation between individual and social learning is conceptually useful, but in practice the cognitive mechanisms involved overlap widely. This is why most scholars now refer to socially biased learning when they refer to the bundle of processes that lead to learning in the presence of knowledgeable conspecifics ("experts"). The social component concerns enhanced exploratory motivation in the presence of group members as well as cognitively more demanding tendencies to copy motor patterns or recognize the goals of others (for instance, through an increase in insight or, in other words, some causal intelligence), but every-

Learning to make and use tools requires observational learning and practice.

thing else involved in social learning is the same as in "regular" individual learning. The overlap in learning mechanisms becomes clear if you consider a concrete example. Think of how a chimp learns to crack nuts; it takes a long time of alternating bouts of practice and bouts of watching others to perfect the technique.[27] If some step-by-step interaction between innovation and social learning were not involved, one wonders how the technique was ever invented in the first place.[28] Our first claim, therefore, is that abilities for both individual (innovation) and social learning will tend to be found in the same species.

Now imagine that this intelligent organism is one in which all learning is transmitted from mother to offspring: it is of the vertical variety. Mother is always there, and youngsters display great curiosity at almost anything the mother does, from feeding to nest building. But mother does not always know best, especially if she is sickly or too busy to be considerate of the youngster's needs because resources are scarce that year. And she could die before the end of the normal period of mother-child association. Would it not be good for offspring to benefit from the inventiveness of all others in the community? One would think so, but of course this can only happen in more egalitarian species. In a rather smart egalitarian species, the bonuses of social learning are great: it allows animals to learn from a large number of smart models rather than from mother only. To put it differently: selection on improved intelligence will be much more effective in egalitarian species, so that over time the smartest, brainiest species will be those that happened to be characterized by egalitarian societies to begin with. This selective process of improving intelligence will lead to a tight correlation across species between sociality, especially of the tolerant or egalitarian variety ("sociability"), and intelligence. Our second claim, then, is that highly intelligent creatures will almost inevitably be highly sociable ones.[29]

Next we can add a twist to this idea. A small increase in social learning abilities will allow an animal in a highly sociable species to capitalize on every individual's inventiveness. An equal increase in individual inventiveness will produce benefits to the animal and its immediate offspring, if they are good social learners, but also to all others in the population. In terms of fitness, then, the carrier of the greater inventiveness may make only modest gains, whereas another individual who became a slightly better social learner benefited a lot more (if group members can benefit from the innovations of all others they encounter). By the cold calculus of natural selection, this means that social learning abilities are much easier to improve than inventiveness, still assuming a species that is socially tolerant, although there must obviously be something worth copying in the population. If the mechanisms that lead to more efficient socially biased learning are rewarded, then innovation ability will automatically be dragged along to some extent. We can therefore add a surprising amendment to the conclusion we had just reached: we can predict that *only* highly sociable species will reach superior levels of intelligence.

The final step in this argument is now obvious. For any species characterized by intelligence and a reliance on social learning during development, culture emerges as a byproduct of these two traits because innovations will be different from place to place, given variation in local conditions and happenstance. We have therefore defined an adaptive suite: highly cultural creatures are highly intelligent, long-lived (as noted before as a precondition for high intelligence) and sociable (specifically, gregarious and socially tolerant).

This amalgam of characters sums up the great apes pretty well. And obviously, it fits us to a tee, since we show all these features in a more extreme form than any great ape. But there are also other creatures that have reached comparable intellectual peaks independently, via separate evolutionary pathways. Elephants, dolphins, ravens, and parrots: all are long-lived, and they also all live in social groups in which close-range observational learning is possible. Many have societies in which support to injured members is routinely shown, illustrating how socially tolerant they are. They should therefore also be cultural, but work is only beginning to document their behaviors.[30]

This new idea is not the same as the popular Machiavellian intelligence hypothesis, which claims that the challenges of social life have provided the more social animals with a selective advantage toward greater intelligence over time.[31] The two ideas predict the same outcome but assume different pathways: Machiavellian intelligence emphasizes the role of social interactions, competition as well as cooperation, rather than that of social learning. We saw before that this theory is not without its detractors and that the orangutan is clearly anomalous. Another major problem is that the Machiavellian intelligence hypothesis has an element of circularity. If living in social groups selects, over time, for increased intelligence, how can we ever test it in a convincing way, especially since some species live in groups but did not manage to become very intelligent (think of many ungulates)?[32] But it does have plausibility and, because it is not an exclusive alternative to the social learning of intelligence hypothesis, it may well be part of a complete explanation.

Although more formal studies still need to be done to test each of these hypotheses and to distinguish between them, at first acquaintance the social learning hypothesis for the evolution of intelligence seems eminently reasonable. Indeed, the correlation between intelligence and sociability is so obvious, at least in retrospect, that its fundamental nature is easily over-looked. Think hard and see if you can think of any truly intelligent crea-ture that is not highly social. Fortunately, the sociable orangutans at Suaq were discovered and studied just in time to refute the idea that wild orang-utans break this rule.

The Cultural Bootstrap The fundamental way in which intelligence and social learning are linked should of course be reflected in how imma-ture animals develop. Our data from Suaq, being observational, could not demonstrate the importance of social learning in development, but they are entirely consistent with it: youngsters are like curious apprentices, anxious to learn from others. Cultural animals simply have to be that way. We can also say it more explicitly: intelligence is, at least in part, socially constructed during development, so that those who happen to grow up in a more sociable environment will show greater technological prowess.[33] Hence, the same correlation between intelligence and sociability also plays out during development.

The fictional Baron von Münchausen may have been history's most cel-ebrated purveyor of tall tales. One story about this character had him pull-ing himself up out of a hole by his bootstraps. The act is physically impossi-ble, but credible enough to give rise to the notion of "bootstrapping"—starting up without external aid. What culture does to the human mind may be very similar to the baron's tour de force: take a creature that is a blank slate but has a superb capacity to absorb cultural knowledge (and a natural bias to absorb some kinds more easily than others) and provide it with a surfeit of knowledge and skills to be adopted, and it may bootstrap itself up to amazing cognitive complexity. Mike Tomasello describes how every human child goes through a long journey of guided discovery of the world; in a three-way interaction between a mentor, objects, and its own budding mind, each child develops effective theories about how the world works.[34] It is as if ontogeny recapitulates phylogeny at lightning speed. This way of developing produces cumulative cultural change: every generation stands on the shoulders of the previous one, looking farther and seeing more, and so on ad infinitum.

Great apes lack language and do not engage in much teaching,[35] if at all, and so are probably less dependent on culturally guided construction dur-ing development, yet the importance of experience and social learning in

During development, intelligence is constructed through interaction with the biotic, social, and physical environment.

the development of cognitive abilities is undeniable. Some form of "enculturation" is no doubt happening. Anne Russon has recently begun to study skill development in orangutans orphaned as young infants and reintroduced into natural habitats after years of life in captivity.[36] Her outcomes will tell us how strong the dependence of intelligence on conditions during development really is, allowing us to compare great apes and humans in this respect.

The dependence on external inputs is no accident. The development of the brain, at least that of primates, is unlike that of any other organ.[37] The target of brain development is not specified in detail. Development happens interactively, with parts of the brain competing with other parts for space, expanding or shrinking depending on their inputs and use. Primate brains have more synaptic connections around adolescence than later in life: selective pruning of connections takes place depending on the details of experience. As a result, some parts of the brains of humans and that of great apes (and perhaps other taxa as well) are truly a blank slate, waiting to be written on. This flexible process allows a customization of software that is unprecedented in nature. Each and every brain can be filled differently, although brains developing in the same place at the same time end up becoming very similar in their actions and memories.

Human evolution, then, is an unprecedented experiment by Mother Nature, unique in the history of the world and perhaps in that of the entire universe. The "hard" adaptations of regular biological evolution—such as superb digging claws, improved color vision, more efficient digestion of a high-fiber diet, or a tendency to avoid predators by avoiding dangerous microhabitats—play only a minor role in the changes we have seen since the ancestral great ape. Even soft adaptations, more flexible developmentally—for instance, the ability to learn the hiding places of predators or the most profitable local foods—are relatively unimportant. Instead, culture has become the key adaptation. Genes are involved, of course, but only in laying the foundation. What is built on that foundation is immensely powerful—a procedure that in a few short years can absorb the hard-won collective wisdom of previous generations. When external conditions change, cultural change is also fast, much, much faster than regular evolution, and the slow upward crawl toward the adaptive peak turns into a fast trot. Culture is as close to the open-ended extreme of the developmental spectrum as can be imagined for any natural organism.

Culture, however, also has a down side. It is a double-edged sword, great for cutting a new swath into uncharted territory but also easy to fall on. Burn our libraries, smash our computers, and stop all teaching for just one generation—break just a single link in the chain of transmission—and it is all gone, only to be regained, if at all, after a long process of carefully building innovation upon invention.[38] Great civilizations disappeared with hardly a trace, their institutions lost, their writing undecipherable, even if the descendants of the people who made it possible are still around.

TRIANGULATING HUMAN NATURE 10

What have we learned from the work on the vanishing red ape? Whenever I travel in Indonesia, and am asked to explain to the people I meet what it is that I do there, by far the most common response is: "Oh, you're trying to prove Darwin's theory!" The question echoes the one posed by the wife of the bishop of Wilberforce, some 150 years ago, when she heard about Darwin's theory. The tone in which it is usually asked betrays the same deep unease, even angst, that motivated her question: Do I really believe that humans evolved from the apes? Would acceptance of this belief not lead us to descend into Nietzschean nihilism and hence toward immorality?[1] I doubt it. Indeed, I am convinced that an evolutionary account of the origins of human nature will yield insights that should allay these fears. It will show that we have both a noble and a savage side, and that it is our own choice to decide which side we're on. In this chapter, I return to our attempt at building an evolutionary account of the origins of human nature with which I began this book. This is of course a massive undertaking, but the work on orangutan technology, culture, and intelligence contributes to an outline of the path we can take.

Let us briefly recapitulate the primatological program laid out in Chapter 2. To know thyself, know thy neighbors. Human nature is part mammal, part primate, part great ape, and part uniquely human. Understanding what it is to be human requires an understanding of all of these layers of human nature, though of course the layers that were added most recently stir up the most excitement. Defining humans by making comparisons is a job that is never finished. It is the stamp-collecting aspect of our work, and

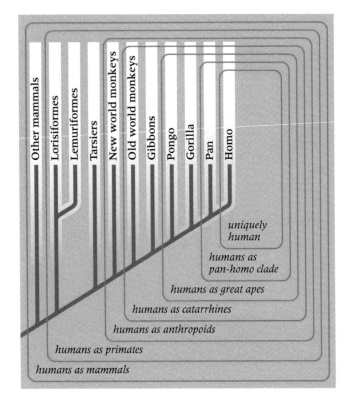

Other mammals

Lorisiformes

Lemuriformes

Tarsiers

New world monkeys

Old world monkeys

Gibbons

Pongo

Gorilla

Pan

Homo

uniquely human

humans as pan-homo clade

humans as great apes

humans as catarrhines

humans as anthropoids

humans as primates

humans as mammals

we must continue to collect new stamps, "as long as we continue to be surprised by the natural history of modern taxa."[2]

New findings from the field generally force us to strike items off the list that were previously thought to be uniquely human, and in this book I have happily contributed to this parlor game. At the same time, though, as we learn new facts about humans, and especially human foragers (extreme, even militant egalitarianism among the most mobile foragers, for instance), we may find reason to prop up the pedestal traditionally reserved for humans.[3]

Documenting contrasts and commonalities among species is a necessary first step. The ultimate aim is an understanding of the origins of the contrasts, and for that we need theories founded on broad-based studies of organisms other than humans. Most of this theorizing builds on studies of a broad array of species, mostly primates, though not necessarily limited to them,[4] but focusing on variability within species, as we have learned for chimpanzees and orangutans, is also a highly effective approach to developing and testing our theories.

I will therefore begin with an exploration of the point of departure for human evolution, by providing a diagnosis of the universal great ape and then pointing out a few features that are only found in chimpanzees and humans. Knowing what great apes are about, we can identify our uniquely derived features, the outermost layer of human nature, the part that arose only and uniquely in the hominin lineage. Once we have these listed, our agenda is set: it is their origin that we need to explain. Leaning on the theoretical insights gleaned from three decades of primatology, we will end with a first stab at reconstructing under what conditions a great ape transmogrified into a human.

Foundation: The Ape in Us Each of the four living species of great ape (chimpanzee, bonobo, gorilla, and orangutan) is so different from the others that the search for common features may seem doomed to failure. It is true that the similarities are not in the easily observed variables: group composition and social organization are all over the map; diet is quite variable; mating systems also vary widely in the degree of female promiscuity. Yet, it is hard to escape the conclusion that Asia's great ape, as it has emerged from the mists of Sumatra's swamps, looks much more like the chimpanzee than the textbook stereotype has it. Orangutans are intelligent, socially tolerant, and technologically adept. They use tools, share meat, forage together in opportunistic parties of all possible compositions, and even display culture. This similarity hints at the possibility that there is a universal great ape nature. Let us review the results of earlier chapters to pick out the features that separate the great apes as a group from their sister group, the Old World monkeys.[5]

An orangutan's back yard: the Sumatran swamp

All great apes are large, as primates go. Large size contributes to slower life histories, and great apes are even slower than one would expect for their body size, a legacy of their descent from arboreal ancestors. Among primates and a few other mammalian lineages, slow-paced life history is linked to large brains. Great apes score higher than monkeys on a broad range of cognitive tests. Unlike monkeys, they can recognize themselves in mirrors, can imitate, engage in pretend play, make tools, occasionally teach, and in a few cases they have been shown to take the other's perspective. In the wild, the large brains are used especially for skill-intensive foraging. I have stressed this connection for orangutans, but even a mountain gorilla, that ultimate herbivore, displays incredible dexterity grabbing and folding nettle leaves just right so as to minimize the number of stings to its hands and lips.[6] Nest building is another expression of intelligence and manual dexterity.

The orangutans of Suaq are highly sociable.

There is also something about the social behavior of great apes that is quite rare among monkeys. Although there are obvious exceptions, by and large dominance relations are much less rigid among great apes than among most monkeys. For instance, we see formal subordination signals in only a few of the possible types of pairs (within and between the two sexes) in the four species.[7] Indeed, great apes display remarkable social tolerance, one expression of which is the tendency to share food. Except from mother to infant, food sharing is not common among primates. We see it in a few species when males have meat and share with their consort of the day. Within same-sex pairs, it is found only in some highly tolerant capuchin monkeys and great apes: chimps, bonobos, and orangutans.[8]

There is a straightforward explanation for this unusual social feature. Two major principles underlie the form of all social organization, animal and human alike: cooperation and competition. For animals to form a gregarious social unit, they must derive a net benefit from doing so, because, at least in mammals, solitary life is the ancestral state. For most primates, the shared benefit of group life is the added protection against predators afforded by more eyes and ears and the opportunities for communal counterattacks. This ubiquitous benefit forms the foundation for all social life in these groups. Ironically, an inevitable upshot of group living is increased competition within the group over access to critical resources such as food or shelter.

The large body size of great apes makes them very sensitive to competition, in particular the extractive foragers, such as chimps and orangutans. It also diminishes their vulnerability to predation, especially the arboreal ones such as the orangutan. Great apes could therefore ill afford to live in permanent groups, except during times of plenty, although those that eat fibrous foods that are abundant may have less trouble. All great apes, therefore, show fission-fusion sociality, albeit to varying extent. Parties in most chimpanzee and some orangutan populations wax and wane in size with food abundance[9] (this is especially true for same-sex association; between sexes the presence of sexually attractive females is the most important factor). Gorilla groups vary in how much space they occupy to accommodate the variation in competition. Among lowland gorillas, groups either spread out over large areas or even fission into smaller units, as do other apes.[10] In other words, great apes cope with competition by increasing their interpersonal distance.

The option of bailing out when the others play rough makes ape social life qualitatively different from that of most monkeys. When subordinates are forced to remain in the group, because going it alone sooner or later means death, dominants can squeeze them like lemons: what alternatives do the poor losers have? But when subordinates can walk away, dominants interested in the company of others had better be nice. Hence the evolution of social tolerance. It may not be the perfect socialist society, but neither is it primate purgatory.

The actual fitness benefit of this social restraint toward subordinates is not hard to spot. Others might have some useful skills or remember something about the environment. Those who look for company whenever they can and tolerate others when they are not too hungry will end up with a greater repertoire of skills in knowledge. This benefit of social life is uniquely important among great apes, the most skill-intensive foragers among the primates. The great apes' technological and cultural prowess is critically dependent on the combined presence of social tolerance and sophisticated intelligence.

Finally, one more social feature may be seen as unique to great apes: their tendency to collaborate with nonrelatives. Collaboration with relatives is common among most animals, including numerous primates, but working together with non-relatives is far less widespread. Great apes, with their slow life history and, in most species, relatively small social spheres, may be forced to choose nonrelatives simply because suitable kin may not be available with whom to form an alliance or exchange relationship. We tend to believe that support of relatives, which is often not reciprocated in full if at all, does not require much calculation. It is therefore possible that this accident of life history has forced great apes to engage in more mental bookkeeping of the give and take in their collaborations than your average monkey.

According to Ernst Mayr, "it is a miracle humans ever happened."[11] It is hard to disagree: there is no way we could have predicted the evolution of a hyper-intelligent bipedal ape from first principles or the known broad patterns in evolution (the "laws" of paleontology). On the other hand, if we know both the organism and the environment and are content to extrapolate forward only a short period of time, then evolution is in fact rather predictable. The universals shared by great apes show a fortuitous confluence of all the elements that favor the evolution of cultural abilities

and human-like hyper-intelligence reviewed in the previous chapter: high intelligence, and more specifically innovative ability, skillful foraging, a capacity for observational forms of social learning, long life span, a reasonable level of social tolerance, and a tendency toward food sharing and exchange. Admittedly, this list does not explain why only a few of the many great apes took that direction, and it hardly makes our evolution inevitable. But it does show that human behavior and intelligence is built on a solid great ape foundation. And now that that foundation is more or less mapped out, we can begin to speculate which elements of the foundation formed the main sources of human nature.

Before we can begin that task, we must examine features that are not universal among the great apes but are limited to chimpanzees and our own species (in fact, this is the part of the foundation that most work to date has focused on). That analysis will reveal what these African apes, with whom we share the most recent common ancestor, have to add to this picture. Not surprisingly, they add quite a bit, but what may spark interest is that the additions concern our social arrangements more than the foundations for culture.

The *Pan–Homo* Clade Chimpanzees *(Pan)* and humans *(Homo)* are the only great apes that share the following unusual features: serious, sometimes lethal, between-group violence,[12] routine hunting of game, and a striking sex difference in both of these activities.[13] In fact, they are the only primates that have these features. That does not necessarily mean that these shared traits are homologous, because in that case we face the problem of explaining their absence in bonobos and quite possibly in some of the now extinct hominins in the ancestral line. An alternative possibility is that humans and the ancestral chimps independently chanced upon this strange social arrangement as a result of being placed in similar conditions with similar cognitive resources. Either way, all these features probably reflect one underlying key variable: male philopatry and bonding.

It probably all began with the establishment of the tendency for males to stay all their lives inside the ranges in which they were born: philopatry (from the Greek for "love of fatherland"). In primates generally, the sex that benefits most from forming strong cooperative bonds (alliances) tends to be the philopatric one. The alliances are about systematic support in fights with others, which allows allies to achieve higher ranks than they would alone. Relatives make the most reliable partners, so you stick with kin through thick and thin. The easiest way to achieve that is by staying near where you were born. But if one sex stays, the other has to go: inbreeding avoidance is one of the strongest forces in mate choice.[14] Usually, the females are the sex staying in their natal groups or ranges.[15] Alliance formation is easier for females, whose competition is mainly about access to food or shelter, than for males, whose competition is mainly about access to mates. Access to mates is not so easily shared—it is a constant-sum game: any mating opportunities I grant my ally to keep him interested in supporting me is so much paternity denied to me! Access to food or shelter is more easily shared. Hence, we expect more alliances among females than among males, and because alliances with relatives are much more durable, females win the conflict over who gets to stay home.[16] Males, therefore, usually migrate away from their group of birth to look for opportunities elsewhere.

Among African apes, there is a clear trend in the opposite direction. In gorillas, both sexes generally leave their natal groups, but males have a somewhat better chance of staying by taking over the family store from their aging father. In chimps and bonobos, the rule, while still not hard and fast, is more rigid. The universal tendency among great apes toward fission-fusion social organization means that coalitionary defense of food sources is not very useful, and females would become largely indifferent to staying or leaving. If—and this is the key condition—if there were some overriding benefit for males to stay at home, the pattern could flip toward male philopatry. In gorillas, the males that stay around tend to inherit the group, which is the best route to genetic immortality for a male.[17] No real flip yet, but when the father stays around for many years or his son inherits, maturing females tend to leave their natal group. In chimpanzees, the males form brotherhoods, alliances much like those among females in other species.[18] Orangutans are the exception here, for males do not form coalitions, and male tenure is not long enough to have sons inherit the mating rights to the females. Females get to stay put; that way, they at least get nicer neighbors.

Why on earth, when we have just shown that males are not likely to form alliances, do male chimps (and humans) form them so readily? We do not know for sure, but the origin may have to do with coalitionary mate guarding. Imagine a situation like the one we saw among orangutans, with females coming into receptivity once every so many years and males just cruising around looking for action. When these males are highly mobile and can cover a lot of ground, the few and far between fertile females will be set upon by a veritable horde of suitors.[19] In orangutans, male mobility is too limited to lead to such mating swarms, although at Suaq they may be getting close, and it is possible that the dominant flanged male occasionally loses control over the situation. If males routinely run around on the ground, on the other hand, mob scenes are almost inevitable. There is no way that even the most ferocious dominant male can maintain exclusive access to the female under such conditions, but if he teams up with one or more friends—or, better still, relatives—the team may be able to defend access to the female. Exactly this coalitionary mate guarding has now been observed in a chimp community with the largest number of males on record.[20]

Once males organize themselves into bonded teams, they are likely to restrict their action to areas with which they are most familiar and in which they can beat the competition, so teams will space out. The next step—keeping other males out systematically—may be linked to a new threat: infanticide. As noted in Chapter 5, infanticide by males is a serious problem among many primates. Most primate females share this basic vulnerability, but for the risk to be acute, the social system has to be such that the killer males actually benefit. This happens in a range of conditions. However, where females have control over when they mate and with whom, they can reduce the risk considerably, especially when strangers show up only rarely. Because great ape males can be pretty coercive, the females must work hard to mate with the males in the right mix, and that is not always possible.[21] But above all they must try to stay away from strange males; and this is also in the interest of all the likely fathers! Once teams had come into existence, therefore, they would become strongly territorial. We would also expect females with dependent offspring to try to avoid the border zones. Both these predictions hold for chimpanzees.

Territoriality is a characteristic of lots of animal species, but rarely do we see lethal violence, certainly nothing approaching systematic slaughter. Here is where the strange solidarity of the chimpanzee brotherhoods comes into play; especially the higher-ranking males in a community form

Subadult male orangutans are more like chimpanzee males than the flanged male orangutans in being both mobile and sociable.

true fraternities that take risks for each other. They hunt together and play complementary roles in capture, and although the meat tends to end up with the top male, he will make sure to share with his buddies.[22] Note that all great apes like to eat meat, but only chimpanzees hunt systematically.[23] And among chimps, variation within communities over time and differences between communities in the mean rate of hunts are directly linked to how much time males can afford to spend together. Hunting, then, is a communal pastime, and the more opportunities that males have to be together the more they hunt. Although the love of meat is what makes this behavior possible, the political gains may outweigh the nutritional ones: eating meat together is more important than eating meat per se.

These warm friendships prepare the males for the riskiest of all endeavors: communal defense of their range. When in the overlap zone with a neighboring group, males in a party may suddenly decide to go on patrol: all march quietly in single file, their tension betrayed by their goose bumps. Kids are not welcome, because their noisy behavior might betray the presence of the patrol and spoil the effect. Often, males form patrols after they have heard calls or other sounds indicating the presence of other chimps. If they come across those others, the outcome depends on the relative numbers. If the others are in a sizeable party, they all make a big ruckus, running around screaming, hugging their buddies nervously—and then it is all over. But if a single neighbor is encountered or the enemy party is grossly outnumbered, the party becomes a lethally efficient chimp panzer division. The attack is silent, swift, and well orchestrated, and the aim is to kill. The victim is subdued communally, beaten and bitten, dismembered and emasculated.[24] Chimpanzee observers have now collected several examples of communities that were systematically exterminated in this way. The term *genocide* comes to mind.

These brutal attacks are made possible by the fission-fusion life style, which can lead to serious discrepancies in the sizes of parties that meet in the overlap zones.[25] But to explain why we see these attacks in chimps and humans, but not in any other primates, we need to remember that chimps and humans have both become social carnivores, in the functional sense: males become team members, willing and able to take risks for each other. Males that hunt together, patrol together.[26] And males that patrol together, kill together: chimpanzee family values.

The third feature unique to chimps and humans is a sex difference in how much they hunt. "Hunting" among all other primates is very much like regular foraging. Orangutans, for instance, go after slow lorises: they search very carefully in places where these small nocturnal primates could be hiding, and if they spot one they quickly grab it by the scruff and deliver a deadly bite. Impressive, but it has little to do with the long deliberate stalk, the chase and the capture, let alone the cooperative effort of a group hunt. It is worth mentioning that in the majority of observed cases, when a slow loris is snatched the forager was a female. Chimp females are just as fond of red colobus meat as males are but rarely participate in the hunts. It is not that they catch no prey at all, but they follow the general primate pattern by catching their prey when the opportunity arises, not after lengthy and deliberate hunts. It is the chimp males that stand out by engaging in these elaborate group hunts, for the high drama of the kill and especially the politics of meat distribution.

These observations throw an interesting light on the often strictly enforced sexual division of labor characteristic among human foragers. Even if hunting is not always the communal affair it is in chimps, we see similarly extensive meat sharing among foragers. Indeed, so little sharing seems to go to the hunter's immediate nuclear family that hunting by male humans is considered by some to be a form of costly signaling—a behavioral peacock's tail.[27] The male advertises his qualities by bringing home large chunks of meat and then generously giving it away to all. Females are supposed to find such generosity irresistible.

If viewed in this historical perspective, the sexual division of labor seems to have little to do with sex differences in nutritional requirements (females' need for a steady stream of high-density food stuffs) or even in hunting ability (females being dragged down by dependent offspring in various ways).[28] These ideas never made too much sense when held against the light of the comparative primate record. This explanation also makes clear why in many foraging societies women are not allowed to hunt, not even those without children or in better physical shape than some of the men. As Craig Stanford put it: "Meat has a gendering influence."[29] The sexual division of labor, in sum, is yet another example of a trait that initially seems ecologically based but upon closer inspection turns out to be about the different reproductive strategies of the two sexes.

Before we knew much about orangutans, primatologists tended to argue that the true foundation for human evolution was laid with the emergence of the *Pan–Homo* clade. The gap between these species and the other primates was just too large. Now the picture has become more complex. The foundation (universal commonalities among great apes) is both broader and older than usually believed. The *Pan–Homo* clade added to this base a set of features that were definitely critical in putting us on the road to humanity, but probably not for the emergence of our most surprising feature: our immersion in culture.

Uniquely Human We have just listed what the first hominins came equipped with—the great ape universals and the *Pan* peculiarities—if not in actuality then at least potentially. Defining humans, in a comparative, zoological sense, is now fairly straightforward. Our focus is on behavior, not on the fact that humans alone are fully bipedal, have much larger brains, have smaller teeth and jaws, and have lost canine teeth that can be used as weapons. To characterize human behavior, we pick hunter-gatherers, or foragers, the very few people who engage in a life style that must be closest to the ancestral life ways of anatomically modern humans as they arose some 50,000 years ago. It does not really matter that many of today's foragers are not direct descendants of an unbroken line of foragers but instead may represent a secondary return to foraging, for whatever reason. From them we learn how a human being equipped with a modern mind and living as a forager in a small community might live.[30] Despite the variability among the different groups, there are enough similarities among at least the so-called immediate-return foragers, who do not store food on a large scale, to map out the key contrasts with great apes with respect to the biological variables that involve or affect behavior. Here is the list.

First, humans have relatively larger and very much fatter babies, who are more dependent and develop more slowly and then go on to live decades longer than our great ape ancestors ever did. These biological facts point to a further slowdown of life history relative to the already quite slow pattern of the great apes. Oddly enough, however, some of our life events occur more quickly: women produce babies at a faster rate than female apes do. They can afford to do so because human babies are weaned much earlier and then fed on specially processed "weaning foods." This break with the ape way of raising offspring is made possible by outside help from female relatives, especially grandmothers and older children, or males. In a

Human infants are not only larger, they are also much fatter than orangutan infants.

unique development, unprecedented among primates and shared only with one or two other mammals, human females experience a complete cessation of breeding (menopause) well before their bodies have aged to the point that reproduction could not be sustained. Perhaps older women gain more fitness by helping their daughters rear their children and so produce many more offspring than they would by trying to continue producing their own children at ever-lower rates and ever-greater risk.[31]

Second, bonobos notwithstanding, we are comparatively deviant in our sexual behavior. The ovarian or menstrual cycles of human females lack the exaggerated cyclical anatomical changes exemplified by the perineal swellings found in the two species of chimpanzee, in which the moment of ovulation is rather unpredictable in chimpanzee females and extremely so in bonobo females.[32] In common with the bonobos, humans engage in sex throughout the menstrual cycle and pretty much throughout the reproductive cycle, including much of pregnancy and lactation, but of course we lack their sexual swellings. Oddly, this sexuality, which might seem to enable a promiscuous life style, is accompanied by the presence of social pair bonds, which tend to produce sexual exclusivity, depending on socioecological conditions and cultural norms. And at least as oddly, sex in humans tends to be a private affair, not practiced in view of others. Pair bonding may have something to do with the greater care lavished on our children, who, even years after weaning, remain clumsy foragers.[33] In Chapter 6, I ascribed the discretion of human sex to the need for the human female to keep one male interested in investing in her and her offspring.

Third, we have a far more complex social organization than any ape. Among mobile tropical foragers, sharing of food is a moral imperative, as is the absolute lack of status differentiation, a tendency called militant egalitarianism by Christoph Boehm.[34] We have seen that great apes often collaborate with nonrelatives. This holds even truer for humans, as Hobbes noted long ago. Exchange may have begun with commodities that were produced irregularly, such as meat (most hunters return empty-handed). As foragers became more sedentary, specialization seems to have developed, especially within families and across age and sex boundaries. This sexual division of labor is often quite strictly maintained: traditionally, males hunted and women gathered. We just saw that the origin of sexual specialization in chimpanzees may have less to do with family economics and more with male mating tactics, an idea also entertained by students of human behavioral ecology.[35] In sum, humans share and trade more than any other primate.

The final uniquely human trait, and the most striking contrast of all, is our hypertrophied brain, more than three times as large as the brains of the great apes, and all the remarkable things we do with it. We work together and deceive, we make and use tools, we adopt and teach cultural values, we undergo rites—all much more than apes do. Above all, we link these behaviors together with a uniquely complex symbolic communication system called language. This distinction may be so familiar to all of us that we tend no longer to notice it, but such a rapid change in brain size is biologically unprecedented. I cannot think of any other lineage in which one species has evolved a brain that is more than three times that of its closest relatives, while maintaining roughly similar body size.[36] We do not yet know in detail how to explain the origin of these other features, but this last set of human characteristics is what truly sets us apart; hence the *sapiens* in our biological name.

When a particular species differs from its close relatives in a set of features, chances are that these characteristics are somehow linked. A compelling reconstruction will have to weave together various themes, perhaps even for a single pacemaker. That is probably true here. Longer life spans and larger brains clearly go together among primates. The pair bonds and provisioning by males may also be linked to the slower life history, as in the embedded capital model. Trading is but one reflection of interdependence that is (as I will argue below) inextricably linked to culture. There is unlikely to be a magic bullet—a single proposition that ties it all together and explains Mayr's miracle. But a satisfactory explanation of the final contrast, the enormous expansion of the human brain—and the novel things it makes possible, including, perhaps most importantly, culture—would take us a long way.

One lineage of bipedal apes rather suddenly became so different from all the others that we need molecular evidence and arcane anatomical details to remind us of our intimate family relationship with the other great apes. Why did one among many leave the great ape mind behind and become the large-brained "symbol-using animal"?[37] If we have any luck solving this one, we can start to think about solid biological explanations for the origin of morality, religion, art, humor, music, sports, and even language.

When orangutans walk bipedally they tend to raise their arms for balance.

What Happened during Hominin Evolution? Some six or seven million years ago, many great apes, steadfast canopy animals, had increasing difficulty traveling through the tree crowns. As the canopies became less continuous in response to persistent drying trends, they were forced to come to the ground more often or wither away in small forest fragments. One lineage among many responded to the new conditions by going bipedal. Their morphology may have been such that traveling on the ground more or less by default eventually led to walking on hind limbs. It is generally believed that these australopithecines led rather conventional great ape lives for several million years: they are often characterized as bipedal apes.[38] Their proudest achievement, which didn't make an appearance until several million years later, was the use of simple stone tools, of the Oldowan type. These tools are generally believed to be outside the range of the possible for living hominoids. Some researchers claim that the stone assemblages that have been unearthed under chimpanzee nut-cracking sites could be mistaken for Oldowan,[39] but most archeologists beg to differ.

Somewhat less than two million years ago, hominins of a different sort emerged. Anatomically, they were larger-brained, taller, and fully adapted for upright locomotion and roaming the open savannas. Behaviorally, they showed evidence of organized hunting, or at least organized scavenging, and use of a more sophisticated kind of tools of the Acheulean type. This species, *Homo erectus,* could soon be found throughout all tropical and subtropical parts of the Old World, all the way to Southeast Asia. Surprisingly, thought, this species' tool kit remained pretty much the same for over a million years, showing little or no geographic variability. This points to a remarkable lack of cumulative evolution.[40]

Out of this lineage evolved, a few hundred thousand years ago, our own species. But although the changes in the tool kit at that time suggested fancier cognitive abilities and more complex culture in the new species, they were nothing compared to what happened a mere 50,000 years ago. Around that time, our species' culture was drastically redesigned, and that in the absence of any morphological change. Rather suddenly, a dazzling array of finely crafted tools makes its appearance, from sturdy to delicate. The tools are made from a variety of materials, from stones to bones to antlers, some of which are found hundreds of kilometers from the sites where their raw materials originated, suggesting the existence of sophisticated trading networks. Many tools display seemingly functionless modifications, objects are treated with pigments, the dead are buried and equipped for their voyage to the other realm. Cave paintings are made that rival the finest recent art. All of this is accompanied by more geographic variation. These, at last, were people completely like us!

This explosion of innovation was a prelude to the invention of agriculture and more complex societies and eventually, to squeeze another 10,000 years of relentless cultural evolution into two words, to writing and the internet. However, we must keep things in perspective: the cultural explosion was indeed a great leap forward, but the new techniques and behaviors were not qualitatively different from what came before. The changes did not occur at a run-away pace or generate ever more complex technological achievements instigating parallel changes in other aspects of culture. It can fairly be argued that the run-away

Human technology developed from such humble beginnings as primate tool use.

phase of cultural evolution was reached only recently, perhaps since the Enlightenment, when we began the systematic pursuit of innovation and its transmission.

There are therefore really two puzzles to solve. The first one is to find out what accident of history put our ancestors on this unusual trajectory toward superior culture and technology. Is there anything we can take from recent revelations about great ape behavior that could tip us off? The different hominin species all no doubt arose in response to different environmental challenges and opportunities and played different ecological roles. That makes it tough to develop a single account for these various events. Nonetheless, they do have a few things in common. Although we have no firm facts at this stage, what we have learned about great ape culture may help to guide us to an answer.

The second puzzle is harder to unravel: how some 50,000 years ago a revolution occurred that produced a dramatically more advanced and complex human culture, as far as we can tell without major changes in the size of our brains or other aspects of our morphology. Here, the insights gained from studying great ape cultures will probably be of less use, but we can nonetheless use them to develop a novel hypothesis.

I will postpone the issue of the great cultural leap forward to the final section and mount an attack on the general problem first. Where is the guiding influence of culture in hominin evolution? Culture must already have been prominently present in the first hominins but not, it seems, significantly much more so than in the most sophisticated great apes of today. There is no denying that the extinct hominins were more cultural than today's great apes, but in a way they seem to be more similar to the great apes than to modern humans. In fact, we can roughly predict from fieldworkers' observations of great apes what may have caused the incremental changes that produced their material culture.

Culture is part private—innovation—and part social—diffusion. Increased cultural complexity may reflect improved innovation, increased social transmission, or (most likely) both. Such improvements may be an immediate outcome of greater exploratory tendencies that arose because habitats changed and traditional techniques no longer worked, or because new opportunities suddenly presented themselves. They may also be the direct result of more favorable social conditions for socially mediated learning, such as increased social tolerance or increased time spent together.

Gracile australopithecines and early members of the genus *Homo* spent more time together around clumped resources, perhaps clusters of tubers that they dug up with tools or large mammals that were butchered with the aid of tools. We may reasonably infer that this new life style provided both the opportunities and incentives for increased tool use and hence expanded culture in general.

As we see in today's great apes, however, changes in conditions produce only so much cultural change: after a while, a ceiling is reached. To move that ceiling up, genetic changes in the underlying abilities are needed. Natural selection can only work on the abilities that underlie the cultural skills if the cultural potential is maximally expressed.

This approach to cultural change, following directly from the interpretation of variation among great apes, provides a plausible scenario for cultural evolution during most of hominin evolution. If, for ecological reasons, animals spend more time together, or if habitat change favors the invention of new skills (which will be guaranteed to stay around in socially tolerant groups), we expect to see cognitive changes that increase inventiveness or improve social learning abilities. These abilities are very much two sides of the same coin, because the same cognitive machinery that makes you creative also tends to make you a good observational learner.

Skills that improve subsistence, including those based on tools, are the kinds of cultural traits that are most easily improved by natural selection: better feeding, especially during times of scarcity, brings fitness rewards. Over time, therefore, tools became fancier and more diverse, and no doubt signal variants and symbols followed suit. But more remarkable than the changes was the fact that once a new repertoire was in place, the new equilibrium turned out to be stable to the point of being static. A conservative force seemed to have stifled innovation. In a stable situation, apparently, individuals are happy to copy what works and averse to experimentation.

It is important to remember that most culture is not of the run-away variety, not truly cumulative. Many chimpanzee and some orangutan populations are highly cultural and rely on sophisticated tools to make a living. I have stressed that the conjunction of this phenomenon in chimpanzees and orangutans implies that it must have been in place for millions of years. If that is right, then culture—while producing adaptations so much faster than regular organic evolution and especially producing fine-tuned local adaptations completely unattainable by natural selection on regular features—remained stuck at some modest level of complexity. I believe this property of cultural systems is explained by inherent conservatism. Young apes and humans explore and experiment, but up to a point. The success of culture, after all, lies in copying what others do and seems worth copying. To a naïve youngster entering a confusingly complex world, almost everything must seem to be worth copying: the adults really seem to know what they're doing, after all.[41] Culture, then, poses this strange paradox: without innovation there is no culture, but if we do not have strong tendencies toward slavish copying and instead try to figure out everything for ourselves, we won't get very far. Hence, the inevitable tension between independent innovation and faithful copying.

In any normal situation, where the adults are well adjusted and successful, the best thing a youngster can do is to copy rather than to invent. Being hard-headed just does not get you very far: better to follow the lead of your elders. The absence of solid theory to inform speculation about conditions favoring increased innovation is deplorable. However, we see a penchant for innovation among otherwise highly conservative copiers such as orangutans in one set of conditions. They can be summarized by Anne Russon's dictum that "no mother is the necessity of invention" based on her work with orangutan rehabilitants (ex-captive orphans) released into the forest. These naïve animals tried all kinds of novel tricks and were remarkably persistent in sticking to techniques that were patently ineffective.[42] They had little choice, after all, but to try to find something to eat in the strange, threatening, dimly remembered place. Their behavior suggests that some modern human communities were thrown into a situation where the regular tricks no longer worked. Many such communities may even have gone extinct, but some hit on major improvements, perhaps along the lines of fishing, that got them out of a pickle.

The upshot of this idea is that cultures can change but not in a manner we would characterize as gradually cumulative. Cultural history may well be like punctuated equilibrium: periods of cultural stagnation, when things go well and no one feels the need for change, alternating with periods of renewal or rapid change or even extinction, when the customary ways stopped working. But even cultural crises marked by feverish experimentation and innovation may be followed by periods of relative calm, when once again copying others is the surest way to success. Institutionalized, permanent cultural revolution did not exist.

This scenario obviously fits cultural evolution from the first cultural organism to early modern humans: for example, some tool-making styles remained constant for over a million years and hardly varied from place to place.[43] But does it apply to our caveman ancestors? Or did they buck the trend? The cultural explosion that started with them was followed, a modest 30–40 thousands years later, by the adoption of agriculture, civilization, metalworking, writing, science, and industrial production methods. Although there has been plenty of cultural stagnation since the great leap forward, there has also been a relentless historical march toward greater cultural complexity. That looks like a fundamental change in the way culture worked: from punctuated equilibrium to autocatalysis and cumulative change.

The Cultural Revolution The technological explosion that gave rise to the Upper Paleolithic and Later Stone Age has long baffled paleoanthropologists. Earlier major changes in material culture had generally been accompanied by changes in the morphology of their makers. But not this time: people before and after the cultural explosion looked just the same—provided you take away the jewelry and other accoutrements of a Cro-Magnon. To explain this exception to the co-evolution of morphology and archeology, Richard Klein has proposed that a macromutation reorganized the brain and made fully modern language possible.[44] Others, however, suggest that the great cultural leap was more evolutionary than revolutionary and do not feel the need to invoke what they consider a *deus ex machina*.[45]

It is tempting to agree with the latter camp. The problem with the macromutation idea is that genetic data suggest that the human species is far older than 50,000 years.[46] If language evolved more recently, not all people should be able to speak in a fully modern way. My guess is that a human being from before the big divide would pick up modern life without skipping a beat if transplanted into modern life, provided that happened at a young enough age. In other words, the change was not in the brain but in the mind—a mind created by cumulative cultural evolution, just as every new human mind is constructed during development. All human development is an interactive process where the existing cultural knowledge is woven into the biological substrate. Our study of culture indicates that an individual who grew up in a cultural vacuum would be unrecognizably different from one who was raised in a rich cultural environment. To explain why it took so long after the birth of our species to reach cultural revolution, we need to realize that cultural evolution, being a cumulative process, takes time and requires the coming together of the right ingredients. Indeed, in an ironic twist on the multiregional model for morphological evolution, many researchers interpret the archeological record as supporting a gradual and parallel emergence of modern culture in multiple regions.[47]

The more gradualist alternative may be more plausible, but it too faces a problem. It fails to explain why cultural evolution had become gradual and cumulative rather than the stop-and-go variety that preceded it. This is where Klein's idea may prove useful, and we may need to blend the two models. Underlying the process of continuous and gradual cultural change is the presence of full-blown language, that most distinctive of human special features. Since all humans speak, the ability for modern speech must be as old as our species, or at least 150,000 years old. Cultural evolution may be changed fundamentally once language is around. No doubt, language was used from the beginning for discussions of social relationships and reputation (in a word, gossip),[48] but that is unlikely to produce interesting cultural evolution. However, language is especially powerful in improving the transfer of skills and knowledge from those who know to those who don't, both within and between generations. Having language also makes innovation more systematic: people can reason about how well things work.[49]

The two models can therefore be reconciled, but there is still one thing missing from this blended model. What are the inducements for innovation or adoption of innovations that the presence of language made possible? I suspect that the cultural revolution is conceivably a consequence of a more sedentary life style, which in turn created major incentives for specialization and trade and, hence, for continued innovation.

Archeologists have noted that the new tools took much longer to make.[50] Almost certainly that implies that they were made by specialists, people who had learned to make these tools and were almost certainly much better at it than most others. Cave paintings, likewise, are so difficult to replicate for unskilled amateurs that they must have been made by well-trained artists. Would these artisans and artists have been full-time participants in hunting or other major (specialized) activities of the tribe? A picture emerges of specialists exchanging goods and services, rather than the jacks-of-all-trades that were characteristic of great apes and earlier hominins. Whereas Jack is best off doing what everybody else is doing, and hence specializes in copying, a production specialist has an incentive to improve his or her products.

Social patterns among recent hunter-gatherers are clearly consistent with the role of specialization in driving cumulative cultural change. Highly mobile foragers, who do not store food and therefore consume it all immediately, can't afford to have (and carry) too much personal property. As a result, there is not much to gain from a superior ability to make things. In the words of Marshall Sahlins, "mobility and property are in contradiction."[51] After all, you can't take it with you.

Indeed, one might even argue that the egalitarian ethos of mobile foragers forces them toward the conservative end of the spectrum: it stifles innovation and the adoption of novel techniques used elsewhere. Much of the gain from making an advance immediately leaks away to the many others who help themselves. Moreover, an entrepreneurial spirit may be viewed as an indication of nascent despotic tendencies, anathema in such a society.

In striking contrast, once foragers become more sedentary and have permanent settlements with satellite field camps, the number of tools used by a group (its tool kit) increases considerably. In addition, present-day collectors have larger and more complex tools, such as fish traps.[52] Where there are many different tools of complex design, there are probably multiple toolmakers. We can deduce a general rule: a more sedentary life style invites specialization. Groups that stay put place a premium on trying new techniques, making better versions of existing tools, and so on—all of which is pretty much impossible when high mobility enforces simplicity.

Foragers can afford to stay put when they are able to exploit resources from their home base or a satellite camp without having to move. There are all kinds of ecological reasons for this life style, but to explain the cultural explosion in the case of modern humans we must look for a more systematic cause, perhaps a shift in how resources are exploited. For instance, the invention of fishing and the exploitation of seafood in productive coastal zones may have provided a push toward a more sedentary life.

The shift may have happened at different times in different places, and indeed it may not have happened at all in most places or may have been temporary only. That would explain why the archeological record suggests various hesitant starts in different places, some of which may have petered out again.[53] However, it is possible that people that have undergone the great cultural leap forward were then able to settle in areas where previously only a mobile life was possible. In a way, then, we expect a mix of extrinsic ecological and intrinsic cultural reasons for the shift, perhaps a pattern similar to what happened some 40,000 years later with the transition to farming and pastoralism.

An interesting parallel development of sedentism may have made specialization even more favorable. Once human foragers settled down, access to the major resources needed to support sedentary life can be defended, and wealth can be accumulated. With storage of food and critical materials, the obligate need to share begins to wane. With the egalitarian ethos out of the way, producers could benefit from the surpluses they produce, whereas a mobile forager gains nothing from producing large resource chunks other than the prestige that comes from making them available to each and all group members. The strongest individuals and alliances could then monopolize these resources or the stores. More successful men have an incentive to become polygynous; more successful women can bear and support more children. Indiscriminate sharing becomes trade, and specialists making useful products or providing important services gain from their inventiveness in a way never seen before. The conditions of sedentary life create strong incentives for improved innovation and adoption of effective new skills or conventions, allowing natural selection to hone these capacities.

Even in the simplest foraging societies, people practice more exchange than chimpanzees. But the amount of trade—exchange of goods or services for other goods or services and later for small, highly valued tokens—must have skyrocketed once people became sedentary. Where specialization is possible, those who are really good at making arrowheads, say, will become specialized weapon makers and trade their products for the foods brought in by others. As this process continued, through settlement and agriculture, we became bakers, butchers, and brewers. Thus was born the division of labor in a market economy.

After specialization had given rise to a division of labor, all members of society needed goods produced by other members. They were all in the same boat and had to row together. Exchange, a luxury in great ape society, had become a necessity in the complex society of modern humans. The only other animals with such obligate dependence on others are the eusocial species (such as bees), in which non-breeding castes specialize on certain essential tasks such as cleaning, provisioning, or defense. Humans, of course, manage to do all this without being eusocial; all of us potentially are breeders ourselves, and very few are lifelong helpers that eschew reproduction.[54] This interdependency, perhaps more than the need to be allies in war, may be the glue that keeps human societies together. It critically depends on specialization, which in turn is made possible by sedentary life.

The next step in cultural evolution is trade and exchange between communities. Archeologists have noted that after the cultural revolution began materials used by the toolmakers are much more likely to have been acquired through long-distance trade. Ester Boserup, who studied cultural complexity among farming societies, found that openness to external influences was more important than the conditions for the appearance of inventions: cultural diffusion is the major engine of change.[55] This makes perfect sense: by being open to new ideas from outside, we effectively increase the pool of possible innovations from which to choose far beyond those we could generate in our own societies. This is especially true of those rare but revolutionary inventions, like the proverbial wheel or the taming of wild beasts. Cultural change can now become a never-ending process of accumulation.

In sum, a more sedentary life, made possible by some key innovations that allowed us to extract more edible food from the same area of land (or, probably more likely, coastline), created the incentives for the invention and production of ever fancier tools. Along with many changes in our social organization, it brought about specialization, which in turn led to trade and continuing incentives for innovation. If this sounds a bit like a commercial for free-market capitalism, I'm afraid it is: Adam Smith's invisible hand may have driven the dramatic expansion of human culture well before it became recognized as the foundation of capitalism.

I should stress of course that this idea is right now a mere working hypothesis suggested by the work on great apes. The value of hypotheses, though, is that they lead to focused observation and comparison. Or, as

Charles Darwin once wrote to a colleague: "How odd it is that anyone should not see that all observation must be for or against some view if it is to be of any service."[56]

The people I would meet on the street were apprehensive about what answers I would come up with when they asked me what I did. I become increasingly confident that they need not have worried. The human beings that evolved from great apes with behavioral capabilities similar to those of orangutans or chimpanzees derive their humanity from culturally constructed cognitive abilities, a process repeated every time a child is raised. Interdependence—and the trade and exchange that underlie it—can override our selfish tendencies, provided societies are organized in a way that exchange can flourish. Religions have merely tried to codify and add resilience to a system that evolution had already put in place. The intelligence-through-culture theory that the Suaq orangutans inspired claims that the specialization and interdependence spawned by culturally based skills of modern humans can thrive only in a society that is socially tolerant and open to innovation and diffusion. Thus, peeking into the evolution of our behavior through our view of the orangutans of Suaq did not induce us to share Nietzsche's nihilism; instead, it made us see the power of culture as a biologically based adaptation that has installed in us an emotional need to be a member of a supportive social network.

EPILOGUE:
LIVING ON BORROWED TIME

Field studies of great apes have now opened a window on cultural evolution in humans. However, the window is at risk of being closed before we are able to peer through it into our distant past. During recent decades, orangutans have suffered dramatic declines (see below), and the African great apes, though still much more numerous, are not in much better shape.[1] The continued presence of great apes in nature is not something we should take for granted.

In this epilogue, I will tell the story of the events that befell our study site, Suaq Balimbing, and the orangutans living there. The story is largely a sad one, but it may yet have a happy ending.

The Story of Suaq When we established Suaq, it was not exactly pristine. Especially along the river, human activities had clearly modified the forest: people cut trees, constructed shelters for overnight stays, and uprooted soils digging for worms to make fishing bait. Much less alteration was evident in the swamp. Fishermen placed traps or nets and cut a few trails, much as we do, but fish and other wildlife, such as otters and tortoises, were still abundant, suggesting that fishing had hardly made a dent in the prey populations. However, one tree species, medang glue,[2] had been the target of bark collecting. To collect the bark, which provides the raw material for insect repellant, the tree is cut down, the bark is stripped, subsequently dried on racks, and taken to market. The efficiency of the collectors was admirable; we knew only one or two mature trees in our study area that had escaped the roving teams of bark collectors (and that in near-featureless terrain that is hard to traverse). Fortunately, many of the stumps had sprouted, so the species might recover in due course (it is an orangutan fruit species).[3]

Suaq Balimbing is part of the Kluet swamp, which is part of the Gunung Leuser National Park, which in turn is part of the Leuser Ecosystem. Most of what is now national park has been protected for decades. The Kluet portion has been protected since 1937.[4] Some visionary nature lovers and big-game hunters had discovered the natural beauty and biological uniqueness of the area and lobbied the colonial Dutch government for some protection. After the local elders had requested protection for the forests along whose edges they made their living, in hopes that they would more or less be left alone, the colonial government gave in and declared a large chunk of land protected. Most of this region was steep mountain terrain, geologically active, with unstable slopes, complete with hot springs, earthquakes, and landslides—not easily exploited for logging and too steep or high for agriculture, and with no commercially interesting mineral riches. A tiny part of it was untrammeled coastal swamp. This part could be included because there were no villages along this stretch of the coast: the surf there was strong and there were no bays or river estuaries that could serve as harbors for fishing boats. This piece of coastline therefore remained unchanged—no development separated the "blang" (dwarf-shrub vegetation) on the peak of Gunung Leuser (3,404 meters above sea level) from the beaches of the Indian Ocean.

Although there was little or no logging inside the national park, the logging concession on the opposite side of the Lembang River was busy working the dryland parts and had stayed out of the swamps. Swamps are hard to get into and even harder to get

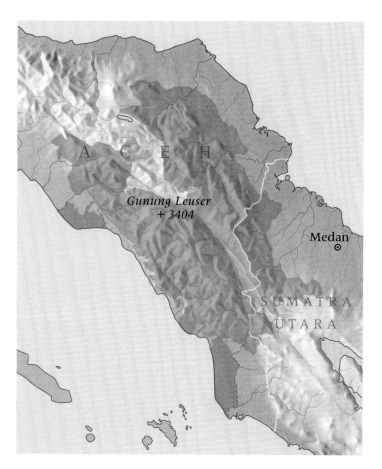

Gunung Leuser National Park, in the Leuser Ecosystem

wood out of with heavy equipment. So, in 1993, the local government reached a deal with the logging concession that the swamp directly opposite of Suaq would be removed from the concession and be logged to make way for rice paddies. How could one reasonably disagree with that? Indonesia needs to produce more rice to feed its burgeoning population. We had just gathered enough data to be able to point out that the 2 meter difference between the lowest and the highest water levels during a normal year would make rice farming difficult without costly dams to control water levels. Moreover, many fields elsewhere in the region were not worked very intensively, and increased investment in raising the productivity in the nearby coastal rice fields would bring better returns. Nonetheless, the deal went ahead. The forest was cut, the valuable timber harvested. Farmers from a nearby village came and worked the land, diligently trudging back and forth some 5 kilometers each day. Predictably, their crops

Within a few years after clearing, the unused parts of the area clear-cut for rice paddies showed solid regeneration, much of it directly from the stumps.

Logging roads open the land to further development.

were washed away, so they gave up. After several years of disuse, the forest began to grow back nicely.

Meanwhile, in the logging concession across the river changes were taking place. A logging concession practices selective logging. According to the strict regulations governing concessions, the company may only take out stems above a minimum size and not on steep slopes, and it must leave some seed trees and the occasional refuge. Some species are also off limits because they are valuable to local collectors—for instance, those that tend to contain bees' nests. The work plans are approved beforehand, logging roads and log yards carefully planned, and the activities continuously monitored by the forestry department. In theory, at least. In practice, things usually did not go quite that way. But in a way it did not really matter, because virtually all parties involved agreed that the law was wrongheaded (the only ones not in the know were some central planners and all foreigners). The reason to favor a carefully controlled selective cut over a complete clear-cut was that such selective logging was sustainable. After some 40 years of regeneration, the concessionaire could return and do a second cut. In practice, I don't know of a single concession where that actually happened.

Everywhere, the following sequence played out instead. The logging company constructed logging roads that opened up erstwhile inaccessible areas, and the logging operations removed the largest trees. These actions were perfect preparation for the next step: conversion. In most places, there would not be enough local inhabitants to turn the area into farmland. Instead, the plan was to turn the logging concessions into industrialized plantations of soft-wood exotic trees, or more commonly of oil palm. It just so happened that numerous transmigration projects were located near the logging concessions. Transmigrants were landless poor from overpopulated central islands, most of them from Java. Over the years, there has been much criticism of the locations selected for these projects, just as there has been criticism of the transgressions in logging concessions. Critics were addressing a phantom situation, however; the areas selected for the transmigrants often were not meant to become self-sustaining agricultural zones. Instead, the transmigrants were to become workers in the new plantations nearby. If the original transmigration project failed because of poor site selection, so much the better.

There was no transmigration project near Kluet. Across the river, then, local entrepreneurs began to set up their own oil palm plantations, small-scale versions of the mega-enterprises elsewhere. Local villagers, not to be left behind, began their own forest gardens, mixtures of fast-growing cash crops and a variety of tree crops that would gradually take over. Such gardens are a tradition in Aceh; the southwestern corner of the province, for instance, is well known for its nutmeg. The main logging road became the new main road to the isolated village of Pucuk Lembang, upriver from Suaq. In the old days, the villagers used to come by Suaq, laboriously pushing their full canoes upriver after a trip to the coastal towns, a trip that would take most of the day. Now the same trip on the back of a truck would take less than two hours when the road was dry! In a few more years, the hill forest between Suaq and the next valley, that of the fertile Kluet River, would be turned into gardens and plantations. Almost everyone was very happy with the way things were going; and the protected area was still left alone.

These developments, however, began to take their toll on the orangutans in Suaq. Although our data are anecdotal, we do not think it is mere coincidence that the northwestern females, Abby, Diana, and Pelet, whose home ranges had been largely across the river from our station before 1994, seemed to have great trouble staying healthy and raising their babies. Abby and Pelet have both had signs of disease: Abby had swollen joints, whereas Pelet and her son Peter had large circular lesions on their wrists that indicate a ringworm infection. Peter was the whiner of Suaq, always hungry, always tired, and both Dedi (Diana's child) and Peter seemed to lag behind in growth. And Abby still had not given birth again by the end of our study, even though we estimated that it had been almost nine years since her last infant Ati was born (eight years is the average interval between births).

These individual cases tell us something unexpected about orangutan females. Once they have settled in their home range, they become very reluctant to leave it. The range may be large, but it may not be stretched beyond its limits. The social system seems shapeless and fluid, with much overlapping among female ranges, and yet it is dif-

Peter, Pelet's son, showed circular wounds on his wrists, characteristic of ringworm infection.

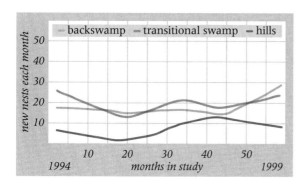

new nests each month

— backswamp — transitional swamp — hills

50
40
30
20
10

10 20 30 40 50

1994   _months in study_   1999

Even though logging gradually encroached on the study area, the number of new nests per month showed only a very slight increase.

ficult for females to pack up and leave one range to settle elsewhere. This tendency was demonstrated dramatically by the following observation. For all the years that our station was active, from 1994 through 1999, we ran monthly transects to count nests, allowing us to estimate how many new nests had been built in any given month. Although there were the usual ups and downs, there was no upward trend over the years in the number of new nests each month, despite the gradual closing in of the logging operations on our study area. Something similar happened around Ketambe in the Alas valley. When that site was established in 1971, Herman Rijksen estimated that the local orangutan density was about five individuals per square kilometer. Some thirty years and virtual deforestation of all the surrounding areas later, the density is still that, or perhaps even a bit less! As in Suaq, no massive influx of strange orangutans has occurred. We do see a modest number of new males showing up, but that is only to be expected. Especially remarkable is the absence of new adult females with babies moving in.

Conservation problems are hard to predict, and even harder to deal with. The situation so far was not perfect, but a new equilibrium would establish itself in due course. By 1997, however, a new threat materialized. Thailand's banks started to fold under the weight of spectacularly bad loans, and its currency, the baht, started to slide against the dollar. The dominoes soon began falling, and the Indonesian rupiah, which had been pegged against the dollar for years, suddenly fell as well. At the worst of Krismon (short for _Krisis Moneter_—Indonesians love acronyms), a year or so later, the rupiah had only about one-sixth its previous value.

The first results were good for the local economy. Export crops were priced in dollars, and suddenly the local growers could buy a lot more with the yield. Patchouli, a small weedy herb from which oil can be pressed to make the Indian perfume, suddenly became the crop of choice. Everybody got into the patchouli business (locally known as nilam). At night, the hills around the coastal towns were suffused in a red glow from all the fires lit to prepare forests for cultivation. The hills across the Lembang River from Suaq also were hit, and more forest was converted.

But the patchouli boom was just a warm-up for the real game. While the Sumatran countryside was booming, factories and banks were going bust,

Fires are set to open the forest for patchouli cultivation *(left)*; ovens are used to extract the patchouli oil *(right)*.

especially on industrialized Java. Companies could no longer pay for their imported raw materials, priced in dollars, nor could they make the payments on their bank loans. At the height of the crisis, two-thirds of Indonesian companies were technically bankrupt. Thousands of workers were laid off. The economic crisis turned into political turmoil. The demonstrations that followed became ever angrier. In May 1998, the unthinkable happened: after 32 years in power, the regime of President Suharto was brought down by mass demonstrations. The collapse of central authority rekindled long-dormant ethnic and religious conflicts, of which those in Irian Jaya, Ambon, East Timor, and Aceh were only the most visible manifestations.

Anarchy swept the nation. The genie was let out of the bottle—and had no desire to return to it. It was payback time. All these years, people had feared the government but not respected it. They had been forced into compliance by a corrupt regime that they considered thugs and thieves out only to enrich themselves. Now that these leaders were gone, it was the people's turn. And the people took to the forest.

No forest was secure. Literally everywhere one looked, timber was being poached out of all accessible forest, with complete disregard of the legal status of the land or the ecological consequences: from steep slopes above roads and villages to national parks. The scale of the poaching surprised

even cynical long-time observers of Indonesia's notoriously corrupt forest sector. Farmers neglected their fields, because they could make much more money by cutting, dragging, or sawing timber than by tending to their rice paddies. Hardscrabble locals formed chain-saw gangs, financed by loans given to them by sly entrepreneurs to pay for supplies.

It was open season on natural resources. Conservation is one of those functions of society that depend on the presence of a central authority that looks out for the common good. Here was a textbook example of the consequences of the collapse of central authority: the national parks were being ransacked.[5]

Commercial logging is capital-intensive. Trees are cut with chain saws, and the raw logs are then dragged by heavy machinery to log yards along the concession roads, where giant trucks pick them up for transport to the big timber yards. Concessions are riddled with all-weather roads, log yards, and big camps. The logs are processed far away, in dedicated factories with precision saws. This process minimizes the loss of commercially valuable wood but creates serious and often long-lasting damage to the forest.

This rice paddy had not been planted for two years.

Timber poaching is much simpler. Trees are felled in the same way, but after that the logs are quartered with chain saws and dragged out of the forest by water buffaloes, or raw muscle power. In the swamps, timbering is even more labor-intensive. The quarters, about 4 meters long, have to be pulled out on sleds ("ongkak") by teams of four strong young men over handmade wooden railroads greased with soap or old motor oil. The logs are piled up on the riverbank and then rafted down to a point where they can be loaded onto a truck and taken to a local sawmill. It is backbreaking,

Growing bolder, the loggers eventually put their log yard right next to our washhouse at our lower camp.

dirty, and dangerous work, and many of the men, some still children, get sick or injured.

This way of processing timber is wasteful with wood but, ironically, may be less destructive to the forest infrastructure in the long run because it does not damage the soil, unless the logging intensity is very high. In the short run, of course, it leads to the loss of much of the canopy, including many major food trees—in the swamps all but one of the top timber species were high on the list of orangutan food species.

Opportunistic timber raiders started to work in the Kluet swamps, along the coastal road, and from the road to Pucuk Lembang. They had left Suaq for last—the only place where there were people standing in their way. For many months, they had been active in the vicinity, but our vigilance had kept them at bay. Why go through the hassle of having your activities reported and facing the threat of action by the conservation service, police, and army when you can cut unimpeded next door? But as the police became increasingly inactive and unwilling to enforce the law, the logging gangs entered the site. They became bold and fearless, strutting confidently past our window and setting up camp right next to our station. They also found strength in numbers: we counted 24 such camps along the river inside our study area alone, providing shelter for some 225 men in all. We also counted 21 "railroads" in use at the time, some of them over a kilometer long. It is hard work to construct these rails, so all commercially interesting trees along them are taken out. Size does not really matter; only sinkers, which can't be floated out, escape exploitation.

Out of the swamp, the quartered logs are rafted to a landing place, where they are loaded onto trucks.

Because the entrepreneurs are politically well connected and let their money speak, it took desperate negotiations to reach a settlement, but by June 1999 we had reached an agreement that the logging at Suaq would stop. Logs that were already cut could be removed, but no more new trees would be cut. This agreement more or less held.

The forest was wounded. About one-third of the study area had been affected, but at least it was still green. Moreover, swamp forest regenerates better than dryland forest: the trees growing into the gaps caused by the tree falls and the skid trails tend to be the same species as those that were cut. There was hope.

The End of Our Road The long-simmering conflict between Acehnese rebels and the Indonesian government had flared up again in the early 1990s. Aceh has a proud history of fierce independence combined with openness to foreigners. A local pun is that Aceh stands for "Arab-Cina-Eropa-Hindia" to indicate the mix of ethnicities that came together on the northern tip of the island. Aceh is also overwhelmingly Muslim, being the first region in today's Indonesia to have embraced, in the early thirteenth century, the religion brought by the Arab traders.[6] The European element is largely derived from the Portuguese traders who came in the fifteenth century, soon to be followed by the Dutch. Both powers were attracted by Aceh's gold and valuable spices, in particular pepper. Aceh's power reached its apogee during the seventeenth century, when its favorite native son, sultan Iskandar Muda, ruled over both Aceh and most of peninsular Malaysia.[7] Ever since then, cultural and family ties are stronger with that part of Malaysia than with the rest of Indonesia.

The Dutch, who arrived as traders but gradually colonized most of what today is Indonesia, had a hard time subduing the proud Acehnese when they tried to consolidate their rule over the archipelago at the end of the nineteenth century. Faced with the toughest resistance they had encountered anywhere in their colony, they established only a few precarious garrisons on the coast, and these were attacked guerrilla-style from the mountains. A violent campaign of "punishment" began in which civilians were massacred throughout the region. By then, it was no longer the spice trade that attracted the Dutch to Aceh. Oil had been found on the East Coast and became a mainstay of the colonial economy. Later, massive gas reserves were discovered and Aceh became one of the world's largest providers of liquefied natural gas. Add gold, some other precious minerals, and timber to the mix, and it is easy to see how outsiders would be interested in this small corner of Sumatra. It is also easy to understand that the people living in regions endowed with great natural wealth are interested in pursuing independence, as this would obviously significantly raise their own standard of living, especially if they are culturally and religiously different from the rest of the country in the first place.

Predictably, Aceh was an enthusiastic supporter of Indonesia's independence struggle at the end of World War II. The Japanese, who had easily driven out the colonial Dutch in 1942, were first welcomed as liberators but were soon regarded as colonizers themselves. When the Dutch came back in 1945 to take up business as usual, a few months after the Netherlands had been liberated from five years of Nazi occupation, skirmishes broke out everywhere. The Acehnese wanted to become part of a federal Indonesia. They even put up the money to buy the very first airplane for the freedom fighters, the Seulaweh, later to serve as the first passenger plane for the new national airline, Garuda. The federal structure never materialized, however, and soon enthusiasm for the new country led to complaints about new colonization.

Just as some Acehnese leaders had never accepted Dutch rule, there was always an undercurrent of resistance against Indonesia. A new round of armed resistance, which began in the late 1970s, became really serious in the early 1990s. The focal points were, not surprisingly, the gas and oil fields on the East Coast and the nearby plantation areas, established mainly in the 1980s and populated with transmigrant workers hailing largely from the overpopulated island of Java. Working on the West Coast, we optimistically thought the unrest would not spread to the quiet backwaters there. But unrest did spread, especially after May 1998, when big demonstrations in Jakarta brought down the centralist Suharto government and plunged much of the country into virtual anarchy. By 1999, the Free-Aceh rebel movement (GAM) had gained solid support down the West Coast. The movement's supporters became bold and openly challenged the army and police. Killings back and forth became near-daily events, and when not in the field, we quickly learned how to respond whenever rumor spread that killers were on the rampage again: people would flee into their houses and board everything up. Within minutes a bustling settlement would look like a ghost town. During the night, no one would venture out, because that's when most mystery slayings would happen.

It was in this tumultuous period, in August 1999, that Yus, Perry, and I were out working, moving about quite cautiously and traveling during daylight only. We were trying to finish up our geographic surveys of cemengang tool use. I was desperately trying to solve this riddle before it was too late: swamps were being clear-cut and drained everywhere, and with the civil war spreading I suspected it was now or never. We did not dare go farther up north, beyond Meulaboh, where we knew there were still a few swamps that I very much wanted to check. Apart from that, we had the main results wrapped up by the end of that month, and Perry and I were happy when it was time to leave and say good-bye to Yus once more, as we had done so often before.

Yus, of course, stayed behind; he lived there. He had moved back to the West Coast, near where he was born, to be near Suaq. I had hired Yus in 1980 as my first field assistant ever, when my wife and I had just started working at Ketambe in the central rift valley. We shared our love of the forest and its inhabitants, and spending many years together in the forest made us more like brothers than boss and employee. So when I roamed around northern Sumatra to do wildlife surveys for the Wildlife Conser-

Yus

vation Society (WCS), Yus was more than happy to join the team, and to lead it whenever I was in the United States. Yus was also on the team when we found Suaq, and he was instrumental in the decision to stay and set up our field site there. His work at the site allowed him to move back to the West Coast to live near Suaq and his extended family.

After a few years, the Leuser Development Programme (LDP) took over the administration of the station, which had become too much for a lone researcher with WCS support to maintain. LDP was a pioneering effort of the Indonesian government and the European Union to preserve the natural riches of Leuser and support sustainable economic development in the densely populated coastal regions. Yus then joined them as their local representative; the time had come for him to support conservation in this way.

In September 1999, he was accompanying two consultants who wanted to visit several of the coastal peat swamps. They were interested in carbon sequestration by thick layers of peat, which after all is undecayed wood and litter. Although the consultants had clear instructions not to travel at night and not to cross an imaginary line on the map, they did both, probably to check a swamp where the three of us had been only about a month before, when it was still safe to go there. Fate had it that a day before their visit there had been another shooting in a village south of Tapaktuan. The police had arrested some alleged ringleaders, and the enraged villagers had moved en masse to the district capital, Tapaktuan, to protest their capture. The demonstration at the police station turned nasty when the embattled police opened fire on the demonstrators, injuring several of them. Locals, afraid to help them, ignored their pleas for help. The villagers made it back home but vowed to take revenge. The next evening, they stopped cars coming from the direction of Tapaktuan and dragged out anyone who was Javanese or a member of the Indonesian armed forces. The car with Yus happened to pass by that night. The consultants and the driver happened to be Javanese. They were taken to the beach. Yus, being a local Acehnese, was told to leave, but he characteristically insisted on staying with his charges. He thought this was all a huge misunderstanding that he could clear up. The whole group of captives—some army personnel, some Javanese ladies selling cosmetics, and the LDP team—were taken to a shed. Later that night, all captives were marched to the beach, hands tied behind their backs, and the captors began systematically slitting their throats. The driver made a desperate dash to escape and jumped into the sea. Miraculously, he made it to a station of the conservation service, some 20 kilometers to the south, past the mouth of the Kluet River, and raised the alarm. By then, however, it was too late. Two years later, the bodies were found in a shallow grave near the beach. I don't think it has ever become clear exactly who was behind the killings. Yus left a wife and two school-age children.

After the events became known, all nonlocal staff of LDP and affiliated projects had to leave. Many were connecting the events near Tapaktuan to LDP and Suaq. Threats to the station, perhaps as payback for our opposition to the logging, were repeated. Rumors had also been flying for months that the army suspected GAM was using our camp as a hiding place and was going to attack the station. Suaq was evacuated in great haste—a good move, it turned out, because in the weeks and months that followed more people disappeared or were shot, and a firefight between army and rebels took place in the village along the coast right near the mouth of the Lembang River.[8] Although our field staff had stayed put for months with allegations and accusations coming from all directions, when the bullets started to fly, they had to flee. Our station has since been burned by the army because it was suspected that rebels were hiding in it.

National Trends We got to know the orangutans at Suaq as individuals with distinct personalities and temperaments. We recorded their life events, the highs and lows—the births, the deaths in the family, the first effective tool use, the defeat of a rival, the gradual loss of influence. Such intimate familiarity breeds the urge to protect. Yet, we failed them. We don't know what happened to our friends—king Arno; Pelet and Peter, her sickly boy; competent Ani; rapidly growing Anika; or teenager Andai, who should have been getting pregnant at the time our observations stopped. None of us has been back to Suaq, and we don't know exactly what happened to our orangutans, although Syamsuar, one of our local assistants, reports that he still spots orangutans in the old study area when he has a chance to sneak in. Apparently, even the loggers felt it was too dangerous to be out in the swamps, so that activity has died down. There is some hope that many of our red friends are still alive.

Personal stories are easier to relate to than dry statistics, but what happened at Suaq played out everywhere, albeit usually less violently. The

Rafts containing thousands of logs are floated down all major rivers— this one in central Borneo.

myriad of personal stories at many sites add up to a major trend. The anarchy that had begun on the streets of Jakarta and toppled a mighty president spread to the countryside, and the tumult finally brought down trees everywhere on the outer islands of the sprawling archipelago called Indonesia.

We did an analysis based on satellite images and our detailed knowledge of the situation on the ground around the entire Leuser Ecosystem (where I had done surveys for LDP for several years up to 1999). This analysis found that during the seven years that closed out the twentieth century, nearly half of the orangutans disappeared from Leuser.[9] To put that in perspective, remember that it takes a female orangutan some seven years to raise a single baby to independence (and eight years to give birth again). Although the government is now reaching some degree of stability, the situation in the field has not changed much. Serge Wich has recently taken the lead on a re-evaluation, the results of which are not reassuring.

Leuser is easily the main population cluster in Sumatra. What happens there determines the fate of the Sumatran mawas. The situation in Borneo is not any rosier. Borneo has witnessed the same dramatic events following the fall of the central government in 1998, but it has also been frequented

by droughts of historic duration and persistence, linked to the most intensive El Niño events of the century. Since time immemorial humans everywhere have used fire to clear land for farming, and small-scale slash and burn is still widely practiced in this region. But the companies that were clearing large parts of the forest to create plantations also used fires, as did the colonists sent into transmigration areas. Almost all the large fires that destroyed several million hectares in 1997 and 1998 were deliberately set fires that ran amok. At the same time, a huge project to drain peat swamps and clear them for agriculture also got underway in southern Central Borneo. The drying peat was easy prey to the flames, and peat fires alternately raged and smoldered for months. Dry-season fires are now becoming something of an annual tradition, a major change on an island where spontaneous forest fires were thought not to occur, except in a thin strip along the East Coast.[10]

It was not always like this. Herman Rijksen and Erik Meijaard made a detailed study of orangutan population trends.[11] Their conservative estimate is that around 1900 some 315,000 orangutans roamed the forests of Borneo and Sumatra. Most of the islands were still clad in forest, with small enclaves of open ground around towns and villages and a few large agricultural zones near the major cities. By the end of the century, barely

Clearing and burning the land to make way for an oil palm plantation.

15 percent of this number remained. In the same period, the human population increased from about 37 million to some 220 million.

Yet, it is not sheer numbers and the space directly occupied by our dwellings and agricultural lands that are doing in the forest and its denizens. During much of the twentieth century, the only serious threat to the orangutans was capture for the cooking pot and for commercial use. Zoos and research institutes ordered orangutans, and a pet market also gradually arose. Being so similar to human babies, orangutan infants make the world's most delightful pets, but after a few years they become strong-willed and even stronger-bodied and virtually impossible to keep around the house. Capture for the pet trade is still taking place and needs to be combated vigorously; unchecked, it may drive the orangutan into extinction. But more insidious threats have meanwhile emerged.

Serious commercial logging started in the sixties. At least in Sumatra, selective logging approximately halves the orangutan density.[12] Its effect is easy to understand because logging also reduces the abundance of succulent fruit by the same amount. Where timber poachers continue logging, orangutan density declines further until no mawas are left when the large trees are all gone and an impenetrable jungle remains. (Fortunately, there are indications that the orangutans from Borneo are less sensitive to logging.)[13] When selective logging is done right, however, it does not destroy the forest matrix, and losses to orangutans and numerous other species should be transient: we did not have time to find out for sure because those forests are gone now.

The nineties saw the big drive to convert forested lands to large-scale industrial estates: endless rows of oil palms planted on the blackened soil. Such plantations are biological deserts, but only a misanthrope would begrudge Indonesia this kind of development. In many countries, prosperity has been built on the mining to exhaustion of natural resources such as timber, coal, or oil. And when intensive production is concentrated in regions that can ecologically support this activity and when a protected area system, as carefully planned and extensive as Indonesia's, is operating as it should, economic development and conservation can coexist. Following the Krismon and the fall of the government, however, people took over all the forests and cut wherever it was economically viable. Pretty much everyone living near the forest took part. The reserves were under siege; many were damaged, some disappeared altogether.

The islands of Sumatra or Borneo still conjure up an image in most westerners' minds of overwhelming greenness. My favorite urban myth is that some Dayak languages in Borneo have up to eleven words for green. Ironically, despite all the forest loss this image may still be an apt one. When the smoke has cleared, and the burned and charred lands either have been replanted with tree crops such as oil palm or pulp trees, or have regenerated into impenetrable jungle, all of this land will once again look a healthy green when seen from above. There are signs that the worst is behind us and that people yearn for a return to some form of order. A return to political stability in Indonesia will therefore bring good news for conservation, despite the potentially damaging devolution of government responsibilities to local levels.

Why Did This Happen? Why this wanton destruction? Why would a people destroy the great natural beauty, along with its long-term economic potential, of their own lands? Part of the answer is simply the greed that goes unchecked when anarchy rules. In a society without checks and balances, such as an effective police force, being a conservationist is maladaptive. Your allegiance is first and foremost to your immediate family, then to your extended family, then to the tribe, but never really to the state. When so many people have found a get-rich-quick scheme through the chain saw, the few whose awareness of the greater good and dedication to society as a whole made them reluctant to run with the herd merely end up poorer than the rest. Stable social organization is not only essential to keep culture from sliding into an abyss, it also enforces the social contract and keeps us from following our more selfish urges.

Stable social organization, unfortunately, is necessary but not sufficient. After all, parks were in trouble even before the fall of the Suharto government, when Indonesia was a very stable, centrally led and planned country. Like so many newly independent countries, Indonesia has struggled to find its bearings. Suharto came to power after a chaotic period in the wake of a purported communist coup in 1965. His government established order. The regime spawned a large bureaucracy, and lack of countervailing democratic controls made corruption endemic.

Like in many other places, much is forbidden in Indonesia, but almost everything is possible. The corruption had reached the point of making effective policing impossible; even when the law enforcement authorities

For the large agricultural estates, land is cleared and burned *(right)*, then planted with new oil palm *(opposite, above)*, and after several years the countryside looks pleasantly green from the air *(opposite, below)*.

could be coaxed into action, the alleged perpetrators would walk free again because they bribed the judiciary and so avoided prosecution.[14] Moreover, prosecution was directed against only the more blatant and visible transgressions. Commercial poaching inside protected areas, the removal of parts of parks for logging concessions, the establishment of plantations inside logging concessions—all of these activities were a legal shade of gray, because the companies involved had acquired at least a few of the numerous permits required and could then begin their activities, claiming that further approvals were on their way.

If corruption is one half of the story, intimidation is the other half. Those who undertook the not-so-legal exploitation were allegedly supported by the armed forces. The army was in the timber business, owning concessions directly or indirectly though subsidiaries.

The regular people were generally excluded from the process, and hence from the profits. They resented their government, but were powerless against it. New Order was the name of the government, but cynicism was the order of the day. This resentment explains the explosion of illegal logging after the fall of the government. Unfortunately, parks in developing countries have few people willing to speak up for them, so it is rather easy to help yourself to whatever resources have commercial value.

Because Indonesia contains over 75 percent of the world's wild orangutans, these recent events add up to a deadly serious threat. If the spontaneous destruction of forest cannot be stopped, it may be all over in a dec-

ade or two for the wild orangutan—and for many other species that thrive
only in old-growth forest. The prospects for the recovery of an economically viable forestry sector are not terribly bright either.

There is, however, also a deeper cultural explanation that goes beyond
corruption and government systems. The forest may be magnificent to
visit, it may hold lots of valuable species, but you can't eat it. And the forest

produces wonderful services, but you can't cash in on them. So, how can one earn a living from an intact forest? We can impose levies on the use of water, for example, but in most societies there is no support for such measures. The temptation is great to make the forest pay for itself by exploiting it. Indeed, virtually all the affluent societies of the world are built on a solid foundation of ecological rubble. America east of the Mississippi was virtually clear-cut in a logging frenzy that lasted some two centuries and fuelled the smokestack industries up and down the East Coast. This sequence of steps has played out all over, and it is difficult to deny its logic: logging pays for opening up the area and supplying the capital for further development.

This frontier mentality of exploitation and extensive use for as long as possible has been widespread in history, and it still reigns in most of the more thinly settled forested regions in the world.[15] A frontiersman is one who has moved away from a dead-end life to make it elsewhere (Indonesian has a verb for this action: *merantau*). A frontiersman is not interested in law and order. Progress is about subduing nature, about clearing the forest and making it produce cash. Local governments in the frontier regions share these sentiments and just do not buy in when the central government insists on conservation. To the locals, the supply of forest seems endless: it can never end, and if it does, why, just move on to the next frontier. At the frontier, government and governed alike share a sense of solidarity against the outsiders who think of regulating its use.

But the frontier does not last forever. It opens up, but inevitably timber extraction, fishing, or trapping becomes commercially unprofitable or marginal. After the easy pioneer period, the profits of extensive farming or ranching likewise diminish. Especially near the growing population centers, more intensive farming practices yield better returns on investment. With no more easy money to be made, people start to leave for the next frontier. In some places, land may also have become degraded. But gradually, the folks who stayed begin to clean up and build profitable businesses. Where population centers are nearby, land use becomes intensified. Elsewhere the wounded land recovers and forests regenerate. The frontier closes.

The future landscape will have enough space for wildlands or recovered wildlands. Having had a taste of the market economy, very few people nowadays want to return to a marginal existence as shifting cultivators or timber poachers, if given a choice. Moreover, shifting cultivation may once have been a great way to make a living on poor land, but with higher densities of people and higher personal aspirations, it is hardly a prescription for sustainability. Hence, if we manage to hang on to some orangutan populations for a few more decades, then we should be able to bring them back from the brink.[16]

This is not an impossible dream. After the frontier closes, people's minds change too. We can be confident that that will happen. It is not just wealthy westerners that become conservationists. My field assistants, farmers originally, all became compassionate conservationists as they became acquainted with the individual histories of the orangutans. If the day arrives that people can afford to care about nature again, many are ready to become involved in conservation.

Not so long ago, America had a frontier. Most of the fierce and tasty animals were locally wiped out. A few species, such as the passenger pigeon, even became extinct. As society grew more affluent, nature became a scarce commodity, and people increasingly turned to it to find relief from their frantic everyday lives. Attempts at restoring the natural riches soon followed. And now, in greater Yellowstone, the whole community of large mammals and their predators has been reassembled: wolverines, coyotes, wolves, grizzly bears, black bears, cougars (a.k.a. pumas or mountain lions). It shows that where the species are still available, even if they have to be brought back through captive breeding efforts or translocation from remote refugia, the natural communities can be restored and thrive again.

Even in a more stable future, however, conservation must be enforced to protect the common good. If parks are unprotected, they become like the proverbial commons. Individuals will always gain from exploiting them, leaving it to future generations to deal with the fallout. The idea that local communities are interested in complete protection of the nature that surrounds them is a tenacious myth, reminiscent of the noble savage happily living the life of Zen affluence. Such an attitude does not make economic sense. We all agree that some protection of the resource base or even biodiversity is necessary, but we often call for protection of our neighbor's turf while exploiting our own. Hence, inevitably, some authority ready to engage in law enforcement is needed in even the most supportive society.

It is just a matter of time for conservation efforts to take root in the countries that we now call developing. Sooner or later, the forest will come back, and the bits now separated will become reconnected. The challenge is to make sure that all the important species are still around somewhere to re-colonize them. That is why continued conservation efforts, even in the face of seemingly overwhelming odds, are so critical. For some species, the task will not be difficult. For others, such as the orangutans, it may not be so easy.

The Future of Orangutan Cultures If my expectations are correct, then at the latest a century from now orangutans may once again roam all the recovered forests. But will these orangutans be as cultured as those we found only a decade or so ago? Our information on great ape cultures is so recent that our answer to this question is speculative, but we know enough about the mechanisms of establishment and maintenance of cultures to make an informed guess. The local repertoire of cultures is a dynamic equilibrium between two opposing processes. Adding to the cultural repertoire is enrichment due to local innovation and diffusion (diffusion is the importation of new variants into communities by immigrants). The countervailing process is extinction due to failure of transmission. A loss in the richness of culture is expected when human-induced processes reduce social transmission, diffusion, or innovation.[17]

To start with social transmission, we know that a higher frequency of opportunities for socially biased learning leads to larger repertoires of cultural skills, especially those requiring careful close-range observation. Any deterioration in the conditions for social transmission, therefore, should in the end reduce the richness of the local cultural repertoire, especially those of skillful behaviors.

All kinds of human activities may disturb the normal transmission process. The loss may be sudden and dramatic, as when transmission is completely interrupted, however briefly. Local extinction of the orangutans of course leads to the complete loss of local cultures. But even if this loss is followed by re-colonization, chances are that by then the locally specific cultures will be gone, most notably the kinds of skills that are habitat-dependent. This kind of loss of culture is easily envisioned. But more subtle erosion of cultures is also possible. Basically, anything that will reduce association time or social tolerance should, over time, lead to a gradual reduction of the local repertoire of cultural variants. The actual cause may be

hunting or logging. Hunting will tend to make orangutans avoid any behavior that attracts the hunter's attention. Many primates that are hunted become more silent and more solitary, and these cryptic behaviors reduce opportunities for social learning. Logging or other forms of exploitation make the forest less productive; and where there is less to eat, orangutans will find it harder to spend time together.

Next consider diffusion. Forests all over the tropics become increasingly fragmented: as more and more tracts are cleared, the original forest is cut up into smaller and smaller islands isolated from the others. Fragmentation should especially affect tree-dwelling mammals that cannot easily move between the forest islands, such as orangutans. In human society, immigrants have historically brought in most of the important innovations.[18] Diffusion, after all, is the process that is responsible for the similarity in cultures among nearby regions. When the traditional connections between areas are severed and diffusion comes to an end, one important engine of local cultural change disappears, and inevitably the equilibrium number of cultural variants will settle at a lower value.

Fragmentation may be the main cause of cultural erosion.

Turning now to innovation, we know very little about the conditions that bring it about, although the absence of knowledgeable role models may be a major stimulating factor. Perhaps where hunting is a serious threat, animals have to be so vigilant that they cannot afford to concentrate as much on solving environmental problems.

As I stressed above, we have no clue whether any of these changes will actually take place in the future. The main problem is that we have not yet been able to develop an intuition about the time scales involved in cultural evolution in great apes. How long does it take for, say, tree-hole tool use to become locally extinct, and how long does it take on average for it to get re-established again?

We also do not know whether cultural erosion has taken place in the past as a result of local extinction and behavioral changes due to hunting by humans. It is quite conceivable, after all, that humans had wiped out orangutans over large areas and that the red apes re-colonized most of the islands only after farmers had replaced the foragers and converted to Islam, a religion with strict rules on diet. If that is so, then orangutan cultures in the past may have been richer, or a new equilibrium may already have been reached.

We need be less circumspect about the future. Our knowledge of the mechanisms leaves little room for optimism: fragmentation, logging, and hunting are of course rampant, and cultural erosion is bound to happen. What is uncertain is how long that will take and how bad it will be. Only time will tell, but recent developments raise the specter of cultural extinction, even if the animals themselves are still around.

NOTES

1
The Great Ape Paradox

1. Galdikas (1982a).
2. Kortlandt and Kooij (1963).
3. Tooby and DeVore (1987).
4. De Waal (1982).
5. Savage-Rumbaugh and Lewin (1994).
6. Tomasello et al. (1993).

2
Planet of the Apes

1. Reynolds (1967). The "most surprizing Creature" mentioned in the heading is from an account of a live chimpanzee brought to London in 1738 (p. 50).
2. Rijksen and Meijaard (1999).
3. Slotkin (1980), quoted in Kuper (1994).
4. Darwin (1859).
5. Huxley (1863).
6. Darwin (1871).
7. Gould (1981); see also Kuper (1994).
8. Montagu (1968).
9. Wallace (1869); Hornaday (1885); Beccari (1904).
10. These finds, and the enormous publicity they received, have also served to create the opposite and equally unjust, romanticized view of fieldwork as a glamorous affair.
11. Ruvolo (1997); Goodman et al. (1998).
12. Huxley (1863).
13. See Cartmill (1990).
14. For instance Goodall (1986); Wrangham and Peterson (1996).

3
Homo sylvestris

1. Kelley (1997).
2. Van Schaik and Deaner (2003).
3. Fleagle (1999).
4. Fleagle (1999).
5. Recent finds suggest that another member of the same clade, cf. *Lufengopithecus chiangmuanensis,* may be a closer relative of the orangutan: Chaimanee et al. (2003).
6. Bacon and Long (2001).
7. See Rijksen and Meijaard (1999) for a full listing.
8. Zhi et al. (1996).
9. Muir et al. (2000).
10. Whitten et al. (1984).
11. Groves (2001).
12. Jablonski (1998).
13. Rijksen and Meijaard (1999).
14. Continuing growth after reaching sexual maturity is known to occur in males in many species, but among elephants and whales females may show it too (Nowak 1999), as do many primates (Pereira and Leigh 2003). The gradual transition from growth to reproduction is evidenced by the smaller final size of females who start reproduction at very young ages, suggesting that reproduction and bodily growth compete for resources among primates, at least in this transition period.
15. Beccari (1904).
16. Go to www.orangutan.org/facts/sounds.php to hear a short part of a long call.
17. Utami et al. (2002).
18. Fleagle (1999).
19. Lovell (1990).
20. Unfortunately, I don't know of any studies that compare the size

of arboreal or terrestrial parties among chimpanzees or bonobos.

21. Lovell (1990).

4
Orangutan Heaven

1. Te Boekhorst et al. (1990).
2. Martin and Bateson (1993).
3. Van Schaik and Mirmanto (1985).
4. Terborgh and van Schaik (1987).
5. There are of course tree squirrels, in fact lots of them, but their biomass is very modest compared with the total biomass of terrestrial seed predators in a dry land forest, and hence their ability to deplete seed crops as they ripen is more limited.
6. Knott (2001).
7. *Tetramerista glabra* (Tetrameristaceae); the fruits look somewhat like the better-known kandis (*Garcinia*, Guttiferae).
8. Donner (1987).
9. Ibid.

5
Arbo-Reality

1. *Neesia cf. aquatica* (Bombacaceae).
2. Van Schaik and Knott (2001).
3. *Polyalthia sumatrana* (Annonaceae), known as banitan at Ketambe, where similar behavior can be seen.
4. Byrne (1999).
5. Van Schaik et al. (1999).
6. Utami and van Hooff (1997).
7. Fox et al. (in press).
8. Singleton and van Schaik (2001).
9. Singleton (2000).
10. *Colocasia esculenta* (Araceae).
11. *Semecarpus heterophyllus* (Anacardiaceae, the family to which poison ivy belongs as well).

12. *Alstonia spathulata* (Apocynaceae).
13. *Dyera* spp. (Apocynaceae), locally known as jelutung and pantung.
14. Knott (1998).
15. The contrast in food metabolism between the orangutans of the two islands, if it exists, may produce an interesting model for human obesity. Furthermore, solving the mystery of obesity among zoo orangutans would help to make the orangutans' lives in captivity more comfortable.

6
Party On (and Off)

1. Mitani et al. (1991).
2. Sugardjito et al. (1987).
3. Van Schaik (1999).
4. Galdikas (1995).
5. See Barrett et al. (2002).
6. Rijksen (1978).
7. Van Schaik and Griffiths (1996).
8. Sugardjito (1983).
9. Singleton and van Schaik (2002).
10. Knott (2001).
11. Kaplan and Rogers (2002).
12. De Waal and Lanting (1997).
13. Indeed, the use of a foreign object to stimulate oneself may be one of the most obvious and thus oldest forms of tool use, albeit not one that we believe has provided a major selective advantage for the ability to manipulate tools (see next chapter for that).
14. Van Schaik, Pradham, and van Noordwijk (in press).
15. Delgado and van Schaik (2000).
16. Fox (2002).
17. Delgado and van Schaik (2000).
18. Utami and Mitra Setia (1995).
19. Fox (2002).
20. Van Schaik and Janson (2000).
21. Van Noordwijk and van Schaik (2004).

22. Reviews in Hrdy (1979); van Schaik and Janson (2000).
23. Van Schaik and Kappeler (1997).
24. Van Schaik, Pradham, and van Noordwijk (in press).
25. When the social situation is such that dangerous strangers never show up, females should minimize their risk by attempting to mate with all potentially dangerous males in the vicinity. This is approximately the situation in bonobos.
26. Van Schaik (2000b).
27. Some of the infanticide cases in chimps arise when females did not manage to mate with the dominant males around conception: Hamai et al. (1992); see also the review in van Schaik (2000a).
28. See the calculations in van Schaik, Pradham, and van Noordwijk (in press).
29. Small (1993); van Schaik et al. (1999).
30. Utami et al. (2002).
31. Beccari (1904).
32. Galdikas (1995).
33. Van Schaik et al. (1999); Paul (2002).
34. Friedl (1994).
35. Goodall (1986).
36. Wilson and Wrangham (2003).
37. Galdikas (1985a).
38. Delgado (2003).
39. Singleton and van Schaik (2002).
40. Singleton and van Schaik (2001).
41. Singleton and van Schaik (2002).
42. They are in fact rather similar to the so-called noyeaux described for nocturnal primates: e.g., Bearder (1987).
43. Delgado (2003).
44. Tatang Mitra Setia, unpublished manuscript.
45. Beccari (1904).
46. Delgado (2003).

7
Life in Slow Motion

1. Knott (2001).
2. Wich et al. (in review).
3. Hill et al. (2001).
4. Cribb (2000).
5. Hooijer (1961); Harrison (1996).
6. Flannery (2001).
7. And how we managed to blame women for it is another story worth telling in more detail.
8. Cribb (2000).
9. Leighton et al. (1995).
10. Hrdy (1999), especially chaps. 12 and 14.
11. Sugardjito (1983).
12. Van Noordwijk and van Schaik (2004).
13. Promislow and Harvey (1990); Charnov (1993).
14. Van Noordwijk and van Schaik (2004).
15. Hawkes et al. (2003).
16. Kaplan et al. (2000).
17. Utami et al. (2002).
18. Wich et al. (in review).
19. Bogin (1988).
20. Maggioncalda et al. (2002).
21. Delgado and van Schaik (2000).

8
The Dawn of Technology

1. Beck (1980).
2. Wilson (1975); Beck (1980).
3. Parker and Gibson (1977).
4. McGrew (1992).
5. Hunt (1996).
6. Ottoni and Mannu (2001).
7. Van Schaik, Deaner, and Merrill (1999).
8. Kappeler (1998).
9. O'Malley and McGrew (2000).
10. *Neesia cf. aquatica* (Bombaceae).
11. Van Schaik and Knott (2001).
12. Adult males at Suaq do something very similar to what their colleagues at Gunung Palung do before the fruits naturally open (dehisce); the hairs are still a sticky mass at that stage, making it easy to pick out the seeds, provided of course that the animal is strong enough to open the fruit! Once the fruits open, these males almost completely switch to tools.
13. Boesch and Boesch-Achermann (2000); E. Vinson (pers. com.).
14. *Jackiopsis ornata* (Rubiaceae).
15. Povinelli and Cant (1995).
16. Fox and bin'Mohammad (2002).
17. For a collection of amazing but true stories, see Russon (2000).
18. Balda et al. (1996).
19. Cheney and Seyfarth (1990).
20. Deaner (2001); Johnson et al. (2002).
21. Byrne (1995); Hare et al. (2000).
22. Yoerg (2001).
23. Aiello and Wheeler (1995).
24. Byrne and Whiten (1988); Whiten and Byrne (1997).
25. De Waal (1982).
26. Hare et al. (2000).
27. Galdikas and Vasey (1992).
28. Tomasello and Call (1997).
29. Byrne (1997).
30. Milton (1988).
31. Van Schaik and Deaner (2003).
32. Deaner et al. (2003).

9
The Culture Club

1. Tylor (1871).
2. McGrew (1998).
3. Tuttle (2001).
4. Imanishi (1952).
5. See especially Custance et al. (1995); Stoinski and Whiten (2003).
6. Russon and Galdikas (1995).
7. Van Schaik and Knott (2001).
8. Whiten et al. (1999).
9. The sites that provided solid long-term data were represented by Suci Utami Atmoko, Serge Wich, Ian Singleton, Michelle Merrill, Cheryl Knott, Biruté Galdikas, Akira Suzuki, and Marc Ancrenaz. Other sites represented but not contributing to the complete cultural comparison were Soraya (Dolly Priatna), Bukit Lawang (Ivona Foitova), and Lokan (David Agee). The retreat was kindly organized and underwritten by the L. S. B. Leakey Foundation.
10. Van Schaik et al. (2003a).
11. Fox and bin'Mohammad (2002).
12. Ingmanson (1996).
13. Galef (1992); Tomasello (1999).
14. Van Schaik (2003).
15. Keesing (1958).
16. Merrill (2004).
17. Van Schaik et al. (2003b).
18. Terkel (1996).
19. Hudson et al. (1999); Galef (2003).
20. King (1994).
21. The geographic method we have used here usually does not identify animals' use of labels because we tend to assume, conservatively, that variation in diet or responses to potential predators have a solid ecological basis. This assumption now needs serious reconsideration and renewed field comparisons.
22. But see a recent attempt by Hohmann and Fruth (2003).
23. Byrne (1995).
24. McGrew et al. (2001).
25. Boesch (1996).
26. Nakamura (2002).
27. Boesch and Boesch-Achermann (2000); Matsuzawa et al. (2001).
28. Kortlandt and Holzhaus (1987)

have argued that chimps learned
these skills by observing humans.
This may be true, but it is unlikely
to hold for many other skilled
techniques, nor does it explain
the maintenance and geographic
patterning of great ape cultures in
general.
29. Van Schaik and Pradhan (2003).
30. See Rendell and Whitehead
(2001) for cetaceans; Hunt (1996)
for crows on New Caledonia.
31. Byrne and Whiten (1988);
Whiten and Byrne (1997); de
Waal and Tyack (2003); and refer-
ences therein.
32. Van Schaik and Deaner (2003).
33. Tomasello (1999).
34. Ibid.
35. Boesch (1996).
36. Russon (2003).
37. Elman et al. (1996).
38. This raises the question of how
predictably the same outcomes
would be re-created—a question
reminiscent of the one asked for
organic evolution. As with organic evolution, the answer is
that it depends on how similar the
starting conditions are. Since the
chances of nearly identical starting conditions before and after a
disastrous loss of culture are reasonably good, strong convergence
may be expected. Examples of
strikingly parallel cultural evolution in human history on different continents (e.g., Keesing
1958; Diamond 1997) support
this conjecture.

10
Triangulating Human Nature

1. Dennett (1995).
2. Moore (1996).
3. Boehm (1999).

4. E.g., chapters in van Schaik and
Janson (2000).
5. Van Schaik, Preuschoft, and Watts
(in press).
6. Byrne and Byrne (1993).
7. Van Schaik, Preuschoft, and Watts
(in press).
8. Feistner and McGrew (1989).
9. See several chapters in Boesch et
al. (2002).
10. D. Doran (pers. com.).
11. Mayr (1988).
12. It is sometimes argued that human foragers do not engage in be-
tween-society violence or warfare, but there are numerous
indications that war goes back to
our Pleistocene past, well before
agriculture and states (Keeley
1996).
13. E.g., Goodall (1986); Boesch and
Boesch-Achermann (2000).
14. Paul (2002).
15. Pusey (1987); Pusey and Packer
(1987).
16. Wrangham (1980); van Schaik
(1989).
17. Watts (2000).
18. Bonobos hardly form brotherhoods, so we must assume that
once male kin bonding exists, it is
not easily lost and that the common ancestors of chimps and
bonobos were very much like
chimps.
19. Cf. Rodman (1984).
20. Watts (1998).
21. Some of the infanticide cases in
chimps arise when females did
not manage to mate with the
dominant males around conception (Hamai et al. 1992).
22. Boesch & Boesch-Achermann
(2000); Mitani and Watts (2001).
23. Stanford (1999).
24. Wrangham (1999); Wilson and
Wrangham (2003).

25. Ibid.
26. Watts and Mitani (2001).
27. Hawkes and Bird (2002).
28. McGrew (1992).
29. Stanford (1999).
30. Hawkes et al. (1997).
31. Hawkes et al. (1998); Hawkes et
al. (2003).
32. Heistermann et al. (1996).
33. Kaplan et al. (2000).
34. Boehm (1999).
35. Hawkes (1996).
36. See also Klein and Edgar (2002).
37. Burke (1996), p. 3.
38. Klein and Edgar (2002).
39. Mercader et al. (2002).
40. Klein (1999); indeed, Richard
Klein argues that hand axes
change rather abruptly at around
600,000 years ago, a development
he links to a punctuational
change in encephalization and
the colonization of Europe (pers.
com).
41. Boyd and Richerson (1985).
42. Russon (2002, 2003).
43. Klein (1999).
44. Klein and Edgar (2002).
45. McBrearty and Brooks (2000);
d'Errico (2003).
46. Klein (1999).
47. D'Errico (2003).
48. Dunbar (1996).
49. Language is therefore older than
cumulative culture; hence, the
mysterious origins of language are
not explained in this way. Here,
we assume it had some solid biological or cultural pacemaker. See
Hauser et al. (2002) for a modern
perspective.
50. Klein and Edgar (2002).
51. Sahlins (1972).
52. Rowley-Conwy (2001); Torrence
(2001).
53. McBrearty and Brooks (2000).
54. It should be remembered that,

while this level of exchange is uniquely developed in humans, the phenomenon itself is based on the ability to exchange information and goods, a common behavior of great apes.

55. Boserup (1981).
56. Charles Darwin's letter to Henry Fawcett, September 18, 1861 (quoted in Shermer 2002).

Epilogue
Living on Borrowed Time

1. Walsh et al. (2003).
2. *Notophoebe* sp. (Laurauceae); several such species are collected around Indonesia's swamps.
3. We gradually learned that such targeted collection of forest resources, responding to a particular demand, is common; it is what is killing the last Sumatra rhinos, argus pheasants, and gaharu trees (*Aquilaria* spp., used for incense in the Middle East).
4. Wind (1996).
5. FWI/GFW (2002); Holmes (2000).
6. Ricklefs (1993).
7. Ibid.
8. In 2003, several mass graves were discovered in the regency of Aceh Selatan.
9. Van Schaik et al. (2001).
10. MacKinnon et al. (1997).
11. Rijksen and Meijaard (1999).
12. Rijksen (1978); van Schaik et al. (1995); Rao and van Schaik (1997).
13. Perhaps because Bornean orangutans are better able to cope with low fruit abundance: Felton et al. (2003).
14. Robertson and van Schaik (2001).
15. Van Schaik and Rao (2002).
16. Conservation is a two-way street: without intact plant communities, there can be no stable populations of orangutans, or indeed most other animal species. However, the diversity of the plant community may in part be maintained by the orangutan, who, as the largest frugivore, facilitates the dispersal of roughly two-thirds of the species it eats (Galdikas 1982b).
17. Van Schaik (2002).
18. Boserup (1981).

REFERENCES

Aiello, L. C., and Wheeler, P. (1995). The expensive-tissue hypothesis; the brain and the digestive system in human and primate evolution. *Current Anthro. 36,* 199–221.

Bacon, A.-M., and Long, V. T. (2001). The first discovery of a complete skeleton of a fossil orangutan in a cave of the Hoa Binh Province, Vietnam. *J. Hum. Evol. 41,* 227–242.

Balda, R. P., Kamil, A. C., and Bednekoff, P. A. (1996). Predicting cognitive capacity from natural history: examples from four species of corvids. *In* V. Nolan, Jr., and E. D. Ketterson (eds.), *Current Ornithology,* vol. 13, pp. 33–66. New York: Plenum Press.

Barrett, L., Dunbar, R., and Lycett, J. (2002). *Human Evolutionary Psychology.* Princeton, NJ: Princeton University Press.

Bearder, S. K. (1987). Lorises, bushbabies, and tarsiers: diverse societies in solitary foragers. *In* B. B. Smuts, D. L. Cheney, R. M. Seyfarth, R. W. Wrangham, and T. T. Struhsaker (eds.), *Primate Societies,* pp. 11–24. Chicago: University of Chicago Press.

Beccari, O. (1904). *Wanderings in the Great Forests of Borneo.* London: Archibald Constable and Co.

Beck, B. B. (1980). *Animal Tool Behavior: The Use and Manufacture of Tools by Animals.* New York: Garland STPM Press.

Boehm, C. (1999). *Hierarchy in the Forest: The Evolution of Egalitarian Behavior.* Cambridge, MA: Harvard University Press.

Boesch, C. (1996). The emergence of cultures among wild chimpanzees. *Proc. Brit. Acad. 88,* 251–268.

Boesch, C., and Boesch-Achermann, H. (2000). *The Chimpanzees of the Taï Forest: Behavioural Ecology and Evolution.* Oxford: Oxford University Press.

Boesch, C., Hohmann, G., and Marchant, L. F. (eds.) (2002). *Behavioural Diversity in Chimpanzees and Bonobos.* Cambridge: Cambridge University Press.

Bogin, B. (1988). *Patterns of Human Growth.* Cambridge: Cambridge University Press.

Boserup, E. (1981). *Population and Technological Change: A Study of Long-term Trends.* Chicago: University of Chicago Press.

Boyd, R., and Richerson, P. J. (1985). *Culture and the Evolutionary Process.* Chicago: University of Chicago Press.

Burke, K. (1996). *Language as Symbolic Action: Essays on Life, Literature and Method.* Berkeley: University of California Press.

Byrne, R. W. (1995). *The Thinking Ape: Evolutionary Origins of Intelligence.* Oxford: Oxford University Press.

——— (1997). The technical intelligence hypothesis: an additional evolutionary stimulus to intelligence? *In* A. Whiten and R. W. Byrne (eds.), *Machiavellian Intelligence II: Extension and Evaluations,* pp. 289–311. Cambridge: Cambridge University Press.

——— (1999). Cognition in great ape ecology: skill-learning ability opens up foraging opportunities. *In* H. O. Box and K. R. Gibson (eds.), *Mammalian Social Learning: Comparative and Ecological Perspectives,* pp. 333–350. Cambridge: Cambridge University Press.

Byrne, R. W., and Byrne, J. M. E.

(1993). Complex leaf gathering skills of mountain gorillas *(Gorilla g. beringei):* variability and standardization. *Am. J. Primatol. 31:* 241–261.

Byrne, R. W., and Whiten, A. (1988). *Machiavellian Intelligence: Social Expertise and the Evolution of Intellect in Monkeys, Apes, and Humans.* Oxford: Clarendon Press.

Cartmill, M. (1990). Human uniqueness and theoretical content in paleoanthropology. *Intern. J. Primatol. 11,* 173–192.

Chaimanee, Y., Jolly, D., Benammi, M., Tafforeau, P., Duzer, D., Moussa, I., and Jaeger, J.-J. (2003). A middle Miocene hominoid from Thailand and orangutan origins. *Nature 422,* 61–65.

Charnov, E. L. (1993). *Life History Invariants: Some Explorations of Symmetry in Evolutionary Ecology.* Oxford: Oxford University Press.

Cheney, D. L., and Seyfarth, R. M. (1990). *How Monkeys See the World.* Chicago: University of Chicago Press.

Cribb, R. (2000). *Historical Atlas of Indonesia.* London: Curzon–New Asian Library.

Custance, D. M., Whiten, A., and Bard, K. A. (1995). Can young chimpanzees imitate arbitrary actions? Hayes and Hayes (1952) revisited. *Behaviour 132,* 839–858.

Darwin, C. (1859). *On the Origin of Species.* London: Murray.

——— (1871). *The Descent of Man and Selection in Relation to Sex.* London: Murray.

Deaner, R. O. (2001). *The Comparative Neuroanatomical Approach to the Evolution of Primate Cognition.* Ph.D. diss., Duke University.

Deaner, R. O., Barton, R. A., and van Schaik, C. P. (2003). Primate brains

and life histories: renewing the connection. *In* P. M. Kappeler and M. E. Pereira (eds.), *Primate Life Histories and Socioecology,* pp. 233–265. Chicago: University of Chicago Press.

Delgado, R. A., Jr. (2003). *The Function of Adult Male Long Calls in Wild Orangutans* (Pongo pygmaeus). Ph.D. diss., Duke University.

Delgado, R., and van Schaik, C. P. (2000). The behavioral ecology and conservation of the orangutan *(Pongo pygmaeus):* a tale of two islands. *Evol. Anthro. 9,* 201–218.

Dennett, D. (1995). *Darwin's Dangerous Idea: Evolution and the Meanings of Life.* New York: Touchstone.

d'Errico, F. (2003). The invisible frontier: a multiple species model for the origin of behavioral modernity. *Evol. Anthro. 12,* 188–202.

de Waal, F. B. M. (1982). *Chimpanzee Politics.* London: Jonathan Cape Ltd.

——— (2001). *The Ape and the Sushi Master: Cultural Reflections of a Primatologist.* New York: Basic Books.

de Waal, F. B. M., and Lanting, F. (1997). *Bonobo: The Forgotten Ape.* Berkeley: University of California Press.

de Waal, F. B. M., and Tyack, P. L. (eds.) (2003). *Animal Social Complexity.* Cambridge, MA: Harvard University Press.

Diamond, J. (1997). *Guns, Germs, and Steel.* New York: W. W. Norton and Company.

Donner, W. (1987). *Land Use and Environment in Indonesia.* Honolulu: University of Hawaii Press.

Dunbar, R. (1996). *Grooming, Gossip, and the Evolution of Language.* Cambridge, MA: Harvard University Press.

Elman, J. L., Bates, E. A., Johnson,

M. H., Karmiloff-Smith, A., Parisi, D., and Plunkett, K. (1996). *Rethinking Innateness: A Connectionist Perspective on Development.* Cambridge, MA: MIT Press.

Feistner, A. T. C., and McGrew, W. C. (1989). Food-sharing in primates: a critical review. *In* P. K. Seth and S. Seth (eds.), *Perspectives in Primate Biology,* vol. 3, pp. 21–36. New Delhi: Today and Tomorrow's Printers and Publishers.

Felton, A. M., Engström, L. M., Felton, A., and Knott, C. D. (2003). Orangutan population density, forest structure and fruit availability in hand-logged and unlogged peat swamp forests in West Kalimantan, Indonesia. *Biol. Cons. 114,* 91–101.

Flannery, T. (2001). *The Eternal Frontier: An Ecological History of North America and Its Peoples.* New York: Grove Press.

Fleagle, J. G. (1999). *Primate Adaptation and Evolution,* 2nd ed. New York: Academic Press.

Fox, E. A. (1998). *The Function of Female Mate Choice in the Sumatran Orangutan (*Pongo pygmaeus abelii*).* Ph.D. diss., Duke University.

——— (2002). Female tactics to reduce sexual harassment in the Sumatran orangutan *(Pongo pygmaeus abelii). Behav. Ecol. Sociobiol. 52,* 93–101.

Fox, E. A., and bin'Mohammad, I. (2002). New tool use by wild Sumatran orangutans *(Pongo pygmaeus abelii). Am. J. Phys. Anthrop. 119,* 186–188.

Fox, E. A., van Schaik, C. P., Wright, D. N., and Fechtman, L. (In press). Intra- and interpopulational differences in orangutan *(Pongo pygmaeus)* activity and diet: implications for the invention of tool use. *Am. J. Phys. Anthro.*

Friedl, E. (1994). Sex the invisible. *Am. Anthropol. 96*, 833–844.

FWI/GFW (2002). *The State of the Forest: Indonesia*, p. 104. Bogor, Indonesia, and Washington, D.C.: Forest Watch Indonesia, Global Forest Watch.

Galdikas, B. M. F. (1982a). Orangutan tool-use at Tanjung Puting Reserve, Central Indonesian Borneo (Kalimantan Tengah). *J. Human Evol. 10*, 19–33.

—— (1982b). Orangutans as seed dispersers at Tanjung Puting, Central Kalimantan: implications for conservation. *In* L. E. M. Boer (ed.), *The Orang Utan: Its Biology and Conservation*, pp. 285–298. The Hague: Dr W. Junk Publ.

—— (1985a). Adult male sociality and reproductive tactics among orangutans at Tanjung Puting. *Folia Primatol. 45*, 9–24.

—— (1985b). Subadult male orangutan sociality and reproductive behavior at Tanjung Puting. *Intern. J. Primatol. 8*, 87–99.

—— (1995). Social and reproductive behavior of wild adolescent female orangutans. *In* R. D. Nadler, B. M. F. Galdikas, L. K. Sheeran, and N. Rosen (eds.), *The Neglected Ape*, pp. 163–182. New York: Plenum Press.

—— (1996). *Reflections of Eden: My Years with the Orangutans of Borneo*. Boston: Little, Brown.

Galdikas, B. M. F., and Vasey, P. (1992). Why are orangutans so smart? Ecological and social hypotheses. *In* F. D. Burton (ed.), *Social Processes and Mental Abilities in Non-Human Primates: Evidence from Longitudinal Field Studies*, pp. 183–224. Lewiston: Edwin Mellen Press.

Galef, B. G., Jr. (1992). The question of animal culture. *Human Nature 3*, 157–178.

—— (2003). "Traditional" foraging behaviors of brown and black rats (*Rattus norvegicus* and *Rattus rattus*). *In* D. M. Fragaszy and S. Perry (eds.), *The Biology of Traditions: Models and Evidence*, pp. 159–186. Cambridge: Cambridge University Press.

Ganzhorn, J. U., Klaus, S., Ortmann, S., and Schmid, J. (2003). Adaptations to seasonality: some primate and nonprimate examples. *In* P. M. Kappeler and M. E. Pereira (eds.), *Primate Life Histories and Socioecology*, pp. 132–144. Chicago: University of Chicago Press.

Goodall, J. (1986). *The Chimpanzees of Gombe*. Cambridge, MA: Harvard University Press.

Goodman, M., Porter, C. A., Czelusniak, J., Page, S. L., Schneider, H., Shoshani, J., Gunnell, G., and Groves, C. P. (1998). Toward a phylogenetic classification of primates based on DNA evidence complemented by fossil evidence. *Mol. Phylogenet. Evol. 9*, 585–598.

Gould, S. J. (1981). *The Mismeasure of Man*. New York: Norton.

Groves, C. P. (2001). *Primate Taxonomy*. Washington, DC: Smithsonian Institution Press.

Hamai, M., Nishida, T., Takasaki, H., and Turner, L. A. (1992). New records of within-group infanticide and cannibalism in wild chimpanzees. *Primates 33*, 151–162.

Hare, B., Call, J., Agnetta, B., and Tomasello, M. (2000). Chimpanzees know what conspecifics do and do not see. *Anim. Behav. 59*, 771–185.

Harrison, T. (1996). The paleoecological context at Niah cave, Sarawak: evidence from the primate fauna. *Bull. Indo-Pacific Prehist. Assoc. 14*, 90–100.

Hauser, M. D. (1996). *The Evolution of Communication*. Cambridge, MA: MIT Press.

Hauser, M. D., Chomsky, N., and Fitch, W. T. (2002). The faculty of language: what is it, who has it, and how did it evolve? *Science 298*, 1569–1579.

Hawkes, K. (1996). Foraging differences between men and women: behavioural ecology of the sexual division of labor. *In* J. Steele and S. Shennan (eds.), *The Archaeology of Human Ancestry*, pp. 283–305. London: Routledge.

Hawkes, K., and Bird, R. B. (2002). Showing off, handicap signaling, and the evolution of men's work. *Evol. Anthro. 11*, 58–67.

Hawkes, K., O'Connell, J. F., and Blurton Jones, N. G. (2003). Human life histories: primate trade-offs, grandmothering socioecology, and the fossil record. *In* P. M. Kappeler and M. E. Pereira (eds.), *Primate Life Histories and Socioecology*, pp. 204–231. Chicago: University of Chicago Press.

Hawkes, K., O'Connell, J. F., Blurton Jones, N. G., Alvarez, H., and Charnov, E. L. (1998). Grandmothering, menopause, and the evolution of human life histories. *Proc. Natl. Acad. Sci. USA 95*, 1336–1339.

Hawkes, K., O'Connell, J. F., and Rogers, L. (1997). The behavioral ecology of modern hunter-gatherers and human evolution. *Trends Ecol. Evol. 12*, 29–32.

Heistermann, M., Möhle, U., Vervaecke, H., van Elsacker, L., and Hodges, J. K. (1996). Application of urinary and fecal steroid measurements for monitoring ovarian function and pregnancy in the bonobo *(Pan paniscus)* and evaluation of perineal swelling patterns in relation to endocrine events. *Biol. Reprod. 55,* 844–853.

Hill, K., Boesch, C., Goodall, J., Pusey, A., Williams, J., and Wrangham, R. (2001). Mortality rates among wild chimpanzees. *J. Hum. Evol. 40,* 437–450.

Hohmann, G., and Fruth, B. (2003). Culture in bonobos? Between-species and within-species variation in behavior. *Curr. Anthro. 44,* 563–571.

Holmes, D. (2000). *Deforestation in Indonesia: A Review of the Situation in 1999.* Jakarta, Indonesia: World Bank.

Hooijer, D. A. (1961). The orang-utan in Niah cave pre-history. *Sarawak Mus. J. 9,* 408–421.

Hornaday, W. R. (1885). *Two Years in the Jungle: The Experiences of a Hunter and Naturalist in India, Ceylon, the Malay Peninsula and Borneo.* New York: Charles Scribner's Sons.

Hrdy, S. B. (1979). Infanticide among animals: a review, classification, and examination of the implications for the reproductive strategies of females. *Ethol. Sociobiol. 1,* 13–40.

—— (1999). *Mother Nature: A History of Mothers, Infants, and Natural Selection.* New York: Pantheon Books.

Hudson, R., Schaal, B., and Bilkó, Á. (1999). Transmission of olfactory information from mother to young in the European rabbit. *In* H. O. Box and K. R. Gibson (eds.), *Mammalian Social Learning,* pp. 141–157. Cambridge: Cambridge University Press.

Hunt, G. R. (1996). Manufacture and use of hook-tools by New Caledonian crows. *Nature 379,* 249–251.

Huxley, T. H. 1863. *Evidence as to Man's Place in Nature.* New York: D. Appleton.

Imanishi, K. (1952). *Man* [in Japanese]. Tokyo: Mainichi-Shinbunsha.

Ingmanson, E. J. (1996). Tool-using behavior in wild *Pan paniscus:* social and ecological considerations. *In* A. E. Russon, K. A. Bard, and S. T. Parker (eds.), *Reaching into Thought: The Minds of the Great Apes,* pp. 190–210. Cambridge: Cambridge University Press.

Jablonski, N. G. (1998). The response of catarrhine primates to Pleistocene environmental fluctuations in East Asia. *Primates 39,* 29–37.

Johnson, V. E., Deaner, R. O., and van Schaik, C. P. (2002). Bayesian analysis of multi-study rank data with application to primate intelligence ratings. *J. Am. Stat. Soc. 97,* 8–17.

Kaplan, G., and Rogers, L. J. (2002). Patterns of gazing in orangutans *(Pongo pygmaeus). Intern. J. Primatol. 23,* 501–526.

Kaplan, H., Hill, K., Lancaster, J., and Hurtado, A. M. (2000). A theory of human life history evolution: diet, intelligence, and longevity. *Evol. Anthro. 9,* 156–185.

Kappeler, P. M. (1998). Nests, tree holes, and the evolution of primate life histories. *Am. J. Primatol. 46,* 7–33.

Kappeler, P. M., Pereira, M. E., and van Schaik, C. P. (2003). Primate life histories and soecioecology. *In* P. M. Kappeler and M. E. Pereira (eds.), *Primate Life Histories and Socioecology,* pp. 1–20. Chicago: University of Chicago Press.

Kay, R. F., Madden, R. H., van Schaik, C. P., and Higdon, D. (1997). Primate species richness is determined by plant productivity: implications for conservation. *Proc. Natl. Acad. Sci. 94,* 13023–13027.

Keeley, L. (1996). *War before Civilization: The Myth of the Peaceful Savage.* New York: Oxford University Press.

Keesing, F. M. (1958). *Cultural Anthropology: The Science of Custom.* New York: Holt, Rinehart and Winston.

Kelley, J. (1997). Paleobiological and phylogenetic significance of life history in Miocene hominoids. *In* D. R. Begun, C. V. Ward, and M. D. Rose (eds.), *Function, Phylogeny, and Fossils: Miocene Hominoid Evolution and Adaptations,* pp. 173–208. New York: Plenum Press.

King, B. J. (1994). *The Information Continuum: Evolution of Social Information Transfer in Monkeys, Apes, and Hominids.* Santa Fe, NM: SAR Press.

Klein, R. (1999). *The Human Career: Human, Biological and Cultural Origins,* 2nd ed. Chicago: University of Chicago Press.

Klein, R. G., and Edgar, B. (2002). *The Dawn of Human Culture.* New York: John Wiley and Sons.

Knott, C. D. (1998). Changes in orangutan caloric intake, energy balance, and ketones in response to fluctuating fruit availability. *Intern. J. Primatol. 19,* 1061–1079.

—— (2001). Female reproductive ecology in apes. *In* P. T. Ellison (ed.), *Reproductive Ecology and Human Evolution,* pp. 429–463. New York: Aldine De Gruyter, Hawthorne.

Kortlandt, A., and Holzhaus, E. (1987). New data on the use of stone tools by chimpanzees in Guinea and Liberia. *Primates 28,* 473–496.

Kortlandt, A., and Kooij, M. (1963). Protohominid behaviour in primates. *Symp. Zool. Soc. London, 10,* 61–88.

Kuper, A. (1994). *The Chosen Primate: Human Nature and Cultural Diversity.* Cambridge, MA: Harvard University Press.

Leighton, M., Seal, U. S., Soemarna, K., Adjisasmito, Wijaya, M., Mitra Setia, T., Shapiro, G., Perkins, L., Traylor-Holzer, K., and Tilson, R. (1995). Orangutan life history and vortex analysis. *In* R. D. Nadler, B. F. M. Galdikas, L. K. Sheeran, and N. Rosen (eds.), *The Neglected Ape*, pp. 97–107. New York: Plenum Press.

Lovell, N. C. (1990). *Patterns of Injury and Illness in Great Apes.* Washington, DC: Smithsonian Institution Press.

MacKinnon, K., Hatta, G., Halim, H., and Mangalik, A. (1997). *The Ecology of Kalimantan (Indonesian Borneo).* Singapore: Periplus Editions.

Maggioncalda, A. N., Czekala, N. M., and Sapolsky, R. M. (2002). Male orangutan subadulthood: a new twist on the relationship between chronic stress and developmental arrest. *Am. J. Phys. Anthrop. 118,* 25–32.

Martin, P., and Bateson, P. (1993). *Measuring Behaviour: An Introductory Guide,* 2nd ed. Cambridge: Cambridge University Press.

Matsuzawa, T., Biro, D., Humle, T., Inoue-Nakamura, N., Tonooka, R., and Yamakoshi, G. (2001). Emergence of culture in wild chimpanzees: education by master-apprenticeship. *In* T. Matsuzawa (ed.), *Primate Origins of Human Cognition and Behavior,* pp. 557–574. Tokyo: Springer.

Mayr, E. (1988). *Toward a New Philosophy of Biology: Observations of an Evolutionist.* Cambridge, MA: Harvard University Press.

McBrearty, S., and Brooks, A. S.

(2000). The revolution that wasn't: a new interpretation of the origin of modern human behavior. *J. Hum. Evol. 39,* 453–563.

McGrew, W. C. (1992). *Chimpanzee Material Culture: Implications for Human Evolution.* Cambridge: Cambridge University Press.

——— (1998). Culture in nonhuman primates? *Annu. Rev. Anthropol. 27,* 310–328.

McGrew, W. C., Marchant, L. F., Scott, S. E., and Tutin, C. E. G. (2001). Intergroup differences in a social custom of wild chimpanzees: the grooming hand-clasp of the Mahale mountains. *Current Anthro. 42,* 148–153.

Mercader, J., Panger, M., and Boesch, C. (2002). Excavation of a chimpanzee stone tool size in the African rainforest. *Science 296,* 1452–1455.

Merrill, M. Y. (2004). *Orangutan Cultures? Tool Use, Social Transmission and Population Differences.* Ph.D. diss., Duke University.

Milton, K. (1988). Foraging behaviour and the evolution of primate intelligence. *In* R. W. Byrne and A. Whiten (eds.), *Machiavellian Intelligence: Social Expertise and the Evolution of Intellect in Monkeys, Apes, and Humans,* pp. 285–305. Oxford: Clarendon Press.

Mitani, J. C., and Watts, D. P. (2001). Why do chimpanzees hunt and share meat? *Anim. Behav. 61,* 915–924.

Mitani, J. C., Grether, G. F., Rodman, P. S., and Priatna, D. (1991). Associations among wild orang-utans: sociality, passive aggregations or chance? *Anim. Behav. 42,* 33–46.

Montagu, M. F. A. (1968). *Man and Aggression.* New York: Oxford University Press.

Moore, J. (1996). Savanna chimpan-

zees, referential models and the last common ancestor. *In* W. C. McGrew, L. F. Marchant, and T. Nishida (eds.), *Great Ape Societies,* pp. 275–292. Cambridge: Cambridge University Press.

Muir, C. C., Galdikas, B. M. F., and Beckenbach, A. T. (2000). mtDNA sequence diversity of orangutans from the islands of Borneo and Sumatra. *J. Mol. Evol. 51,* 471–480.

Nakamura, M. (2002). Grooming-hand-clasp in Mahale M group chimpanzees: implications for culture in social behaviours. *In* C. Boesch, G. Hohmann, and L. F. Marchant (eds.), *Behavioural Diversity in Chimpanzees and Bonobos,* pp. 71–89. Cambridge: Cambridge University Press.

Nowak, R. M. (1999). *Walker's Mammals of the World,* 6th ed. Baltimore: Johns Hopkins University Press.

O'Malley, R. C., and McGrew, W. C. (2000). Oral tool use by captive orangutans *(Pongo pygmaeus). Folia Primatol. 71,* 334–341.

Ottoni, E. B., and Mannu, M. (2001). Semifree-ranging tufted capuchins *(Cebus apella)* spontaneously use tools to crack open nuts. *Intern. J. Primatol. 22,* 347–458.

Parker, S. T., and Gibson, K. R. (1977). Object manipulation, tool use and sensorimotor intelligence as feeding adaptations in Cebus monkeys and great apes. *J. Hum. Evol. 6,* 623–641.

Paul, A. (2002). Sexual selection and mate choice. *Intern. J. Primatol. 23,* 877–904.

Pereira, M. E., and Leigh, S. R. (2003). Modes of primate development. *In* P. M. Kappeler and M. E. Pereira (eds.), *Primate Life Histories and Socioecology,* pp. 149–176. Chicago: University of Chicago Press.

Povinelli, D. J., and Cant, J. G. H. (1995). Arboreal clambering and the evolution of self-conception. *Q. Rev. Biol. 70,* 393–421.

Promislow, D. E. L., and Harvey, P. H. (1990). Living fast and dying young: a comparative analysis of life-history variation among mammals. *J. Zool. (Lond.) 220,* 417–437.

Pusey, A. E. (1987). Sex-biased dispersal and inbreeding avoidance in birds and mammals. *Trends Ecol. Evol. 2,* 295–299.

Pusey, A. E., and Packer, C. (1987). Dispersal and philopatry. *In* B. B. Smuts, D. L. Cheney, R. M. Seyfarth, R. W. Wrangham, and T. T. Struhsaker (eds.), *Primate Societies,* pp. 250–266. Chicago: University of Chicago Press.

Rao, M., and van Schaik, C. P. (1997). The behavioral ecology of Sumatran orangutans in logged and unlogged forest. *Trop. Biodiv. 4,* 173–185.

Rendell, L., and Whitehead, H. (2001). Culture in whales and dolphins. *Behav. Brain Sci. 24,* 309–382.

Reynolds, V. (1967). *The Apes: The Gorilla, Chimpanzee, Orangutan, and Gibbon—Their History and Their World.* New York: Harper Colophon Books.

Ricklefs, M. C. (1993). *A History of Modern Indonesia since c. 1300,* 2nd ed. Stanford: Stanford University Press.

Rijksen, H. D. (1978). *A Field Study on Sumatran Orang-utans (Pongo pygmaeus abelii Lesson 1827).* Wageningen: H. Veenman and Zonen, B.V.

Rijksen, H. D., and Meijaard, E. (1999). *Our Vanishing Relative: The Status of Wild Orang-utans at the Close of the Twentieth Century.*

Wageningen: Tropenbos Publications.

Robertson, J. M. Y., and van Schaik, C. P. (2001). Causal factors underlying the dramatic decline of the Sumatran orang-utan. *Oryx 35,* 26–38.

Rodman, P. S. (1984). Foraging and social systems of orangutans and chimpanzees. *In* P. S. Rodman and J. G. H. Cant (eds.), *Adaptations for Foraging in Nonhuman Primates,* pp. 134–160. New York: Columbia University Press.

Rowley-Conwy, P. (2001). Time, change and the archaeology of hunter-gatherers: how original is 'Original Affluent Society'? *In* C. Panter-Brick, R. H. Layton, and P. Rowley-Conwy (eds.), *Hunter-Gatherers: An Interdisciplinary Perspective,* pp. 39–72. Cambridge: Cambridge University Press.

Russon, A. E. (2000). *Orangutans: Wizards of the Rain Forest.* Toronto: Firefly Books.

——— (2002). Return of the native: cognition and site-specific expertise in orangutan rehabilitation. *Intern. J. Primatol. 23,* 461–478.

——— (2003). Developmental perspectives on great ape traditions. *In* D. M. Fragaszy and S. Perry (eds.), *The Biology of Traditions: Models and Evidence,* pp. 329–364. Cambridge: Cambridge University Press.

Russon, A., and Galdikas, B. (1995). Constraints on great apes' imitation: model and action selectivity in rehabilitant orangutan *(Pongo pygmaeus)* imitation. *J. Comp. Psychol. 109,* 5–17.

Ruvolo, M. (1997). Molecular phylogeny of the hominoids: inferences from multiple independent DNAS sequence data sets. *Mol. Biol. Evol. 14,* 248–265.

Sahlins, M. (1972). *Stone Age Economics.* Chicago: Aldine.

Savage-Rumbaugh, E. S., and Lewin, R. (1994). *Kanzi: The Ape at the Brink of the Human Mind.* New York: Wiley and Sons.

Shermer, M. (2002). *In Darwin's Shadow: The Life and Science of Alfred Russel Wallace.* Oxford: Oxford University Press.

Singleton, I. S. (2000). *Ranging Behaviour and Seasonal Movements of Sumatran Orangutans* (Pongo pygmaeus abelii) *in Swamp Forests.* PhD diss., Durrell Institute of Conservation and Ecology.

Singleton, I. S., and van Schaik, C. P. (2001). Orangutan home range size and its determinants in a Sumatran swamp forest. *Int. J. Primatol. 22,* 877–911.

——— (2002). The social organisation of a population of Sumatran orangutans. *Folia Primatol. 73,* 1–20.

Slotkin, J. S. (1965). *Readings in Early Anthropology.* London: Methuen.

Small, M. F. (1993). *Female Choices: Sexual Behavior of Female Primates.* Ithaca: Cornell University Press.

Stanford, C. B. (1999). *The Hunting Apes: Meat Eating and the Origins of Human Behavior.* Princeton: Princeton University Press.

Stoinski, T., and Whiten, A. (2003). Social learning by orangutans *(Pongo abelii* and *Pongo pygmaeus)* in a simulated food processing task. *J. Comp. Psych. 117,* 272–282.

Sugardjito, J. (1983). Selecting nest sites by Sumatran orang-utans *(Pongo pygmaeus abelii)* in the Gunung Leuser National Park, Indonesia. *Primates 24,* 467–474.

Sugardjito, J., te Boekhorst, I. J. A., and van Hooff, J. A. R. A. M. (1987). Ecological constraints on the grouping of wild orang-utans

(*Pongo pygmaeus*) in the Gunung Leuser National Park, Sumatra, Indonesia. *Intern. J. Primatol. 8,* 17–41.

te Boekhorst, I. J. A., Schürmann, C. L., and J. Sugardjito, J. (1990). Residential status and seasonal movements of wild orang-utans in the Gunung Leuser Reserve (Sumatra, Indonesia). *Anim. Behav. 39,* 1098–1109.

Terborgh, J., and van Schaik, C. P. (1987). Convergence vs. non-convergence in primate communities. *In* J. H. R. Gee and P. S. Giller (eds.), *Organization of Communities: Past and Present,* pp. 205–226. Oxford: Blackwell Scientific Publications.

Terkel, J. (1996). Cultural transmission of feeding behavior in the black rat *(Rattus rattus). In* C. M. Heyes and B. G. Galef, Jr. (eds.), *Social Learning in Animals: The Roots of Culture,* pp. 17–47. San Diego: Academic Press.

Tomasello, M. (1999). *The Cultural Origins of Human Cognition.* Cambridge, MA: Harvard University Press.

Tomasello, M., and Call, J. (1997). *Primate Cognition.* New York: Oxford University Press.

Tomasello, M., Kruger, A., and Ratner, H. (1993). Cultural learning. *Behav. Brain Sci., 16,* 495–511.

Tooby, J., and DeVore, I. (1987). The reconstruction of hominid behavioral evolution through strategic modeling. *In* W. G. Kinzey (ed.), *The Evolution of Human Behavior: Primate Models,* pp. 185–237. New York: SUNY Press.

Torrence, R. (2001). Hunter-gatherer technology: macro- and microscale approaches. *In* C. Panter-Brick, R. H. Layton, and P. Rowley-Conwy (eds.), *Hunter-Gatherers: An Interdis-* *ciplinary Perspective,* pp. 73–98. Cambridge: Cambridge University Press.

Tuttle, R. (2001). Culture and traditional chimpanzees. *Curr. Anthro. 42,* 407–409.

Tylor, E. B. (1871). *Primitive Cultures.* London: Murray.

Utami, S. S., and Mitra Setia, T. (1995). Behavioral changes in wild male and female Sumatran orangutans *(Pongo pygmaeus abelii)* during and following a resident male takeover. *In* R. D. Nadler, B. F. M. Galdikas, L. K. Sheeran, and N. Rosen (eds.), *The Neglected Ape,* pp. 183–190. New York: Plenum Press.

Utami, S. S., and van Hooff, J. A. R. A. M. (1997). Meat-eating by adult female Sumatran orangutans *(Pongo pygmaeus abelii). Am. J. Primatol. 43,* 159–165.

Utami, S. S., Goossens, B., Bruford, M. W., de Ruiter, J. R., and van Hooff, J. A. R. A. M. (2002). Male bimaturism and reproductive success in Sumatran orangutans. *Behavioral Ecology 13,* 643–652.

van Noordwijk, M. A., and van Schaik, C. P. (2004). Development of ecological competence in Sumatran orangutans. *Am. J. Phys. Anthro.*

van Schaik, C. P. (1989). The ecology of social relationships amongst female primates. *In* V. Standen and R. A. Foley (eds.), *Comparative Socioecology,* pp. 195–218. Oxford: Blackwell.

——— (1999). The socioecology of fission-fusion sociality in orangutans. *Primates 40,* 73–90.

——— (2000a). Infanticide by male primates: the sexual selection hypothesis revisited. *In* C. P. van Schaik and C. H. Janson (eds.), *Infanticide by Males and Its Implications,* pp. 27–60. Cambridge: Cambridge University Press.

——— (2000b). Vulnerability to infanticide: patterns among mammals. *In* C. P. van Schaik and C. H. Janson (eds.), *Infanticide by Males and Its Implications,* pp. 61–71. Cambridge: Cambridge University Press.

——— (2002). Fragility of traditions: the disturbance hypothesis for the loss of local traditions in orangutans. *Intern. J. Primatol. 23,* 527–538.

——— (2003). Local traditions in orangutans and chimpanzees: social learning and social tolerance. *In* D. M. Fragaszy and S. Perry (eds.), *The Biology of Traditions: Models and Evidence,* pp. 297–328. Cambridge: Cambridge University Press.

van Schaik, C. P., and Deaner, R. O. (2003). Life history and cognitive evolution in primates. *In* F. B. M. de Waal and P. L. Tyack (eds.), *Animal Social Complexity,* pp. 5–25. Cambridge, MA: Harvard University Press.

van Schaik, C. P., and Griffiths, M. (1996). Activity periods of Indonesian rain forest mammals. *Biotropica 28,* 105–112.

van Schaik, C. P., and Janson, C. H. (eds.) (2000). *Infanticide by Males and Its Implications.* Cambridge: Cambridge University Press.

van Schaik, C. P., and Kappeler, P. M. (1997). Infanticide risk and the evolution of male-female association in primates. *Proc. Roy. Soc. Lond. B 264,* 1687–1694.

van Schaik, C. P., and Knott, C. D. (2001). Geographic variation in tool use on *Neesia* fruits in orangutans. *Am. J. Phys. Anthro. 114,* 331–342.

van Schaik, C. P., and Mirmanto, E. (1985). Spatial variation in the structure and litterfall of a Sumatran rain forest. *Biotropica 17,* 196–205.

van Schaik, C. P., and Pradhan, G. R. (2003). A model for tool-use traditions in primates: implications for the evolution of culture and cognition. *J. Hum. Evol. 44,* 645–664.

van Schaik, C. P., and Rao, M. (2002). The frontier model of development and its relevance to protected area management. *In* J. Terborgh, C. P. van Schaik, L. Davenport, and M. Rao (eds.), *Making Parks Work: Strategies for Preserving Tropical Nature,* pp. 424–440. Washington, DC: Island Press.

van Schaik, C. P., and van Noordwijk, M. A. (1985). Interannual variability in fruit abundance and reproductive seasonality in Sumatran long-tailed macaques *(Macaca fascicularis). J. Zool. 206,* 533–549.

van Schaik, C. P., Ancrenaz, M., Borgen, G., Galdikas, B., Knott, C. D., Singleton, I., Suzuki, A., Utami, S. S., and Merrill, M. Y. (2003a). Orangutan cultures and the evolution of material culture. *Science 299,* 102–105.

van Schaik, C. P., Azwar, and Priatna, D. (1995). Population estimates and habitat preferences of orangutans based on line transects of nests. *In* R. D. Nadler, B. F. M. Galdikas, L. K. Sheeran, and N. Rosen (eds.), *The Neglected Ape,* pp. 129–147. New York: Plenum Press.

van Schaik, C. P., Deaner, R. O., and Merrill, M. Y. (1999). The conditions for tool use in primates: implications for the evolution of material culture. *J. Hum. Evol. 36,* 719–741.

van Schaik, C. P., Fox, E. A., and Fechtman, L. T. (2003b). Individual variation in the rate of use of tree-hole tools among wild orang-utans:

implications for hominin evolution. *J. Hum. Evol. 44,* 11–23.

van Schaik, C. P., Monk, K. A., and Robertson, J. M. Y. (2001). Dramatic decline in orang-utan numbers in the Leuser Ecosystem, northern Sumatra. *Oryx 35,* 14–25.

van Schaik, C. P., Pradhan, G. R., van Noordwijk, M. A. (in press). Infanticide by males, sex, and harassment by males. *In* P. M. Kappeler and C. P. van Schaik (eds.), *Sexual Selection in Primates: New and Comparative Perspectives.* Cambridge: Cambridge University Press.

van Schaik, C. P., Preuschoft, S., and Watts, D. P. (in press). Great ape societies: structures, bonds and cognition. *In* A. Russon and D. Begun (eds.), *The Great Apes.* Cambridge: Cambridge University Press.

van Schaik, C. P., van Noordwijk, M. A., and Nunn, C. L. (1999). Sex and social evolution in primates. *In* P. C. Lee (ed.), *Comparative Primate Socioecology,* pp. 204–240. Cambridge: Cambridge University Press.

Wallace, A. R. (1869). *The Malay Archipelago: The Land of the Orang-utan and the Bird of Paradise.* London: Macmillan.

Walsh, P. D., et al. (2003). Catastrophic ape decline in western equatorial Africa. *Nature 422,* 611–614.

Walther, G. R., Post, E., Convey, P., Menzel, A., Parmesan, C., Beebee, T. J. C., Fromentin, J.-M., Hoegh-Guldberg, O., and Bairlein, F. (2002). Ecological responses to recent climate change. *Nature 416,* 389–395.

Watts, D. P. (1998). Coalitionary mate guarding by male chimpanzees at Ngogo, Kibale National Park, Uganda. *Behav. Ecol. Sociobiol. 44,* 43–56.

——— (2000). Causes and consequences of variation in male mountain gorillas' life histories and group membership. *In* P. M. Kappeler (ed.), *Primate Males: Causes and Consequences of Variation in Group Composition,* pp. 169–179. Cambridge: Cambridge University Press.

Watts, D. P., and Mitani, J. C. (2001). Boundary patrols and intergroup encounters in wild chimpanzees. *Behaviour 138,* 299–327.

Whiten, A., and Byrne, R. W. (eds.) (1997). *Machiavellian Intelligence II: Extensions and Evaluations.* Cambridge: Cambridge University Press.

Whiten, A., Goodall, J., McGrew, W. C., Nishida, T., Reynolds, V., Sugiyama, Y., Tutin, C. E. G., Wrangham, R. W., and Boesch, C. (1999). Cultures in chimpanzees. *Nature 399,* 682–685.

Whitten, A. J., Damanik, S. J., Anwar, J., and Hisyam, N. (1984). *The Ecology of Sumatra.* Yogyakarta: Gajah Mada University Press.

Wich, S. A., Utami-Atmoko, S. S., Mitra Setia, T., Rijksen, H. D., Schürmann, C., van Hooff, J. A. R. A. M., and van Schaik, C. P. (in review). Life history of wild Sumatran orangutans *(Pongo abelii).*

Wilson, E. O. (1975). *Sociobiology.* Cambridge: Belknap Press.

Wilson, M. L., and Wrangham, R. W. (2003). Intergroup relations in chimpanzees. *Annu. Rev. Anthropol. 32,* 363–392.

Wind, J. (1996). Gunung Leuser National Park: history, threats, and options. *In* C. P. van Schaik and J. Supriatna (eds.), *Leuser: A Sumatran Sanctuary,* pp. 4–27. Jakarta: YABSHI Press.

Wrangham, R. W. (1980). An ecological model of female-bonded primate groups. *Behaviour 75*, 262–299.

——— (1999). Evolution of coalitionary killing. *Yearbk. Phys. Anthro. 42*, 1–30.

Wrangham, R. W., and Peterson, D. (1996). *Demonic Males: Apes and the Origins of Human Violence*. Boston: Houghton Mifflin Company.

Yoerg, S. I. (2001). *Clever as a Fox: Animal Intelligence and What It Can Teach Us about Ourselves*. New York: Bloomsbury.

Zhi, L., Karesh, W. B., Janzewski, D. N., Frazier-Taylor, H., Sajuthi, D., Gombek, F., Andau, M., Martenson, J. S., and O'Brien, S. J. O. (1996). Genomic differentiation among natural populations of orang-utan *(Pongo pygmaeus). Current Biol. 6*, 1326–1336.

INDEX